eLmL 2020

The Twelfth International Conference on Mobile, Hybrid, and On-line Learning

November 21 – 25, 2020

Valencia, Spain

eLmL 2020 Editors

Alexander Mikroyannidis, The Open University, UK
Maiga Chang, Athabasca University, Canada
Stephen White, The University of Huddersfield - Queensgate, UK

Printed from e-media with permission by:

Curran Associates, Inc.
57 Morehouse Lane
Red Hook, NY 12571

Some format issues inherent in the e-media version may also appear in this print version.

International Academy, Research, and Industry Association (IARIA)
412 Derby Way
Wilmington, DE 19810

Phone: (408) 893-6407
Fax: (408) 527-6351

petre@iaria.org

Additional copies of this publication are available from:

Curran Associates, Inc.
57 Morehouse Lane
Red Hook, NY 12571 USA
Phone: 845-758-0400
Fax: 845-758-2633
Email: curran@proceedings.com
Web: www.proceedings.com

Table of Contents

eLmL 2020

Forward

The Twelfth International Conference on Mobile, Hybrid, and On-line Learning (eLmL 2020), focused on the latest trends in e-learning and also on the latest IT technology alternatives that are poised to become mainstream strategies in the near future and will influence the e-learning environment.

eLearning refers to on-line learning delivered over the World Wide Web via the public Internet or the private, corporate intranet. The goal of the eLmL 2020 conference was to provide an overview of technologies, approaches, and trends that are happening right now. The constraints of e-learning are diminishing and options are increasing as the Web becomes increasingly easy to use and the technology becomes better and less expensive.

eLmL 2020 provided a forum where researchers were able to present recent research results and new research problems and directions related to them. The topics covered aspects related to tools and platforms, on-line learning, mobile learning, and hybrid learning.

We take this opportunity to thank all the members of the eLmL 2020 Technical Program Committee as well as the numerous reviewers. The creation of such a broad and high-quality conference program would not have been possible without their involvement. We also kindly thank all the authors who dedicated much of their time and efforts to contribute to the eLmL 2020. We truly believe that, thanks to all these efforts, the final conference program consists of top quality contributions.

This event could also not have been a reality without the support of many individuals, organizations, and sponsors. We are grateful to the members of the eLmL 2020 organizing committee for their help in handling the logistics and for their work to make this professional meeting a success.

We hope that eLmL 2020 was a successful international forum for the exchange of ideas and results between academia and industry and for the promotion of progress in eLearning research.

eLmL 2020 Chairs

eLmL 2020 Steering Committee

Stephen White, The University of Huddersfield - Queensgate, UK
Maiga Chang, Athabasca University, Canada

eLmL 2020
Committee

eLmL 2020 Steering Committee
Maiga Chang, Athabasca University, Canada
Stephen White, The University of Huddersfield – Queensgate, UK

eLmL 2020 Publicity Chair
Jose Miguel Jimenez, Universitat Politecnica de Valencia, Spain

eLmL 2020 Advisory Committee
Herwig Mannaert, University of Antwerp, Belgium
Hironori Washizaki, Waseda University, Japan
Christian M. Stracke, Open University of the Netherlands, The Netherlands
Ivan Ganchev, University of Limerick, Ireland / Plovdiv University "Paisii Hilendarski", Bulgaria
Mudasser Wyne, National University - San Diego, USA

eLmL 2020 Technical Program Committee
Khadidja Bakhti, Algerian Space Agency, Algeria / Beijing Institute of Technology, China
Tina Boyle Whyte, Marquette University, USA
Egle Butkeviciene, Kaunas University of Technology, Lithuania
Mauro Callejas Cuervo, Universidade Pedagógica y Tecnológica de Colombia, Colombia
Djordje Cantrak, University of Belgrade, Serbia
Cristina M.R. Caridade, Coimbra Polytechnic - ISEC, Portugal
Maiga Chang, Athabasca University, Canada
Lorraine Cleeton, Northcentral University / Walden University, USA
Najima Daoudi, École des sciences de l'information, Morocco
Debzani Deb, Winston-Salem State University, USA
Angel P. del Pobil, Jaume I University, Spain
Rafael del Vado Vírseda, Universidad Complutense de Madrid, Spain
Soumyabrata Dev, ADAPT SFI Research Centre, Dublin, Ireland
Mounim A. El Yacoubi, Telecom SudParis, France
Ramon Fabregat, University of Girona, Spain
Ivan Ganchev, University of Limerick, Ireland / University of Plovdiv "Paisii Hilendarski", Bulgaria
Leonardo Garrido, Tecnológico de Monterrey, Mexico
Odeese Ghassa-Khalil, Duquesne University, USA
Henrique Gil, Age.Comm - Instituto Politécnico de Castelo Branco, Portugal
Rawad Hammad, King's College London, UK
Feifei Han, Griffith University, Australia
Oriel Herrera, Univ. Católica de Temuco, Chile
Tsunenori Ishioka, The National Center for University Entrance Examinations, Japan
Tomayess Issa, Curtin University, Australia
Katerina Kabassi, Ionian University, Greece

Keiichi Kaneko, Tokyo University of Agriculture and Technology, Japan
Jai W. Kang, Rochester Institute of Technology, USA
Ilias Karasavvidis, University of Thessaly, Volos, Greece
Komalpreet Kaur, Salem State University, USA
Carsten Kleiner, University of Applied Sciences&Arts in Hannover, Germany
Miroslav Kulich, Czech Technical University in Prague, Czech Republic
Amruth N. Kumar, Ramapo College of New Jersey, USA
Monica Landoni, Università della Svizzera italiana, Switzerland
Cynthia Y. Lester, Perimeter College - Georgia State University, USA
Beibin Li, Paul G. Allen School of Computer Science and Engineering - University of Washington, Seattle, USA
Andreas Lingnau, Ruhr West University of Applied Sciences, Germany
George Liodakis, Hellenic Mediterranean University (formerly Technological Educational Institute of Crete - TEI of Crete), Greece
Martin Llamas Nistal, Universidade de Vigo, Spain
Matteo Lombardi, Griffith University, Australia
Josue Aaron Lopez Leyva, CETyS University, Mexico
Luca A. Ludovico, University of Milan, Italy
Herwig Mannaert, University of Antwerp, Belgium
Sathiamoorthy Manoharan, University of Auckland, New Zealand
Daniela Marghitu, Auburn University, USA
Alke Martens, University of Rostock, Germany
Paulo Martins, INESC TEC / University of Trás-os-Montes e Alto Douro, Portugal
Bruce R. Maxim, University of Michigan-Dearborn, USA
Natarajan Meghanathan, Jakson State University, USA
José Carlos Meireles Monteiro Metrolho, Polytechnic Institute of Castelo Branco, Portugal
Alexander Mikroyannidis, The Open University, UK
Begoña Montero-Fleta, Universitat Politècnica de València, Spain
Umberto Nanni, Universita' di Roma "La Sapienza", Italy
Jari Palomäki, Tampere University, Finland
Arna Peretz, Ben-Gurion University of the Negev, Israel
Matin Pirouz Nia, California State University, USA
Maja Pušnik, University of Maribor, Slovenia
Sonja D. Radenkovic, University of Belgrade, Serbia
Thurasamy Ramayah, Universiti Sains Malaysia, Malaysia
Laura Rayón Rumayor,University of Alcala, Spain
Fernando Reinaldo Ribeiro, Polytechnic Institute of Castelo Branco, Portugal
Ilaria Renna, ISEP - LISITE laboratory, France
Marina Rui, University of Genova, Italy
Demetrios Sampson, Curtin University, Australia
Carol Savill-Smith, Education Support Partnership, UK
Jacopo Soldani, University of Pisa, Italy
Francesco Sovrano, University of Bologna, Italy
Melissa Stange, Lord Fairfax Community College, USA

Exploring Blockchain for Public Sector Recruitment

Konstantinos Siassiakos, Foteini Bompoti, Thanos Papaioannou, Kalliopi Stagka,
Panagiotis Zarafidis, and Anna Pavli
ASEP
Athens, Greece
e-mails: {k.siassiakos, f.mpompoti, c_antiproedros, k.stagka, pzarafidis, a.pavli}@asep.gr

Abstract **- Enhancing the management of human capital resources in the Greek public sector addresses the challenges of optimizing the civil personnel recruitment process, increasing public integrity while enforcing the principles of transparency, participation, accountability, effectiveness and efficiency. The objective is the design and activation of a central, unified Human Resources Management System (HRMS) both in terms of procedures, methods and Information Technology (IT) infrastructure. The blockchain technology adopted for the needs of public administration recruitment in Greece and the expected results are described. The importance of working within an established legislative framework in which merit is well defined, job requirements reflect occupational requirements and illustrate the assessment practices from the Greek public service are set out.**

Keywords – Blockchain; Public sector recruitment; Qualification; Verification; Evaluation.

I. INTRODUCTION

Public sector organizations are expected overtime to fulfill mandates revolving around objectives such as qualitative and cost-effective service delivery, as well as accountability in the management of various types of resources. To achieve that, effective assessment in recruitment of the most qualified personnel is of the essence. Carrying out this complex procedure with the use of multiple assessment tools and information collected from diverse sources is expected to provide a more comprehensive approach of the candidates being assessed and further added value to the recruitment system overall. Securing access to the candidates' work and educational background as well as performance reviews in a credible way is argued that it will, the least, improve the current recruitment process in view of the aforementioned mandates. Blockchain technology is regarded as a game-changer in several sectors including the domain of Human Resources (HR) and recruitment, mainly because of its inherent characteristics of decentralization, transparency and immutability. There are currently numerous business and research, private and public sector endeavors, to explore both the theoretical and practical implications (technical, political, socio-economic, legal and cultural) of the blockchain technology. The purpose of this paper is to report on the development of an innovative assessment tool being designed whilst making most use of the blockchain technology that will ultimately provide ASEP, Greece, with the means to optimize the personnel recruitment process for the Greek public sector it has been entrusted with.

II. PUBLIC SECTOR RECRUITMENT IN GREECE

A. Legal framework

ASEP (Supreme Council for Civil Personnel Selection) is an independent body provided under the Greek constitution, entrusted with performing public administration recruitment processes for project agreements as well as fixed-term and short-term employment agreement positions at all levels. ASEP is supported by a high-end electronic information system managing the vast volume of applications, vacancies, news releases, results and, most importantly, candidates involved in ASEP selection processes records. Candidates are evaluated based on the score they achieve in written exams, the outcome of their interview, and their qualifications overall. Some of the tools missing from ASEP's day-to-day business are functionalities that could relieve the public from the bureaucratic burden (such as achieving validation, i.e. confirmation of authenticity, of university degrees) and further enhance qualitative and cost-effective service delivery and accountability (by way of, amongst others, simplifying the already complex recruitment process of Highly Qualified Civil Personnel).

Under the current legal framework, ASEP is entrusted with performing public administration recruitment processes in Greece, apart from certain exceptions provided by law. More specifically, certain Greek public entities are empowered by the said legislation to proceed with recruitment of personnel, either supervised by ASEP or not. It should be noted that ASEP's competence to supervise the recruitment process of such a public entity does not, in any way, overlap with the entity's competence to deliver that recruitment process.

B. Process

Vacancies in the civil sector are made public by ASEP through newsletters, its official website (www.asep.gr) and the press, in a non-personalized way. Citizens can make queries via its website about announced vacancies looking for those that better match their qualifications. Following the announcement, citizens sign into the ASEP Registry where they fill in their qualifications and submit an e-application regarding the announced vacancies. The e-application itself does not suffice as the candidates are further expected to print out their e-application and send it to ASEP along with the hardcopies of all supporting documents and certificates. ASEP's Central Committee then issues and publishes interim results in the form of tables containing all necessary information (eg. name, ID number, credits collected per qualification etc.) which may be appealed by those with vested interest. ASEP's Council Members in composition review the appeals and the interim results, issue and publish the final results.

Vacancies in the public sector addressed to highly qualified candidates, although announced and handled similarly with the rest (application process, interim and final results and so forth), is significantly more complex to the extent one more step in the recruitment process, just before the issue of the interim results, is added. More specifically, ASEP's Evaluation Committee issues (for internal use only) an initial ranking based on candidates' declared qualifications and assessment methodology that varies as it is left by law to the Committee's discretion to decide upon this each time. The candidates ranking high are then called for an interview and the Committee, upon evaluation, issues and publishes interim results in the form of tables containing all necessary information (eg. name, ID number, credits collected per qualification etc.) which may be appealed by those with vested interest. ASEP's Council Members in composition review the appeals and the interim results, issue and publish the final results.

Following the announcement of the final results in both scenarios as described herein above, the public entities who triggered the recruitment process proceed with hiring the prevailing candidates as per ASEP's results and validating their qualifications. In case of fraud detection, public entities may submit, within three years from the final results publication, a request to ASEP for replacement.

C. *Drawbacks in the current process*

Qualifications' evaluation by ASEP (initially by the Central Committee or the Evaluation Committee as per the case and later by the Members in composition) is a time-consuming process as it is performed in a non-automated way. Qualifications' validation by the public entities that trigger the recruitment process and ultimately hire the prevailing candidates as per ASEP's results is also performed in a non-automated way. Both processes are apparently time-consuming, notably the validation of qualifications requires exchange of letters and, in certain cases, circulation of hardcopies, with all the cost that the stakeholders at issue incur with regard to time, money and manhours. The replacement process itself is time-consuming and linked with both direct and indirect costs.

III. QualiChain Potential

QualiChain targets the creation, piloting and evaluation of a decentralised platform for storing, sharing and verifying education and employment qualifications and focuses on the assessment of the potential of blockchain technology, algorithmic techniques and computational intelligence for disrupting the domain of public education, as well as its interfaces with private education, the labour market, public sector administrative procedures and the wider socio-economic developments.

IV. Public Administration Recruitment Pilot

Qualichain pilot goals in relation to public sector recruitment are the following:

- Demonstrate and assess the QualiChain concept and technological solution, by piloting the combination of disruptive technologies involved in the context of staffing the public sector.
- Assess the impact, i.e. the benefits and risks of the QualiChain technological solution on the full spectrum of stakeholders towards which it is addressed in public administration.

A. *Stakeholders*

The stakeholders involved in the ASEP use case are the following:

1) ASEP Council Members and Employees: As publishers, evaluators, validators, and decision makers with regard to the candidates' qualifications and the entire selection process in general.

2) Citizen/Candidate: As the main participant of a selection process and the owner of qualifications.

3) Public Entity: As "customer" of ASEP selection process and the future employer of the candidate.

4) Qualifications' issuing/accrediting institutions and their personnel: As (indirect) providers of qualifications or on the receiving end of requests for verification, by public entities.

B. *Expectations*

The recruitment and competency management services of QualiChain will be exploited to enhance not just the check of the candidates' declared qualifications, but also their screening, leading to a short list of those to be interviewed and, ultimately, to the identification of the best possible applicant for the role.

Specifically, this pilot has the following main expectations, as illustrated in Figure 1:

- To provide personalised candidate notifications for job vacancies by matching individual profiles with available jobs in the civil sector.
- To utilise the solution's Blockchain based digital ledger in order to validate academic and professional qualifications of individual candidates.
- To improve efficiency of the selection process in terms of time and credibility.

C. *Use case steps*

The Highly Qualified Civil Personnel recruitment process steps are the following:

1) The issuing organization issues a qualification component (either an academic qualification or a work experience certificate) for a citizen.

2) The isssuing Organization, after obtaining the candidate's consent, uploads the qualification component in QualiChain and sends it to the Citizen.

3) ASEP announces positions/vacancies on QualiChain.

4) Citizen/Candidate gets notified of new vacancies via a Data Analytics Tool embedded in QualiChain.

5) Candidate signs up to ASEP's Registry (if not already registered), fills in his qualifications, uploads the relevant proof of qualifications declared (e.g. university degree) and applies for the vacancy they are interested in.

6) ASEP confirms the validity of the proof of qualification declared and potentially its metadata (e.g. year of graduation).

7) ASEP marks the qualification, the validity of which has been confirmed to its Registry, as a Level 6 qualification. A Level 6 registered qualification means that this process does not have to be repeated for this qualification.

8) ASEP uses QualiChain ´s MCDSS (Multi Criteria Decision Support System) to get an initial ranking of candidates.

9) Based on this initial ranking, ASEP proceeds to the stage of interviews.

10) ASEP uses QualiChain MCDSS to get the final ranking and ultimately the interim results.

D. Challenges

Several challenges have been identified from the beginning, as follows:

- Friendliness and usability of user interface provided by Qualichain, given that it will be, mainly, used by ASEP'S members and employees, with no technical background whatsoever.
- Pilot planning and integration with internal ASEP procedures.
- Semantic interoperability between Greek terms used by ASEP information systems (e.g. institution names, qualifications, certifications, job descriptions and so forth) and QualiChain terminology.
- Compliance with Greek and EU regulation e.g. General Data Protection Regulation (GDPR) [1].

V. CONCLUSION

In order to achieve effective assessment in recruitment of the most qualified personnel in the public sector, methods and tools must be constantly developed and tested to educate and train everyone in line with new developments, in our case, with the blockchain technology, so that their benefits can be fully realized by all stakeholders. The opportunity to explore an area that has not had much attention academically, i.e. public sector recruitment process from a different angle, that of embedding highly sophisticated tools, enables this effort to be treated as a breakthrough in contemporary recruitment processes, not necessarily restrained in the civil sector.

ACKNOWLEDGMENT

This work has received funding from the European Union's Horizon 2020 research and innovation programme under grant agreement No 822404 (QualiChain).

REFERENCES

[1] General Data Protection Regulation (GDPR), http://eur-lex.europa.eu/legal-content/EN/TXT/PDF/?uri=CELEX:32016R0679&qid=1522240823531&from=EN

[2] ASEP's founding law 2190/1994 (Official Government Gazette nr. 28/B/1994)

Figure 1. Pilot objectives.

Blockchain Applications in Education: A Case Study in Lifelong Learning

Alexander Mikroyannidis
Knowledge Media Institute
The Open University
Milton Keynes, United Kingdom
e-mail: Alexander.Mikroyannidis@open.ac.uk

***Abstract*—This paper presents a pilot case study of the QualiChain project, aiming at supporting lifelong learning through the combined use of Smart Badges and personalised recommendations. The pilot case study uses Blockchain technology as a means to decentralise lifelong learning and provide lifelong learners with transparent and immutable educational accreditation. At the same time, lifelong learners are provided with personalised recommendations that help them reach their personal and professional learning goals.**

Keywords-lifelong learning; blockchain; decentralisation; smart badge; personalised recommendation.

I. INTRODUCTION

Education today is still controlled mostly by educational institutions, which offer quality, credibility, governance, and administrative functions. This model is not flexible enough and poses difficulties in recognising the achievements of a lifelong learner in informal and non-formal types of education. As a result, a lifelong learner's transition from formal to informal education and vice versa can be hindered, as the achievements acquired in one type of education are not easily transferable to another [1][2]. Generally, lifelong learners have limited control and ownership over their learning process and the data associated with their learning.

This indicates the need for a decentralised model across all types of education, offering learners a framework for fully controlling how they are learning, how they acquire qualifications and how they share their qualifications and other learning data with third parties, such as educational institutions or employers [3][4]. In this paper, we investigate how Blockchain technologies can help realise this vision via a pilot case study for offering support to lifelong learners in various stages of their learning journeys and of their career trajectories.

The remainder of this paper is organised as follows. In Section 2, we introduce the overall framework of the QualiChain project. We then proceed in Section 3 to present the pilot case study for supporting lifelong learning, its scope, the stakeholders involved, the main scenario, as well as the outcomes of a series of consultation workshops about this pilot. Finally, in Section 4 we conclude the paper and outline the next steps of this work.

II. THE QUALICHAIN PROJECT

The emergence of the Blockchain promises to revolutionise not only the financial world, but also education in various ways. Blockchain technology offers a decentralised peer-to-peer infrastructure, where privacy, secure archiving, consensual ownership, transparency, accountability, identity management and trust are built-in, both at the software and infrastructure levels. This technology offers opportunities to thoroughly rethink how we find educational content and tutoring services online, how we register and pay for them, as well as how we get accredited for what we have learned and how this accreditation affects our career trajectory.

The QualiChain research and innovation project focuses on the assessment of the technical, political, socio-economic, legal and cultural impact of decentralisation solutions on education. As shown in Figure 1, QualiChain is targeting four key areas for exploring the impact of decentralisation: (i) lifelong learning; (ii) smart curriculum design; (iii) staffing the public sector; (iv) providing HR consultancy and competency management services.

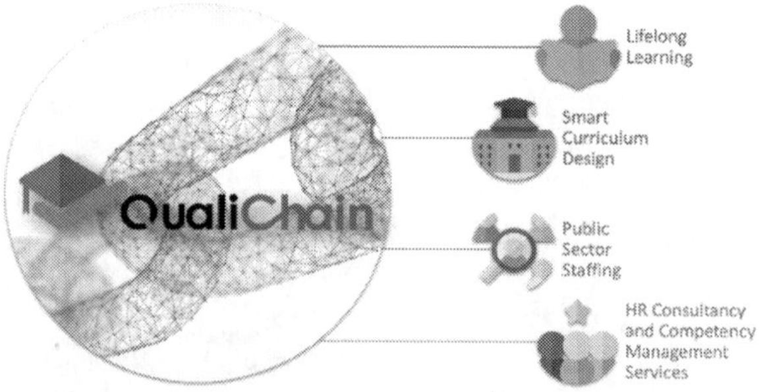

Figure 1. The key areas targeted by the QualiChain project.

QualiChain investigates the creation, piloting and evaluation of decentralisation solutions for storing, sharing and verifying education and employment qualifications and focuses on the assessment of the potential of Blockchain technology, algorithmic techniques and computational intelligence for disrupting the domain of public education, as well as its interfaces with private education, the labour market, public sector administrative procedures and the wider socio-economic developments.

III. Supporting Lifelong Learning

As outlined in the previous section, lifelong learning is a key area targeted by the QualiChain project. We are, therefore, aiming to provide support to lifelong learners in various stages of their learning journeys and of their career trajectories. In the context of this pilot case study, we investigate how Blockchain technologies can support lifelong learners in their learning journey and in advancing their career. Figure 2 illustrates the main goals of this pilot, which are the following:

- Awarding lifelong learners with **transparent and immutable educational accreditation.**
- Offering lifelong learners **personalised recommendations** based on their learning achievements.
- Supporting lifelong learners in reaching **their personal and professional learning goals.**

The next sections describe the scope, stakeholders and main scenario of this pilot, as well as the outcomes of a series of consultation workshops about this pilot.

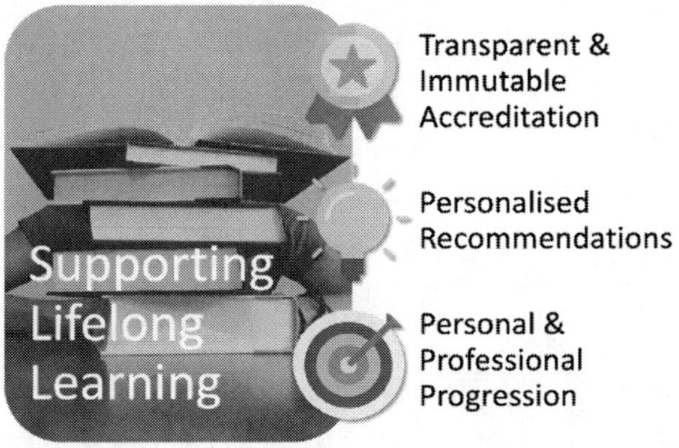

Figure 2. The overall goals of the pilot on supporting lifelong learning.

A. *Scope*

The scope of this pilot case study spans across the following:

- We are targeting both **formal and informal learning**. While formal learning typically happens inside the classroom, for example in a traditional university lecture, informal learning happens outside of the classroom, for example by studying free online courses.
- We are targeting both **academic degrees and other forms of educational accreditation**. For example, open badges have emerged as a new form of certifying that someone has acquired certain skills and has gained specific knowledge upon fulfilling certain criteria, e.g. by completing an online course.
- We are supporting the **learning journey and career trajectory of learners**. We are aiming to support the whole learning journey of learners by offering them recommendations on what to study next. We are also offering recommendations about their next career steps, based on the educational credentials they have acquired.

B. *Stakeholders*

The two main categories of stakeholders involved in this pilot are the following:

Lifelong learners. The concept of "lifelong learning" is based on the fact that learning is not confined to childhood or the classroom, but can take place throughout life and in a range of situations. Lifelong learners pursue learning throughout their lifetime, for either personal or professional reasons. They may study to develop new skills that they need in their professional life, for example to advance their career by finding a new job or by being promoted in their current job. They may also study to acquire skills and knowledge for personal reasons, for example as a hobby of theirs. Lifelong learners may engage in either formal or informal education, or both, depending on their current learning goals and personal or professional circumstances.

Lifelong learners face various challenges associated with the recognition of their learning achievements, for example when transitioning from formal to informal education or vice versa. In this pilot, we seek to support them in various ways, for example by verifying their learning achievements on the Blockchain, or by offering them personalised recommendations about what to study next or which job position might be suitable for them. In this way, we aim to help lifelong learners reach their personal or professional learning goals.

Educational institutions. These are institutions that provide education or training services, either paid ones or free. The offerings of educational institutions can vary from conventional offline degrees to online free or paid courses, such as Massive Open Online Courses (MOOCs) or Open Educational Resources (OERs) [5].

In the context of this pilot, we seek to make the awarding of accreditation by educational institutions transparent and immutable with the use of Smart Badges [6]. Smart Badges are dynamic records of accreditation that follow the same principles as Open Badges [7] and offer the same benefits in recording accreditation. However, Smart Badges are immutable and easily verifiable as they are stored on the Blockchain. The other novelty of Smart Badges lies in their dynamic features. For example, apart from just recording a learning achievement, a Smart Badge can also offer job or course recommendations, as described in the next section.

C. *Scenario*

In this section, we present the interactions between stakeholders in the context of the main scenario of this pilot, as illustrated in Figure 3. Let us consider a lifelong learner, Michelle, who is looking to expand her knowledge and skills on data science, and has thus enrolled in a number of courses offered online, including MOOCs and OERs. Each time she completes a course, she is awarded a Smart Badge by the educational institution that offers the course. This Smart Badge includes data about the skills that Michelle has acquired upon completion of the course. Each Smart Badge

Michelle earns is verified and stored on the Blockchain as part of her personal ePortfolio.

After studying for several months, Michelle has mastered some basic data science skills, including various computer science topics such as databases. Based on these skills, the Smart Badges generate recommendations about jobs that may be suitable for Michelle. Michelle receives personalised recommendations about jobs that fully match her skills, as well as about jobs that match her skills partially. Michelle may also further personalise these recommendations and filter them according to her specific criteria, such as the location of the job, salary, employer, etc.

Michelle is interested in one of the jobs that matches her skills partially. She then receives recommendations about courses that will give her the additional skills required for this job. Michelle enrols for these courses, in order to acquire the needed skills. When she has acquired them, she proceeds to apply for her desired job and allows the prospect employer to access the relevant Smart Badges from her ePortfolio. By using this Blockchain-based infrastructure to support her in her studies, Michelle has adopted a more efficient and targeted approach to learning, towards achieving her desired career trajectory.

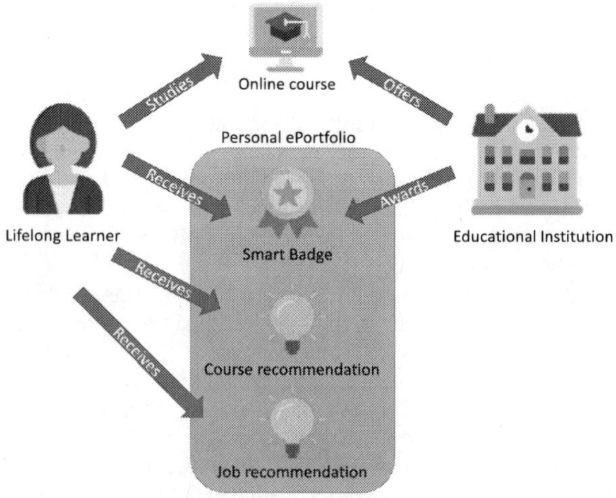

Figure 3. Stakeholder interactions in the main scenario of the lifelong learning pilot.

Our early work on implementing this scenario can be found in [6]. This implementation has been based on the use of Smart Contracts for the Ethereum Blockchain platform [8]. Smart Contracts are defined as "automatable and enforceable agreements" [9] and they constitute one of the main features of current Blockchain platforms, including Ethereum. In order to collect job market data, we are harvesting datasets of current job offers and their associated skills from a job aggregator that has been developed by the European Data Science Academy (EDSA) project [10]. These datasets are placed in Smart Contracts on the Ethereum Blockchain and are then used for matching jobs with a learner's badge-based skills. In this way, the awarded badges are smart, in the sense that they are being used to offer recommendations to learners.

D. Consultation workshops

In order to further develop our pilot case study and to better understand the current needs of our stakeholders, we have performed a series of consultation workshops (Figure 4). These workshops have targeted different audiences in the context of renowned international conferences on open education and educational technology. So far, the workshop series has been delivered in the context of the following events:

- The EATEL Summer School on Technology Enhanced Learning (JTELSS 2019), 3-7 June 2019, Bari, Italy.
- The Association for Learning Technology Conference (ALTC 2019), 3-5 September 2019, Edinburgh, UK.
- The Online, Open and Flexible Higher Education Conference (OOFHEC2019), 16-18 October 2019, Madrid, Spain.
- The Open Education Global Conference (OE Global 2019), 26-28 November 2019, Milan, Italy.

Figure 4. Snapshots from the consultation workshop series.

Participants in these workshops have been early and late career researchers, lecturers, technologists and professionals from the educational sector. During the workshops, participants were introduced to the overall framework of the QualiChain project, as well as the scenarios that apply Blockchain technologies in education. In particular, participants explored the ways that ePortfolios, accreditation, tutoring, as well as other aspects of teaching and learning can evolve within a decentralised ecosystem based on the Blockchain.

E. Findings

In order to document requirements for the further development of our pilot case study, we asked participants of our consultation workshops to produce learning scenarios that make use of Blockchain technologies in the context of lifelong learning. More specifically, participants were asked to work in small groups in order to brainstorm the following aspects of learning scenarios:

- *Persona(s):* Who are the typical users in this scenario and what do they wish to accomplish?
- *Requirements:* Documented in the following format: As Persona "X", I want to do "Y", so that I achieve "Z".
- *Use of Blockchain:* How can the Blockchain be used in this scenario?
- *Related resources:* Any links/publications/other resources that are relevant to this scenario.

These group brainstorming activities were followed by plenary discussion sessions, where participants presented and discussed their scenarios. Figure 5 summarises the main findings from the group activities and discussion sessions. These findings are presented in the form of requirements derived from the learning scenarios produced by participants of the workshops, as well as from the main takeaway points of the discussion sessions.

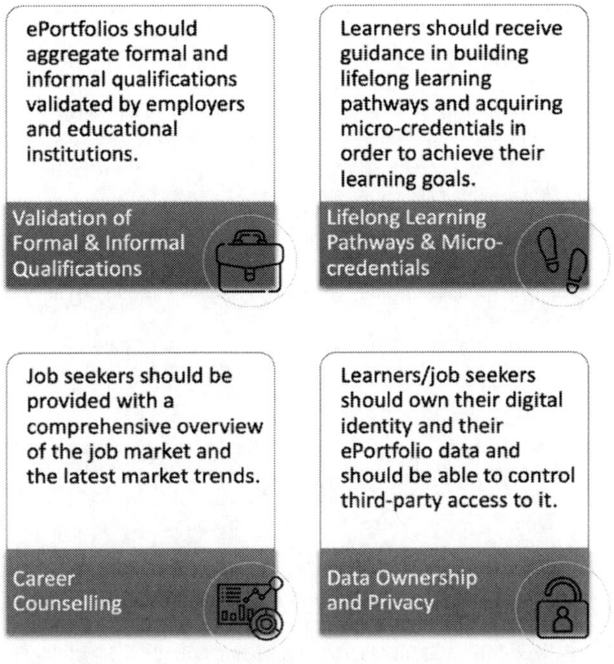

Figure 5. Requirements collected from the participants of the consultation workshop series.

First of all, participants pointed out the need for ePortfolios to aggregate both formal and informal qualifications that will be easily validated by employers and educational institutions. This will help streamline the admission processes in universities and the hiring processes by employers, as well as eliminate falsified qualifications.

Participants also highlighted the need for learners to be guided on how to build lifelong learning pathways in order to achieve their learning goals. These learning goals can be aligned with job market needs for improving the learner's employability, or they can be associated with the learner's personal progression ambitions. Acquiring micro-credentials can help lifelong learners achieve these goals by studying short online courses and earning professional or academic credentials [11][12]. Micro-credentials are rapidly emerging and gaining popularity among lifelong learners, as they address their needs for granular certified learning. Renowned educational institutions from around the world are currently offering a continuously increasing range of micro-accredited courses, thus providing opportunities to pursue further study in a variety of specialised fields [13]-[16].

Career counselling was also featured in the learning scenarios and discussions of participants of the workshops. It was pointed out that job seekers are in need of acquiring a comprehensive overview of the job market and the latest market trends, so that they can make informed decisions about the next steps in their careers.

Finally, data ownership and privacy requirements were deemed quite important by participants of the workshops. It was highlighted that learners and job seekers should own their digital identity and the data in their ePortfolio. Additionally, they should be able to control who accesses their identity and their ePortfolio, which data are accessed and for how long.

These requirements largely validate the scope of the QualiChain lifelong learning pilot, while helping us further expand it. In particular, we will be addressing the validation of both formal and informal qualifications in the form of Smart Badges. We will also be facilitating the building of lifelong learning pathways via personalised course recommendations, which will help learners choose their next online or offline course, towards achieving their learning goals. Additionally, the personalised course recommendations will include micro-accredited courses, in order to facilitate the acquisition of micro-credentials by lifelong learners.

With regards to the career counselling requirement, personalised job recommendations will provide job seekers with advice on their next career steps. We are also contemplating offering detailed overviews of the job market and its latest trends via interactive dashboards, based on the ones we have developed in the context of the EDSA project [10].

We will be extending our pilot case study to address data ownership and privacy requirements by employing decentralisation solutions, such as the Solid platform [17] and the FAIR TRADE framework [18]. Solid is a decentralised platform for social web applications, where the data of users is managed independently of the applications that create and consume this data. This approach enables users to choose where their data resides and who is allowed to access it. The FAIR TRADE framework builds on top of the Solid approach by defining a set of dimensions relevant to data management in decentralised contexts. The framework can therefore be used for describing and evaluating the management of decentralised data solutions, as well as for the development of best practices in the developing field of decentralised data management.

Finally, we will be looking into ways of implementing Self-Sovereign Identity (SSI) for learners and jobs seekers. SSI is a technology that adds a layer of trust to digital interactions, thus allowing individuals to own and manage their digital identity [19]. There are several implementations of SSI in the literature, largely based on the use of Blockchain technology [20]-[22].

IV. Conclusions and Next Steps

This paper has presented a pilot case study for supporting lifelong learning via Smart Badges and personalised recommendations. The pilot case study employs Blockchain technology for providing lifelong learners with transparent and immutable educational accreditation. It also uses personalised recommendations for helping lifelong learners reach their personal and professional learning goals. This pilot is part of the QualiChain initiative for decentralising education and employment qualifications using Blockchain technologies.

Engaging the communities of stakeholders has provided us with a valuable insight into the lifelong learning challenges they face and their proposed solutions. This insight will help us further shape the requirements and the implementation of our pilot. We will continue consulting with the communities of stakeholders throughout the different implementation phases of our pilot, so as to better understand and address their needs.

Acknowledgment

This work has received funding from the European Union's Horizon 2020 research and innovation programme under grant agreement No 822404 (QualiChain).

References

[1] J. Harris and C. Wihak, "To what extent do discipline, knowledge domain and curriculum affect the feasibility of the Recognition of Prior Learning (RPL) in higher education?," *International Journal of Lifelong Education*, pp. 1-17, 2017.

[2] B.-Å. Lundvall and P. Rasmussen, "Challenges for adult skill formation in the globalising learning economy–a European perspective," *International Journal of Lifelong Education*, vol. 35, pp. 448-464, 2016.

[3] A. Mikroyannidis, A. Third, and J. Domingue, "Decentralising online education using blockchain technology," in *Proc. The Online, Open and Flexible Higher Education Conference: Blended and online education within European university networks*, Madrid, Spain, 2019.

[4] A. Mikroyannidis, J. Domingue, M. Bachler, and K. Quick, "A Learner-Centred Approach for Lifelong Learning Powered by the Blockchain," in *Proc. EdMedia: World Conference on Educational Media and Technology*, Amsterdam, Netherlands, 2018, pp. 1403-1408.

[5] D. E. Atkins, J. S. Brown, and A. L. Hammond, "A Review of the Open Educational Resources (OER) Movement: Achievements, Challenges, and New Opportunities," The William and Flora Hewlett Foundation 2007.

[6] A. Mikroyannidis, J. Domingue, M. Bachler, and K. Quick, "Smart blockchain badges for data science education," in *Proc. 2018 IEEE Frontiers in Education Conference (FIE)*, 2018, pp. 1-5.

[7] Mozilla Foundation, Peer 2 Peer University, and The MacArthur Foundation, "Open Badges for Lifelong Learning," https://wiki.mozilla.org/images/5/59/OpenBadges-Working-Paper_012312.pdf, 2010. Retrieved: February 2020.

[8] V. Buterin, "Ethereum white paper," in *GitHub repository* https://github.com/ethereum/wiki/wiki/White-Paper, 2013. Retrieved: February 2020.

[9] C. D. Clack, V. A. Bakshi, and L. Braine, "Smart contract templates: foundations, design landscape and research directions," *arXiv preprint arXiv:1608.00771*, 2016.

[10] A.-S. Dadzie, E. M. Sibarani, I. Novalija, and S. Scerri, "Structuring visual exploratory analysis of skill demand," *Journal of Web Semantics*, vol. 49, pp. 51-70, 2018.

[11] D. Ifenthaler, N. Bellin-Mularski, and D.-K. Mah, "Foundation of digital badges and micro-credentials," *Switzerland: Springer International Publishing*, 2016.

[12] P. A. Lemoine and M. D. Richardson, "Micro-credentials, nano degrees, and digital badges: New credentials for global higher education," *International Journal of Technology and Educational Marketing (IJTEM)*, vol. 5, pp. 36-49, 2015.

[13] J. Caudill, "The emerging formalization of MOOC coursework: Rise of the MicroMasters," in *Proc. EdMedia+ Innovate Learning*, 2017, pp. 1-6.

[14] T. Hunt, R. Carter, L. Zhang, and S. Yang, "Micro-credentials: the potential of personalized professional development," *Development and Learning in Organizations*, 2019.

[15] P. A. Lemoine, W. M. Wilson, and M. D. Richardson, "Marketing Micro-Credentials in Global Higher Education: Innovative Disruption," in *Marketing Initiatives for Sustainable Educational Development*: IGI Global, 2018, pp. 182-204.

[16] B. Mischewski and A. Christie, "Understanding the feasibility of micro-credentials in engineering education," in *Proc. 29th Australasian Association for Engineering Education Conference 2018 (AAEE 2018)*, 2018, pp. 758.

[17] A. V. Sambra et al., "Solid: a platform for decentralized social applications based on linked data," Technical report, MIT CSAIL & Qatar Computing Research Institute 2016.

[18] J. Domingue, A. Third, and M. Ramachandran, "The FAIR TRADE Framework for Assessing Decentralised Data Solutions," in *Proc. WWW 2019 workshop: Linked Data on the Web and its Relationship with Distributed Ledgers (LDOW/LDDL)*, San Francisco, USA, 2019, pp. 866-882.

[19] A. Mühle, A. Grüner, T. Gayvoronskaya, and C. Meinel, "A survey on essential components of a self-sovereign identity," *Computer Science Review*, vol. 30, pp. 80-86, 2018.

[20] D. Baars, "Towards self-sovereign identity using blockchain technology," University of Twente, 2016.

[21] A. Othman and J. Callahan, "The Horcrux protocol: a method for decentralized biometric-based self-sovereign identity," in *Proc. 2018 International Joint Conference on Neural Networks (IJCNN)*, 2018, pp. 1-7.

[22] Q. Stokkink and J. Pouwelse, "Deployment of a blockchain-based self-sovereign identity," in *Proc. 2018 IEEE International Conference on Internet of Things (iThings) and IEEE Green Computing and Communications (GreenCom) and IEEE Cyber, Physical and Social Computing (CPSCom) and IEEE Smart Data (SmartData)*, 2018, pp. 1336-1342.

Using Blockchain, Semantics and Data Analytics to Optimise Qualification Certification, Recruitment and Competency Management: a Landscape Review

Christos Kontzinos
Decision Support Systems Lab
National Technical University of Athens
Athens, Greece
email: ckon@epu.ntua.gr

Ourania Markaki
Decision Support Systems Lab
National Technical University of Athens
Athens, Greece
email: omarkaki@epu.ntua.gr

Panagiotis Kokkinakos
Decision Support Systems Lab
National Technical University of Athens
Athens, Greece
email: pkokkinakos@epu.ntua.gr

Vagelis Karakolis
Decision Support Systems Lab
National Technical University of Athens
Athens, Greece
email: vkarakolis@epu.ntua.gr

Stavros Skalidakis
Decision Support Systems Lab
National Technical University of Athens
Athens, Greece
email: sskalidakis@epu.ntua.gr

John Psarras
Decision Support Systems Lab
National Technical University of Athens
Athens, Greece
email: john@epu.ntua.gr

Abstract—**In the era of digitisation, innovative technologies and Information & Communication Technology (ICT) systems have transformed many areas and domains. The same cannot be said for Higher Education, especially as this concerns the certification of degrees, qualifications and other accreditations of students and job seekers that are still largely in paper form and require manual and time-consuming processes. Given that such documents are pertinent not only for education purposes but also for the job market and Human Resources-related (HR) processes of private and public organisations, there is a growing need for automatic and trustworthy systems that can handle qualification certification while at the same time providing added value for the job market. This paper is written under the context of the European Union (EU)-funded project QualiChain that aspires to investigate the impact of disruptive technologies, such as blockchain, semantics, data analytics and gamification in the domain of public education, as well as the interfaces of the latter with the fields of private education, the labour market, and public sector administrative procedures.. The scope of this publication is to perform a landscape analysis on commercial tools and frameworks that operate in the aforementioned domains and compare them to the projected functionality of the QualiChain platform.**

Keywords-blockchain; semantics; data analytics; state-of-the-art; qualification certification; human resources management.

I. INTRODUCTION

When referring to qualification certification, the most common thought is a higher education diploma, a piece of paper that states the knowledge that has been acquired in a certain scientific field, or the skill to develop a task. The certification body is the entity that provides a certification for this diploma and is the legal recogniser of the knowledge. A typical, paper-based education certificate is a document that states that a person has received specific education and/or evidence of achievement of expected learning outcomes. Education certificates are used for a variety of purposes, such as the recognition of the completion of a specific learning experience by a student; or the achievement of a defined amount of knowledge achieved in a specified area; the acquisition of skills or the attainment of a particular excellence criterion.

Despite the fact that education certificates find use in various educational and work related processes (individuals' further admission in other educational and training programmes, personnel recruitment, etc.), they are largely resisting the pull of technology, as they are still held in diverse formats in siloed databases, often involving paper documentation and extremely time-consuming manual processes for their verification [1]. Additionally, most higher education institutions operate in isolated environments with no connection to the respective labour market that their graduates are projected to follow. As such, in most cases there are no tools that can ease the transition of a person from being a student to a job seeker and the connection between academia and the labour market is in most cases non-existent. Consequently, there is a clear lack of a trustworthy and automatic solutions when it comes to archiving, managing and verifying educational qualifications that can operate in various settings and provide added value to its users.

The slow digitisation of the education sector [2] coupled with the lack of suitable ICT solutions for education credentials' verification, means that holders of such titles are dependent from issuing/accrediting authorities every time they want to verify their degrees. This fact does not only affect academic institutions but also private and public organisations in their HR-related tasks. For example, recruitment in an organisation requires combing through hundreds of candidates' résumés, weeding out the unqualified ones and narrowing down the rest into a group of potential recruits', whose qualifications and academic degrees have to be checked and validated on a case-by-case basis. However, difficulties in the public and private sector do not limit to the actual task of recruiting but extend to a wider set of processes that follow contracting activities, indicatively encompassing personnel allocation and re-allocation, staff mobility, and skills' development and evaluation.

Solutions to these difficulties require fundamental changes in work practices and processes that extend beyond the transformation of the recruitment procedure itself and trace back to the way education and employment credentials and qualifications themselves are archived, managed and used and thereby to the way the educational and other accrediting organisations operate. Disruptive technologies, such as blockchain, algorithmic techniques, data analytics and semantics and innovative concepts like gamification may offer solutions to these challenges. Particularly, blockchain, as a decentralised, permanent, unalterable store of information can help with the archiving and trust issues, as well as provide a frictionless method for transacting with others, whereas computational intelligence found in the technological domains of algorithmic techniques, data analytics and semantic analysis may facilitate decision making and optimise work practices and procedures.

To assess the added value that this combination of technologies might provide to the aforementioned challenges, it is imperative to assess and evaluate similar frameworks and tools that operate in the domains of education and the labour market and provide solutions for qualification certification, recruitment and competency management. Under these circumstances, this paper presents a state-of-play analysis on 19 tools and frameworks that were identified in these domains. This analysis was performed under the context of the EU funded project QualiChain that aims to combine blockchain, semantics and other innovative technologies to provide a holistic, trustworthy and automatic solution in the challenges presented above.

Section I introduces the scope of this paper by presenting the current situation and challenges arising from the lack of technical solutions for qualification certification. Section II introduces the QualiChain project and the platform's functionalities. Section III outlines the criteria used for the analysis and provides a short description of each tool and framework that was analysed. Finally, Section IV presents the conclusions of the analysis.

II. The QualiChain Concept

QualiChain is a project that aspires to investigate the impact of disruptive technologies, such as blockchain, semantics, data analytics and gamification in the domain of public education, as well as the interfaces of the latter with the fields of private education, the labour market, and public sector administrative procedures. The project concept lies in applying the aforementioned technologies for the design, implementation, piloting and thorough evaluation of the QualiChain technological solution, a distributed platform targeting the storage, service, and verification of academic and employment qualifications [3]. Apart from educational and professional certificates verification, QualiChain aims to develop various added-value tools that can provide solutions to major challenges in the domains of education and the labour market. In fact, QualiChain services are structured along two main pillars, i.e., baseline and value adding services. The first pillar is grounded upon QualiChain main technological foundations, namely blockchain and semantics, enabling educational awards' and other qualifications' archiving and storing, awards' verification, the latter incorporating, if needed, certificates' translation and equivalence verification, as well as qualifications' portfolio management. The second pillar will build upon QualiChain baseline services to offer with the help of the computational intelligence, embodied in data analytics and decision support algorithms, as well as gamification techniques, a set of more advanced services, including career counselling, intelligent profiling, and competency management and within the context of the latter recruitment and evaluation support, and consulting.

III. Related Tools and Frameworks

A. Comparison Criteria

The comparative analysis in the following sections pertains to the current state of practices regarding tools, methods and frameworks, similar to QualiChain that are used in education and public administration, as well as commercial applications, and that all the tools presented therein are released for use and are not under development. In addition, the tools and frameworks described are not expected to include every projected function of QualiChain given that their scope is much more specific. What is useful though, is to perform a comparison on the state-of-play of functionalities and technical capabilities included in such systems to identify innovative ideas or potential shortcomings of existing solutions. Consequently, for this comparison the criteria for the analysis largely represent the high-level technical capabilities of the various modules of the QualiChain platform and are the following:

1. Target users: This part of the analysis will help assess if the list of stakeholders identified for the projected QualiChain platform is as complete as possible.
2. Blockchain usage/Data security: Identify the solutions that employ blockchain or other data security methods
3. Personalisation approach: This criterion will help compare the various approaches that make the tools more user-centric
4. Use of Semantics/data interoperability: Distil the tools that provide the capability for data analytics and in less innovative solutions other searchable interfaces as well as the available pool of data.

5. Gamification approach: Identify approaches that increase user engagement
6. Qualification certification and Multilinguality: This criterion pertains to the tools that certify qualifications. Two important sub-criteria here further divide the tools into automatic and non-automatic as well as the capability to translate degrees in multiple languages
7. Recruitment & Competency Management: This criterion pertains to the solutions that offer to organisations the ability to perform various HR related tasks.
8. Open source/APIs: This criterion will help identify the openness of each tool and the potential to create synergies with QualiChain.

B. Selected Tools & Indicative Analysis Tables

The tools and frameworks analysed under the context of this publication were the following:

1. Qualification Check [4] (tool): Qualification Check offer a global solution for qualification verifications, supported by a team of multilingual education experts. Qualification Check provides qualification validation to help stop the damaging and costly effect credentials fraud has on organisations.
2. Recognition Finder [5] (tool and framework): Recognition Finder is a tool for the recognition of foreign professional qualifications in Germany. It presents important information about the legal foundations, the recognition procedures for individual occupations and the available counselling services in a concise form. The tool in not automatic but rather finds the competent authority that the user needs to contact for the respective occupation.
3. European Credit Transfer & Accumulation System [6] (credit and grading system): ECTS is a credit system designed to make it easier for students to move between different countries. Since credits are based on the learning achievements and workload of a course, a student can transfer their European Credit Transfer System (ECTS) credits from one university to another, so they are added up to contribute to an individual's degree programme or training.
4. UHR Recognition of foreign qualifications [7] (tool and framework): The Swedish Council for Higher Education evaluates foreign qualifications to provide support for people looking for work in Sweden, people who wish to continue studying, or for employers who wish to employ someone with foreign qualifications. The tool includes an online application to apply for an evaluation and recognition of qualifications; however, the validation is not performed automatically.
5. ServiceNow [8] (tool): The ServiceNow module offers an expansive portfolio of training offerings across IT, HR, Customer Service and other departments that cover the Now Platform (HR and workflow organisation platform for enterprises). Moreover, it provides certifications upon mastering new features offered in the latest release of the platform, micro-certification on a variety of subjects as well as verification of certifications received through the ServiceNow platform.
6. Teacher Certification [9] (framework): The Teacher Certification framework of the British Columbia is a framework that provides a number of services to UK Ministry-certified educators. Among them are certification services, criminal record checks and fee information. The framework includes complete instructions regarding certification offices, pertinent e-mail addresses and the complete methodological steps that a teacher should follow to complete a certain task.
7. DegreeVerify [10] (tool): DegreeVerify provides immediate online verifications of college degrees and attendance. It provides prompt access to many degree and attendance records and eliminates the complications and delays associated with manual processing through individual schools. It can also reduce the risk and cost of making bad hiring decisions as well as ensure only verified eligible student customers are eligible for receiving offers from prospective employers.
8. WES Degree Equivalency Tool [11] (tool): The WES Degree Equivalency Tool compares a user's education credentials to Canadian standards. It allows a user to select the country he/she studied in, enter his/her credentials and the tool shows the degree equivalency. The Degree Equivalency tool doesn't replace an official evaluation, but rather estimates the degree equivalency.
9. Higher Education Degree Datacheck [12] (tool): HEDD is UK's official degree verification hub, used by organisations, institutions and universities to verify degrees. HEDD cannot be used by students or graduates to verify their own rewards, which means that the organisation using the tool's services will have to request a proof of consent from the individual.
10. NOKUT Recognition of foreign education in Norway [13] (framework): NOKUT if a framework that helps institutions, organisations and universities to validate foreign higher education degrees, vocational education and training certifications. It includes an exhaustive list of regulated professions and industries and a pertinent list of recognition authorities that users of the system will have to contact to get recognised in Norway.
11. Vitnemalsportalen Diploma registry [14] (tool): The Diploma registry is a Norwegian service that helps users automatically collect results from higher education institutions in Norway and share them with potential employers, educational institutions and other relevant recipients. Moreover, all transmissions are encrypted and only the sender can decide who he/she wants to share the data with.
12. e-CF 2.0 Profiling tool [15] (tool): The objective of the tool is to bring to life the content of e-CF version 3.0 and provide linkage to the EU ICT Professional profiles. It helps users build their profiles based on their

preferred orientation (e.g., job profile or education profile) and provides comparisons between user created profiles and established ICT professional profiles to support skill gap identification. The tool also supports multiple languages.

13. CEPIS e-Competence Benchmark [16] (tool): CEPIS is a free online tool that helps assess ICT professionals' skills, based on the e-CF. This tool provides ICT professionals with a personal competence gap analysis that compares their competences against those required for a range of European ICT professional profiles. This enables individuals to plan their career development and make informed decisions about further education.
14. e-Competences assessment and certification assessment [17] (tool): This tool lets users compose their own professional profile, find the best matching ICT profiles and choose the certificates that could help them meet their aspirations. It provides users with three distinct functionalities: a self-assessment tool, comparison of e-competence related certificates and an e-competence demand and supply calculator.
15. IT Staffing Nederland [18] (tool): IT Staffing is embedding the European Competence Framework in their recruiting and matching systems, for the sake of better transparency and quality on this process. The tool takes advantage of semantics for translation of ICT texts into digital e-competences and provides transparency to better interpret job descriptions, vacancy texts, incoming CVs and training materials.
16. Blockcerts [19] (tool): Blockcerts is an open standard for creating, issuing, viewing, and verifying blockchain-based certificates. These digital records are registered on a blockchain, cryptographically signed, tamper-proof, and shareable. The goal is to give to individuals the capacity to possess and share their own official records.
17. Diplome [20] (tool): Diplome is a blockchain-powered credential evaluation service that generates a "certificate wallet", in which it is possible to upload one's qualifications, making it easier for a student, graduate or professional to enrol in a foreign university or enter the labour market in a foreign country. Diplome is a global ecosystem, which can be used by authorities and institutions to securely and unchangeably register education/training documents, guaranteeing their transferability and authenticity.
18. LinkChain [21] (tool): LinkChain is a Blockchain-enabled Linked Data Platform catered to data publishers and consumers that provides certificate equivalence verification, credential auditing & verification while supporting multi-lingual capabilities as well.
19. Blockchain for Education [22] (tool): The available blockchain tool (part of a platform that is in development) enables learners to present their digital certificates while also supporting certification authorities in the management and archiving of digital certificates. The tool relies on blockchain to enable tamper-proof archiving of certificates and their correct and permanent allocation to the learners. The existing in-use tool relies on Open Badges and uses JSON/JSON-LD for metadata and as a basis for querying (verification purposes).

For the analysis of the tools and frameworks that are presented above, the following tables (see TABLE I) were used to describe the general functionality of each tool, the technologies implemented in it and the added value that they provide to users.

TABLE I. ANALYSIS TABLE

<table>
<tr><td>Tool/method name</td><td colspan="3">Recognition Finder[5]</td></tr>
<tr><td>Category (tool, product, framework)</td><td>Tool and framework</td><td>Current version</td><td>Released</td></tr>
<tr><td colspan="4">Description</td></tr>
<tr><td colspan="4">Recognition Finder is a tool for the recognition of foreign professional qualifications in Germany. Moreover, those seeking advice only need a few clicks and this online tool will name the competent authority for their application. In addition, it presents important information about the legal foundations, the recognition procedures for individual occupations and available counselling services in a concise form. Recognition Finder does not automatically verify the user's qualifications but finds the competent authority that the user needs to contact for the respective occupation.</td></tr>
<tr><td colspan="4">Implemented technologies and functionalities</td></tr>
<tr><td colspan="4">• Recognition check allows users to see whether their professional qualifications are recognised in Germany
• The portal is available in German and English, as well as Arabic, French, Greek, Italian, Polish, Romanian, Russian, Spanish and Turkish.
• For mobile use, there is also the "Recognition in Germany" app, which offers the information in seven languages
• The database currently contains more than 1,500 different contact addresses for the recognition procedures of occupations</td></tr>
<tr><td colspan="4">Added Value</td></tr>
<tr><td colspan="4">• In the "Recognition Finder", the user can enter his or her profession and use the occupational profile displayed to determine the German vocational certificate that matches the qualifications acquired abroad.
• Just a few clicks are sufficient to get the address where an application for an assessment of equivalence can be submitted.
• All the information that is important for submitting an application is summarised – for example the documents required for an application.</td></tr>
</table>

Following that, a comparison table was created that analyses each tool based on the criteria described in Section III.A. An indicative section of the comparison table can be seen in TABLE II.

TABLE II. COMPARISON TABLE

Name	Version	Target users	Blockchain/ Transaction Records/	Personalisation	Semantics/ Interoperability/ Analytics/	Gamification	Qualification Certification/ Multilinguality	Recruitment/ Competency management	Open Source/ APIs
Qualification Check	Released	Businesses, public agencies, regulators, education providers, professional bodies, recruitment firms, HR teams,	No Blockchain Full audit trail and record for verification	No	No	No	Automated qualification verification, worldwide education verification, electronic transcripts/ degree certificates to outside bodies/ Multilinguality	No	QCheck API allows queries from integrated systems
Recognition Finder	Released	Students, job seekers	No	No	No	No	Allows users to see whether their professional qualifications can be recognised in Germany, not automatic, finds the competent authority/ 11 languages	No	No

The full table will not be presented in this body of work in its entirety, due to space limitations. However, the main purpose of the table was to help draw the conclusions that will be presented in the following section (Section IV).

IV. DISCUSSION

This section will conclude on the approaches that were analysed and the potential/projected position of QualiChain in the domains of Qualification Certification and Human Resource Management. The conclusions will be based on the eight criteria that were defined for the comparative matrix as well as the overall added value of the presented tools.

The target users constitute the only criterion where no significant differences among the various approaches can be noted. In fact, given that the tools presented are tailored for the stakeholders either in the domain of education, or that of the job market/HR management or a combination of both, it stands to reason that the target users are like those of QualiChain. Identified target users include students, job seekers, employers, private and public organisations, government agencies, education providers, regulators, HR teams and recruitment firms among others. This fact gives credence to QualiChain's approach for stakeholder identification and proves that the list of QualiChain stakeholders is as exhaustive and complete as it needs to be.

Moving on to other criteria, the analysis showed that only 4/19 (Blockcerts, Diplome, LinkChain, Blockchain for Education) tools take advantage of Blockchain ledgers and decentralised standards for the purposes of record keeping, issuing and verification of certifications. While, it is a fact that blockchains are harder to implement compared to more traditional databases, their capabilities for secure distribution of certificates, security, data privacy and immutability are considered to be of paramount importance for minimising fraud around educational and other certificates. Moreover, considering the approaches that did not use blockchain, only 2/19 (Qualification Check, DegreeVerify) keep any records of transactions and 1/19 (Vitnemalsportalen) provides any level of security by adding digital signatures on documents.

Concerning semantics and data interoperability approaches, of all the tools that were described, only 4/19 took it into account. Specifically, IT Staffing Nederland applies semantic software that translates ICT texts into digital e-competencies while Diplome applies other standards of interoperability on the data. On the other hand, Blockchain for Education, offers JSON-LD support which can therefore provide the required verification methodology. Furthermore, LinkChain is projected to be fully semantic and support public and private RDF. Moreover, 4/19 solutions had minor data analytics capabilities, mainly for the purpose of matching between a student's/ job seeker's profile and the skills required for a given position. Finally, 6/19 approaches provided some data structure coupled with searchable registries for the user's convenience. Such searches are only applied on static data and do not provide any automatic capabilities for analysis except for LinkChain that provides a federated searchable Linked Data Platform.

Another criterion studied, was the level of personalisation that each tool provides for a more user-centric experience. The results here are more encouraging given that 8/19 approaches provide some level of personalisation for a user's profile. For example, tools like ECTS make learning more user-centred via use of credits as currency. In addition, WES offers digital badges used to display verified credentials on social media sites like LinkedIn. Moreover, tools that are powered by the European e-Competence Framework, provide users with the capability to develop their profiles based on preferred orientation and competence gap analyses. Finally, the approaches that take advantage of Blockchain (Blockcerts, Diplome and LinkChain) provide each user with a valid and verified certificate/ qualifications wallet.

Concerning gamification, there are no tools that provide a clear solution. While there are some tools that provide some degree of informal gamification with credits and digital badges, the overall conclusion is that the community does not consider it to be that important for the developed tools. However, given that most of the tools are free of charge and offer solutions of low technical capabilities that are realistically applied in Niche markets, it makes sense that gamification cannot be a priority in such systems.

The main criteria of the analysis revolve around the two main high-level functionalities that QualiChain will also provide, i.e., Qualification Certification and Recruitment/ Competency Management. One clear division between the various tools, has to do with the level of automation that they provide. Only 4/19 solutions are non-automatic meaning that they do not automatically certify/validate users' qualifications but rather help them navigate through the various procedures that they will have to follow in order to get certified in a given country or domain.

The rest of the solutions provide various levels of automation and will be assessed based on the actual added value that they offer on the entire end-to-end procedure of either Qualification Certification or Recruitment/ Competency Management. Starting from Recruitment/ Competency Management, no tools were found that offer holistic solutions in a pan-European level. Specifically, while most solutions offer solid functionalities for organisations that can help their HR teams make staffing and strategic decisions, tools like NOKUT (Norway) mainly apply for their own country and other tools (e-CF 2.0 profiling tool, CEPIS e-Competence benchmark, e-Competences assessment and certification assessment and IT staffing Nederland) have application only for ICT positions and organisations. On the other hand, platforms like LinkChain do not directly offer such functionalities but support external analytics and can serve as a data backend for qualification analysis, opportunity identification, competency development & evaluation, etc.

On the contrary and concerning the domain of Qualification Certification, there are a number of solutions that provide added value in every step of the process. Tools like Qualification Check, ECTS, Blockcerts, Diplome, LinkChain and Blockchain for Education are holistic solutions that automatically handle every step of the process while some of them have been adopted by multiple countries. However, there are still solutions that are country specific (Vitnemalsportalen, DegreeVerify) that do not offer the full range of functionalities for every type of user (HEDD) and others like the ServiceNow module that offer micro-accreditations for expertise in specific platforms and tools. In addition, only five approaches support Multilinguality and only three of them (NOKUT, Diplome, LinkChain) offer functionalities for both Qualification Certification and Recruitment/ Competency Management. One of the key suggestions of QualiChain is that having both services operate in a single platform seamlessly will further connect high-level education with the job market so that each domain can learn from the other and help students, job seekers and organisations make more informed decisions. Finally, the fact that 8/19 tools have APIs that allow them to connect with other systems can potentially help QualiChain synergise with them.

V. CONCLUSIONS

The scope of this paper was to perform a state-of-play analysis on tools, applications and frameworks used in the domains of Qualification Certification or Recruitment/ Competency Management. All in all, most of the tools that were analysed are either commercial applications or country/domain-specific and are usually focused on specific functionalities that are useful in some steps of the processes required by students, job seekers, educational institutions and organisations of all types. This gives credence to QualiChain's holistic approach and proves that there is a vacuum on the market of the domains tackled by the project. In fact, not only does QualiChain aim to fill a void in the market but also to advance the state-of-the-art by developing a holistic platform that provides open semantic interoperability and data privacy by extending the research in blockchain, semantics, data analytics and gamification.

ACKNOWLEDGMENT

This work has been co-funded by the European Union's Horizon 2020 research and innovation programme under the QualiChain project, Grant Agreement No 822404.

REFERENCES

[1] M. Turkanovic, M. Holbl, K. Kosic, M. Hericko and A. Kamisalic, "EduCTX. A Blockchain-Based Higher Education Credit Platform," IEEE Access, pp. 5112-5127, 2018, https://doi.org/10.1109/ACCESS.2018.2789929.

[2] Association of Universities in the Netherlands (VSNU): "Digitisation in academic education. Our agenda for a future-proof range of degree programmes," 2017.

[3] C. Kontzinos et al., "University process optimisation through smart curriculum design and blockchain-based student accreditation," In Proceedings of 18th International Confernece on WWW/Internet 2019, Cagliari, Itali 7-9 November 2019 [to be published].

[4] Qualification Check, Qualification Check. https://www.qualificationcheck.com/ [retrieved: February, 2020]

[5] Federal Institute for Vocatiomal Education and Training, Recognition Finder. https://www.anerkennung-in-deutschland.de/tools/berater/en/ [retrieved: February, 2020]

[6] European Higher Education Area, European Credit Transfer and Accumulation System (ECTS). https://ec.europa.eu/education/resources-and-tools/european-credit-transfer-and-accumulation-system-ects_en [retrieved: February, 2020]

[7] Swedish Council for Higher Education (UHR), Recognition of foreign qualifications. https://www.uhr.se/en/start/recognition-of-foreign-qualifications/ [retrieved: February, 2020]

[8] Service Now, Service Now Verification/Certification service. https://www.servicenow.com/ [retrieved: February, 2020]

[9] British Columbia – Ministry of Education, Teacher Certification. https://www.bcteacherregulation.ca/CertificateServices/CertificateServicesOverview.aspx [retrieved: February, 2020]

[10] National Student Clearinghouse Verification Services, DegreeVerify. https://nscverifications.org/degreeverify/ [retrieved: February, 2020]

[11] World Education Services, WES Degree Equivalency Tool. https://applications.wes.org/ca/degree-equivalency-tool/ [retrieved: February, 2020]

[12] Higher Education Funding Council for England (HEFCE), Higher Education Degree Datacheck (HEDD). https://hedd.ac.uk/#section-what-we-offer [retrieved: February, 2020]

[13] Norwegian Agency for Quality Assurance in Education (NOKUT), Recognition of foreign higher education in Norway. https://www.nokut.no/en/ [retrieved: February, 2020]

[14] Unit – The Norwegian Directorate for ICT and Joint Services in Higher Education and Research, Vitnemalsportalen Diploma registry. https://www.vitnemalsportalen.no/english/ [retrieved: February, 2020]

[15] European e-Competence Framework, e-CF 2.0 Profiling tool. http://www.ecompetences.eu/e-cf-3-0-and-ict-profiles-on-line-tool/ [retrieved: February, 2020]

[16] Council of European Professional Informatics Societies (CEPIS), CEPIS e-Competence Benchmark. https://www.cepisecompetencebenchmark.org/ [retrieved: February, 2020]

[17] e-Competence Quality, e-Competences assessment and certification assessment. http://www.e-competence-quality.com/ [retrieved: February, 2020]

[18] ICT-mastery, IT Staffing Nederland. https://www.ict-mastery.eu/index.php/en/#finding-the-best-ict-applicant [retrieved: February, 2020]

[19] Blockcerts - The Open Standard for Blockchain Credentials, Blockcerts. https://www.blockcerts.org/ [retrieved: February, 2020]

[20] CIMEA, Diplome. http://www.cimea.it/en/projects-list/diplome-blockchain4people/home-page-blockchain-2.aspx [retrieved: February, 2020]

[21] LinkChain, LinkChain. https://linkchain.supply/ [retrieved: February, 2020]

[22] Fraunhofer FIT, Blockchain for Education. https://www.fit.fraunhofer.de/en/fb/cscw/projects/blockchain-for-education.html [retrieved: February, 2020]

Decentralised Qualifications' Verification and Management for Learner Empowerment, Education Reengineering and Public Sector Transformation: The QualiChain Project

Christos Kontzinos
Decision Support Systems Lab
National Technical University of Athens
Athens, Greece
Email: ckon@epu.ntua.gr

Ourania Markaki
Decision Support Systems Lab
National Technical University of Athens
Athens, Greece
Email: omarkaki@epu.ntua.gr

Panagiotis Kokkinakos
Decision Support Systems Lab
National Technical University of Athens
Athens, Greece
Email: pkokkinakos@epu.ntua.gr

Vagelis Karakolis
Decision Support Systems Lab
National Technical University of Athens
Athens, Greece
Email: vkarakolis@epu.ntua.gr

Stavros Skalidakis
Decision Support Systems Lab
National Technical University of Athens
Athens, Greece
Email: sskalidakis@epu.ntua.gr

John Psarras
Decision Support Systems Lab
National Technical University of Athens
Athens, Greece
Email: john@epu.ntua.gr

***Abstract*—In today's society, formal and non-formal education credentials play an important role not only for holders of such diplomas and degrees but also for human resource management processes in public and private organisations. However, the degree of digitization in the sector is lagging, as certificates are still paper based and verification processes are very time-consuming. While the first Information & Communication Technology (ICT) solutions in these domains have been developed, they are still dependant on issuing organisations and manual processes. Blockchain is one technology that can be considered for developing trustworthy solutions for digital certificates, given its native characteristics for decentralisation, visibility and verification of transactions. Additionally, the computational intelligence found in analytics and decision support can help develop added value services while gamification can help develop more personalised approaches for the stakeholders of such domains. Under this context, the present publication presents QualiChain, an European Union (EU)-funded project that aims to revolutionise the domain of public education, as well as its interfaces with the labour market, policy making and public sector administrative procedures by disrupting the way accredited educational titles and other qualifications are archived, managed, shared and verified.**

Keywords-higher education; public sector; certification; human resource management; blockchain.

I. INTRODUCTION

In an era that every single piece of information around us is digitised and being exploited via innovative technological solutions in a variety of value adding ways, education certificates are largely resisting the pull of technology, as they are still held in diverse formats in siloed databases, often involving time consuming manual processes for their verification [1]. In education, certificates confirm the achievement of certain learning outcomes and are until today mostly issued on paper or other physical formats [2]. Paper certificates have their advantages, such as being easy to store and difficult to forge due to built-in security features. However, they also create several issues, such as dependence from accrediting authorities for their issuing and verification as well as vulnerability to loss and damage [3]. Additionally, lying about education and employment credentials is a common problem, as it has become very easy to counterfeit academic diplomas and certificates, or even "buy" degrees from fake degree websites [4]. According to a survey by CareerBuilder [5], a staggering 58% of employers have caught a lie on a resume, whereas 33% of them have seen an increase in resume embellishments and fabrications. Similar findings arise from another survey by StatisticBrain [6], according to which over half of resumes and job applications contain falsifications and over three quarters are misleading. Under these circumstances, and although fraud is not limited to educational awards, trust in the educational certification system is receiving significant blows [7][8].

The aforementioned challenges create problems when education credentials are requested as a means of ratifying decisions regarding either personnel recruitment or individuals' further admission in other educational programmes. The recruitment of personnel by an organisation is a lengthy process that comes along with combing through hundreds of candidates' résumés, weeding out the unqualified ones and narrowing down the rest into a group of potential recruits', whose qualifications and academic degrees have to be checked and validated on a case-by-case basis. These challenges do not limit to the actual task of recruiting but extend to a wider set of processes indicatively encompassing personnel allocation and re-allocation, staff mobility, and skills' development and evaluation, most of which fall under the notion of competency management.

Disruptive technologies, such as blockchain, algorithmic techniques, data analytics and semantics and innovative concepts like gamification may offer solutions to these challenges. Particularly, blockchain technology, as a decentralised, permanent, unalterable store of information can help with the archiving and trust issues, as well as provide a frictionless method for transacting with others [9] [10], whereas computational intelligence found in the technological domains of algorithmic techniques, data analytics and semantic analysis may facilitate decision making and optimise work practices and procedures. Moreover, gamification practices can help with user engagement and in developing a more user-centric solution. Under these circumstances, this publication presents QualiChain, a project targeting the creation, piloting and evaluation of a distributed platform for storing, sharing and verifying academic and employment qualifications that will focus on the assessment of the potential of the aforementioned combination of technologies for disrupting the domain of education.

Section I of this publication introduces the scope of the document and describes the challenges revolving around the verification of education certificates. Section II introduces the QualiChain concept and the high-level functionalities that it is projected to have. Section III describes the platform's architecture and introduces the pilot use cases, in which the platform will be applied. Finally, Section IV concludes the document.

II. THE QUALICHAIN CONCEPT

QualiChain is a project that aspires to investigate and provide evidence on the transformative impact of disruptive technologies, such as blockchain, semantics, data analytics and gamification in the domain of public education, as well as the interfaces of the latter with the fields of private education, the labour market and public sector administrative procedures. The concept and focus of the project lie more specifically in the design, implementation, piloting and thorough evaluation in terms of benefits, risks and other potential implications of the QualiChain technological solution, a distributed platform targeting the storage, sharing and verification of academic and employment qualifications. At this point, attention has to be drawn to the fact that although originally inspired from the field of public education and the need to transform certificates' archiving and management, as well as to fight fraud around education awards, QualiChain concept has practically a much larger scope, as its services transcend the mere validation of training certificates and bring forward solutions to major challenges of both public and private interest, such as those of lifelong learning, recruitment, mobility, better linking education with the labour market, etc., thereby accommodating the needs of several stakeholders (see Figure 1).

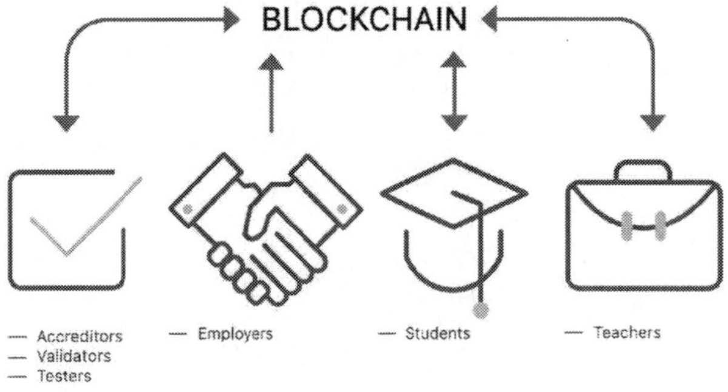

Figure 1. The value of blockchain to QualiChain stakeholders [3]

In fact, QualiChain services will be structured along two main pillars.

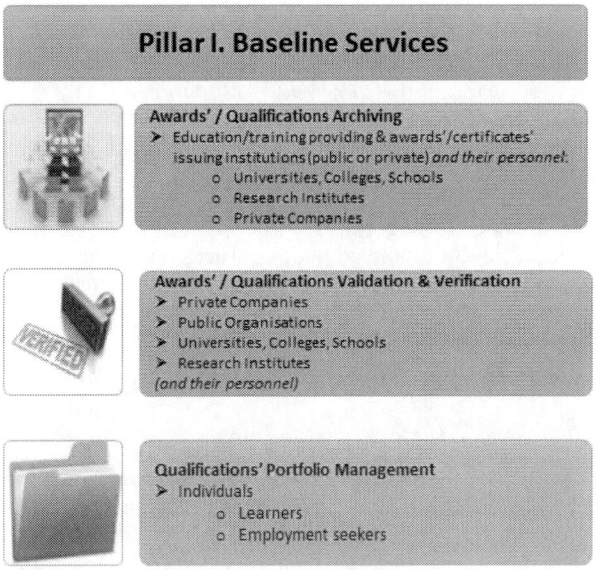

Figure 2. QualiChain Baseline Services

The first pillar (see Figure 2) will be grounded upon QualiChain main technological foundations, namely blockchain and semantics, enabling educational awards' and other qualifications' archiving and storing, awards' verification, the latter incorporating equivalence verification, as well as qualifications' portfolio management.

Figure 3. QualiChain Value Adding Services

The second pillar (see Figure 3) will build upon QualiChain baseline services to offer with the help of the computational intelligence, embodied in data analytics and decision support algorithms, as well as gamification techniques, a set of more advanced services, including career counselling, intelligent profiling, and competency management and within the context of the latter recruitment and evaluation support, and consulting.

III. Architecture and Pilot Cases

A. *QualiChain High-Level Architecture*

QualiChain will deliver an open source solution, comprising of stand-alone components and an integrated environment to facilitate its adoption by the different stakeholders according to their needs. To deliver the services and functionalities prescribed in the QualiChain concept in the previous section, the envisaged QualiChain platform logic layer consists of 3 main components, namely a *Validation and Verification Engine*, a *Profiling and Career Management Engine* and a *Recruitment and Competency Management Engine*, composed in turn by 11 modules (see Figure 4).

The *Validation and Verification Engine* will be responsible for registering from scratch newly awarded certificates and achievements as well as for ratifying claims around the possession of certain awards and qualifications. Thus, it will feature an *Awards' Registration Interface* that will enable issuing and accrediting organisations to register new verified qualifications' records in blockchain's distributed ledger, as well as a *Validation Query Builder*, through which all issuing institutions, public and private organisations, as well as individual users can set up appropriate validation queries. In greater detail, the Validation and Verification Engine is made up of the following sub-components: i. an *Equivalence Verification Module* that supports the identification and verification of equivalent degrees (or even skills, achievements and training courses), issued by different institutions, ii. a *Translation Module*, capable of translating certificates from one language to another, in case a both validated and translated version of a certificate is required, and iii. a *Credentials' Auditing and Verification Module*, responsible for accommodating new awards' registrations and thus adding new blocks to the blockchain database, as well as for receiving users' queries on the validation of awards and other qualifications.

The *Profiling and Career Management Engine* will be responsible for the functionalities required for the management of individual users' digital portfolio, aka digital learning ledger where the latter can archive and access their achievements, qualifications and work experience with the purpose of showcasing them to third parties. The specific component's functionalities are made accessible through a *Portfolio Manager Interface* and are brought to life with the help of the following modules: i. a *Verification Request Module*, enabling individuals to submit to accrediting organisations requests for the confirmation and formal verification of their achievements, ii. a *Career Advisor Module*, capable of crawling world wide web resources and applying data mining techniques with the goal of identifying and bringing into the individuals' attention job vacancies that match their profile, and iii. an *Intelligent Profiling Module*, that leverages job vacancies' elicited requirements and synthesises accordingly individuals' base profile information to deliver multiple, customised versions of their curriculum vitae.

Finally, the *Recruitment and Competency Management Engine* will include functionalities for competency management at both strategic and tactical level addressed to corporate users, the latter including not only education providing institutions, but also public authorities, private companies and policy makers. The Recruitment and Competency Management Engine exposes its functionality through the *Competency Management Advisor Interface* which makes up the entry point to the following sub-components: i. a *Recruits' Profile Designer Module*, enabling recruiters to designate the criteria that candidates should meet, and thereby specify the type and level education, work experience and the rest of qualifications that they should possess as well as any other conditions and requirements they ought to fulfil, ii. a *Qualifications' Screening and Matching Module*, capable of retrieving applicants' credentials and juxtaposing these with recruiters' criteria to sort out a subset of appropriate candidates, iii. a *Selection and Recruiting Module*, applying advanced decision support algorithms on the subset of qualified candidates, to optimise candidate selection and allocation in corporate positions, iv. a *Competency Development, Evaluation and Gap Identification Module*, responsible for keeping track of employees' qualifications records and identifying competency deficit in relation to organisations' mid and long-term horizon goals and v. an *Advanced Decision Support Module*, featuring a variety of sophisticated data analytics, i.e., data mining, statistics' calculation, pattern/ trend recognition, data visualisation and other functionalities of both descriptive and prescriptive character, to support insights acquisition and informed decision making.

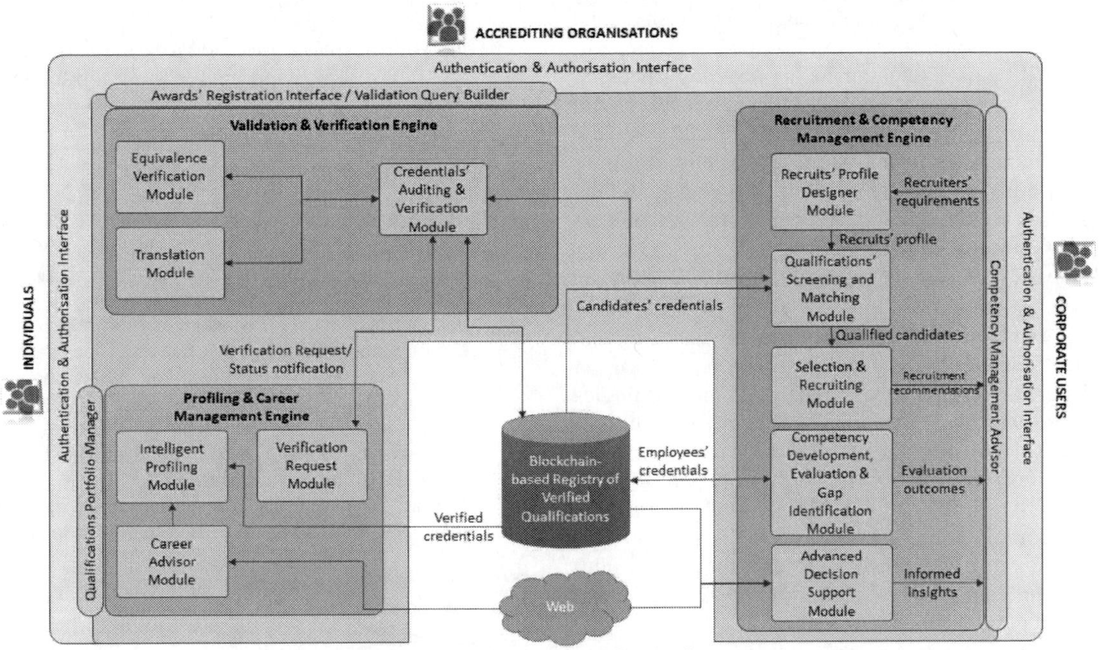

Figure 4. QualiChain Value Adding Services

From an end-user perspective and regarding the QualiChain platform presentation layer, the solution lays emphasis on intuitiveness and features beside the aforementioned management interfaces, appropriate authentication and authorisation interfaces for all targeted stakeholder groups, namely accrediting institutions, individuals and corporate users. Finally, the QualiChain data access layer envisages storage and retrieval of data from blockchain records regarding awards and qualifications, as well as from the web to the extent related statistics, job postings and other learning and career development opportunities are concerned.

B. *QualiChain Pilot Use Cases*

To test and validate the projected platform in its respective domains, it will be implemented in four distinct pilot use cases split between academia, private and public organisations. Specifically, the QualiChain pilots are the following:

1) Cross University Degree Equivalence Verification

Within this pilot use case, QualiChain will develop a methodology for representing the semantics of educational credentials, to support cross-institution and cross-context mapping between different forms of certifications. Existing vocabularies that describe learning goals and topics will be reused and extended to build a detailed knowledge model describing the entities relevant to educational accreditation and their relationships to each other, in the form of an ontology. This pilot will engage lifelong learners, students, job seekers and educational institutions.

2) Smart Curriculum Design and University Process Optimisation

This use case will be implemented in the School of Electrical and Computer Engineering of the NTUA. It will take advantage of QualiChain's analytics and decision support capabilities to analyse the current skill level of students, the school's curriculum and the labour market's requirements for the school's graduates to provide decision support for optimising the school's curriculum. Additionally, this pilot will leverage the blockchain ledger to verify student skills and qualifications with smart badges. This pilot will engage undergraduate and Ph.D. students of the school as well as professors and administrative bodies.

3) Staffing the Public Sector

This pilot use case lies in using the QualiChain platform and services for supporting and simplifying public sector recruitment and competency management procedures. Given that recruitment in public administration must be based on the principles of impartiality, transparency and fairness, this pilot will leverage the platform's blockchain to manage and verify the applications and other supporting documents submitted by candidates. Additionally, the recruitment and competency management services of QualiChain will be used to automate applications' checking and candidates' assessment and selection procedures, and respectively for supporting decisions related to the allocation of human resources within the public sector or employee mobility issues. This pilot will engage public administrations, recruitment firms, employees, job seekers and issuing organisations.

4) Provision of HR Consulting and Competency Management Services

This pilot will explore blockchain for easily checking and ensuring the availability of certain competencies in an individual curriculum. Also, data analytics methodologies and algorithms will be applied for the effective matching of skills, qualifications and competencies with job description requirements, not only for external selection, but also for internal mobility. Semantic technologies will be used to support corporate training and carrier management, throughout the entire individuals' job evolution. This pilot will engage public entities looking for new applicants, candidates and public workers.

IV. CONCLUSIONS

This publication presented QualiChain, a project aiming to develop a decentralised platform for storing, sharing and verifying academic and employment qualifications. Despite the fact that the project is still at an early stage, it has gathered the interest of the research community due to the innovative combination of technologies that it will leverage and the fact that it aims to create value to all stakeholders in the domains tackled. This is also reflected in the complexity of QualiChain's technical solution and the number of distinct pilot cases in which it will be implemented. The innovation potential of QualiChain is very strong, as it focuses on a domain, that of education credentials, that has largely resisted the pool of technology and where the improvement potential in the processes of certificates' archiving, management and verification, the information flow amongst stakeholders and the opportunity for offering value adding services on top of the aforementioned processes and developing new business and education models is literally huge. Disrupting any (or even more than one) of the aforementioned aspects can lead to substantial efficiency, productivity and transparency impacts, which should in turn have noticeable positive societal, economic, political and cultural effects.

ACKNOWLEDGMENT

This work has been co-funded by the European Union's Horizon 2020 research and innovation programme under the QualiChain project (https://qualichain-project.eu/), Grant Agreement No 822404.

REFERENCES

[1] M. Turkanovic, M. Holbl, K. Kosic, M. Hericko and A. Kamisalic, "EduCTX. A Blockchain-Based Higher Education Credit Platform," IEEE Access, pp. 5112-5127, 2018.

[2] W. Gräther et al., "Blockchain for education: lifelong learning passport," Proc. 1st ERCIM Blockchain Workshop 2018. European Society for Socially Embedded Technologies (EUSSET), pp. 1-8, 2018.

[3] A. F. Camilleri, A. Grech and A. Inamorato dos Santos, "Blockchain in education". Publications Office of the European Union, Luxembourg, 2017.

[4] J. Bear, "Degree mills: The billion-dollar industry that has sold over a million fake diplomas," Prometheus Books, 2012.

[5] CareerBuilder. https://www.careerbuilder.com/ [retrieved: February, 2020]

[6] StatisticBrain: Resume Falsification Statistics. https://www.statisticbrain.com/resume-falsification-statistics/ [retrieved: February, 2020]

[7] G. Mohamedbhai, "The Scourge of Fraud and Corruption in Higher Education," IHE, pp. 12-14, 2016. https://doi.org/10.6017/ihe.2016.84.9111.

[8] D. W. Chapman and S. Lindner, "Degrees of integrity. The threat of corruption in higher education," Studies in Higher Education, pp. 247-268, 2014. https://doi.org/10.1080/03075079.2014.927854.

[9] M. Sharples and J. Domingue, "The Blockchain and Kudos. A Distributed System for Educational Record, Reputation and Reward," European conference on technology enhanced learning, pp. 490–496, 2016.

[10] P. Devine, "Blockchain learning: can crypto-currency methods be appropriated to enhance online learning?", ALT Online Winter Conference 2015, pp. 7-10, 2015.

Towards A Blockchain-based Decentralised Educational Landscape

Niaz Chowdhury, Manoharan Ramachandran, Allan Third,
Alexander Mikroyannidis, Michelle Bachler and John Domingue
Knowledge Media Institute, The Open University
Milton Keynes, United Kingdom
email:{niaz.chowdhury, manoharan.ramachandran, allan.third,
alexander.mikroyannidis, michelle.bachler, john.domingue}@open.ac.uk

Abstract—**Institutions in the current educational landscape operate independently. They exhibit reluctance in sharing their teaching and qualifications with others due to the fear of damaging individuality. This practice, however, is counterproductive for the students as they suffer from various difficulties and get deprived of certain benefits. In this paper, we explore the possibility of finding a solution to this deadlock. We argue that Blockchain-based decentralisation can offer a passageway where educational institutions get to keep their individuality but participate in collaborations to help overcome the problems students face. Our principal contribution in this paper is a conceptual educational landscape to show how institutions could potentially manage record-keeping, credential verifications, and continued career support in a decentralised environment.**

Keywords–blockchain; decentralisation; verification; education.

I. Introduction

The primary role of educational institutions is to offer governance, teaching, qualifications and support towards a successful career of their graduates in the post-study period. In this practice, they exhibit a standalone, scattered and remote model. They do not show interest in sharing their teaching methods or qualifications with others due to the fear of damaging their goodwills and reputation. The roles of the institutions can also vary broadly. Some provide both tuition and degrees while others only teach and the degree comes from issuing authorities who do not offer teachings. The practice of universities issuing qualifications for other institutions having no right to confer the degree on their own is not rare either. In addition to maintaining their individuality, the complex nature of types and roles heavily contributed against decoupling educational institutions from their standalone model, making the education system inherently isolated.

This current model is inadequate, backdated and sometimes damaging. It cannot see the full academic history of a student; hence, institutions fail to act appropriately. This model is also unsupportive towards lifelong learners and students receiving micro-credentials. Amongst many shortcomings, the following are three prominent problems that students frequently encounter. First, students need to verify their qualifications every time they join a new job or a new course, which is time-consuming and expensive. Second, the centralised governance puts students records in danger as such practice increases the chances of corruption, manipulation and privacy violation. Third, and finally, institutions fail to give adequate career support, particularly for a more extended period when students achieve multiple qualifications from more than one institution.

While a universal institution is not a practical concept, students' miseries are genuine intricacies that need solving. In this paper, we show that employing Blockchain technology can help decentralising qualification verification, data governance and career support. We demonstrate how existing technologies and methods can be put together to offer a reasonable solution to these problems.

The remaining paper is organised into six sections. Section II presents the current educational landscape and identifies the problems, Section III reviews the technologies to be used in the proposal and Section IV describes potential decentralisation models. Finally, Section V presents the proposed Blockchain-based decentralised educational landscape before concluding the paper in Section VI.

II. Current Educational Landscape

Historically, education is an isolated system centred around teachers or teaching schools [1]. Before the establishment of formal institutions, pupils used to go to teachers' homes to receive an education. This practice gradually evolved, and both pupils and teachers started to gather at common locations, often at renowned places. This move began to establish the concept of school, although still not as a formal institution [2]. Raphael's celebrated fresco the School of Athens on the wall of Apostolic Palace in Vatican City is an excellent depiction of how the school used to look like in the ancient period (shown in Figure 1). Ancient Greece, Ancient Rome, Ancient India and Ancient China have well-documented histories of such schools [3]. By the time the University of Bologna opened its door to students in Europe roughly a millennium ago, the need for institutional education had echoed at different places across the continent and the universities of Paris, Oxford and Cambridge were established.

In this journey of evolution from teachers' home to formal institutions, one element remains common – the standalone and remote nature of the institutions. There are many lobby groups and collaborations between institutions for promoting their names and values, such as Ivy league (US), Russell Group (UK), U15 (Canada), G8 (Australia), Coimbra Group (Europe) and so on, but not many initiatives in giving joint teaching and degrees. Educational institutions have always been protective to safeguard their reputation as they fear sharing teaching

Figure 1. Raphael's celebrated fresco the School of Athens on the wall of Apostolic Palace in Vatican City.

practice and qualifications with others might put their goodwill in danger. Even institutions of the same status can have severe reluctance in joining such a union [4]. For instance, Imperial College London and University College London, two world-renowned universities from England, initiated a merger in a bid to form a large university capable of attracting twice the research fund universities such as Oxford or Cambridge can allure [5]. Although the alliance could help them achieve many benefits, it did not come through due to opposition from management and students of both universities [6].

In the present days, educational institutions play a broad role. Some provide governance, teaching, qualifications and career support. In contrast, others may provide a subset of these duties, such as awarding bodies confer qualifications while institutions without the right of giving their own degree contribute in teaching and governance. With the rise of the World Wide Web, online-based education and micro-credentials have recently become popular. Most of these qualifications come from distance learning and online institutions. The size and functional scope of these institutions are limited, making them provide slow verification assistance and almost no career support in the post-study period.

The current educational landscape shows us the practice has three broad problems. These are as follows:

A. Problem P1

It is a common practice that all educational institutions maintain individual databases of their own to store and hold students' records including their personal information. In most cases, students have no or limited control over their data and often remain oblivious to what exactly their institutions keep on their behalf. This centralised approach, in general, has been a subject of mounting concern as social awareness surrounding how users control their data continues to grow. Such an approach can cause alteration of data for numerous reasons including updates by mistakes, corruption and most importantly deliberate manipulation by the controlling administrators leading to tempering or removal of data without the owner's consent or knowledge. Privacy could be another solicitude as data can be viewed, shared or sold by the possessors.

B. Problem P2

Educational institutions maintain an old tradition of carrying trust through badges, diplomas and certificates. It used to work when there were fewer institutions, and people recognised the certificate issued by a specific university or school. However, as time passed by, people started to lose faith in paper certificates due to the availability of handy technology that can produce fraudulent documents. Instead, it became a new trend for the bearers of certificates, transcripts and other educational records to establish the authenticity of their papers. Sometimes they need to send documents to another school or an employer using official email of the providers, while some test scores, such as the International English Language Testing System (IELTS) or Graduate Record Examinations (GRE) need to come directly from the issuers by post. What seems to be the biggest irony in the education sector is that even the educational institutions that once proudly developed the convention of issuing certified documents now do not trust them and ask for verification at the time of admitting new students.

C. Problem P3

The existing education system is mainly scattered, where educational institutions operate standalone failing to provide continued career support for their students. There indeed exists a practice of helping current students and alumni to obtain jobs through arranging networking sessions in universities and colleges. Still, the impact of such events is limited, and the process lasts for a few years in the post-graduation period. Furthermore, institutions generally have access to records and degree information of the qualification they provide only and cannot access or verify their students' skills and diplomas obtained from other institutions. This limitation prevents them from adequately assessing one's potentials and helping them to apply for the right job and guide them to their career paths.

III. Technology Review

While forming alliances amongst the universities sharing their student records, teaching, and qualification does not seem practical under the current landscape, the problems P1, P2 and P3 desperately need solving. We, therefore, argue that it is time to look for a resolution elsewhere and propose a solution in this paper using existing technologies, such as Blockchain, distributed storage and linked data. Before we present the explanation of how these technologies offer the answers to the problems, we introduce them briefly below.

A. Blockchain Technology

A Blockchain is an immutable distributed ledger secured by cryptographic techniques, as shown in Figure 2, and managed by a decentralised community over a peer-to-peer network through incentivisation [7]. Each member of the community is commonly known as *node* who distributedly maintains the storage of the Blockchain. No node has the authority to make changes unless agreed by the majority of the network. The process of this agreement is called *consensus* [8].

The transactions of a Blockchain are called *immutable* because once inserted, they become permanent and cannot be

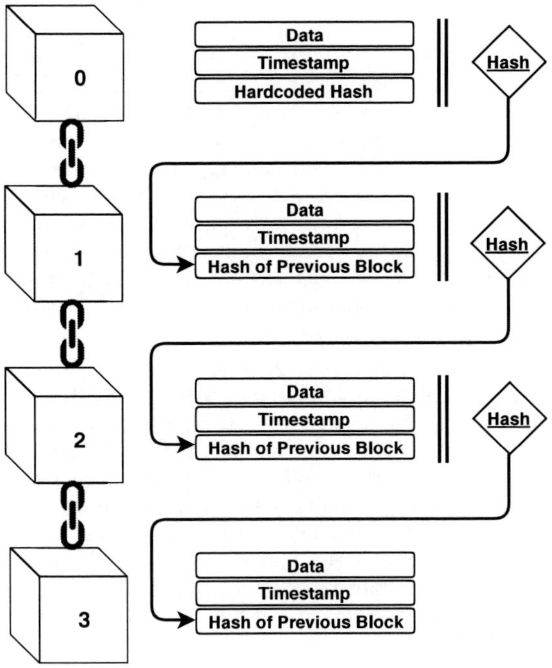

Figure 2. Each block in a Blockchain is chained to one another using cryptographic hashes creating the ultimate bond to develop the chain.

modified retroactively, not even by the authors, without the alteration of all subsequent transactions. The first block of the chain is called genesis block with subsequent blocks added through consensus between nodes. Various consensus methods, such as proof of work, proof of stake, proof of authority etc. are used in different protocols that allow nodes to compete for a pole position enabling them to insert the new block. The design of a Blockchain ensures that, once entered, contents of the blocks cannot be changed as long as no entities control more than 50% of the nodes. This property of Blockchain makes it trustworthy.

The progress in the development of Blockchain has taken the technology beyond the storage of records and includes distributed computing in the form of smart contracts. These are blocks of executable source code stored on a Blockchain with a published interface describing the methods and their parameters. The code gets executed when the corresponding transaction is added on the distributed ledger. Because the code fulfils the same requirements of the immutability of Blockchain data, smart contracts form trustworthy distributed computation [9].

B. Linked Data

Linked Data is a form of structured data interlinked with other data to become useful through semantic queries of associative and contextual nature. It extends the capability of Web data originally meant for only human readers to share information in a way that can be read automatically by machines [10]. Linked Data plays a vital role in integrating data in the presence of multiple data sources, making them interoperable.

Sir Berners-Lee, the founder of the World Wide Web, first coined the term in his note Linked Data. He also outlined four principles known as four rules for Linked Data. These rules state that Lined Data, i) Uses Uniform Resource Identifiers (URIs) as names of things, ii) Uses HTTP URIs to look up those names, iii) At the time of looking up a URI, provides useful information using the standards, such as Resource Description Framework (RDF) and SPARQL [11], and iv) Includes links to other URIs to discover more things [12].

C. Distributed Storage

Distributed Storage is a decentralised approach of storing data in one or multiple servers. HyperText Transfer Protocol, or more commonly known as HTTP, is considered the biggest distributed database where peers can access particular data from anywhere in the world. HTTP became outdated due to its centralised nature. Peer to Peer (P2P) file system, such as BitTorrent, took its place. Although BitTorrent comes with a lot of advantages, several drawbacks, such as unstable downloading, unverified publisher and a lack of incentive mechanism restricted its use [13].

After the arrival of Blockchain, a combination of the distributed file system and Blockchain becomes a promising solution where the former provides the storage facilities while the latter ensures the integrity of the data and provides a way to achieve incentives. Interplanetary Filesystem (IPFS) [14], Swarm [15], and FileCoin [16] are some of these modern distributed storages.

D. Solid: SOcial LInked Data

Sir Berners-Lee originally viewed the World Wide Web as a decentralised network. It was close to a peer-to-peer network assuming each user of the Web would be an active editor and contributor, creating and linking content to form an interconnected web of links [17]. The Internet, however, gradually turns out to be the opposite - an ideal example of the centralised paradigm. Sir Berners-Lee's response to this evolution of the World Wide Web is Solid. Solid, derived from **SO**cial **LI**nked **D**ata, is a set of rules and tools for developing decentralised social applications based on Linked Data. It uses as much as possible the existing W3C standards and protocols [18].

Solid aims to modifying the centralised client-server paradigm, improving peer-to-peer networking in a manner that adds more control and performance features than its traditional concept, such as BitTorrent. Its central focus is to enable the discovery and sharing of information in a way that preserves privacy. It allows users to store personal data in Pods (Personal online data stores) hosted at the location of users' desire. They also have the flexibility to distribute data among several pods; allowing them to organise various types of data (personal, contact, health, financial) in multiple pods with varying degree of access control. In a nutshell, Solid allows users to retain complete ownership of their data, including where to store the data and who has permission to access it [19].

IV. DECENTRALISED MODELS

Disintegrating educational institutions from their isolation does not necessarily have to come through sharing teaching or credentials. Decentralising their governance can potentially make them open to the authorised parties who can access information without any formal union. This approach establishes a trade-off where institutions get to keep their individuality but participate in collaborations to help overcome the existing problems.

Decentralisation means the transfer of authority from one or more central controlling body to local representatives – in the context of web technology, these representatives are generally users. In an educational landscape, the institutions act as the central controlling bodies while students are users. Decentralisation gives students the authority over their data. They get to decide the storage location of their data and can grant access to specific entities while disallowing such access to others. There are several ways to achieve decentralisation. The following describes three models that can be used to decentralise the educational landscape.

A. Model M1: Pure Blockchain-based Decentralisation

Blockchain is decentralised by nature and a distributed ledger that can be used as data storage; hence, it acts as a useful tool for decentralisation. By design, data on a Blockchain are immutable; therefore, no further actions are required to ensure data integrity. There are different ways available to store data on Blockchain. The most efficient way of storing data on a Blockchain requires a smart contract. This model provides a fully distributed storage with a firm guarantee of data integrity. The tradeoff is, however, the cost as it requires payment for every contract deployment. The cost varies based on the size of the smart contract; the longer the contract, higher the fees required to deploy it. Amongst other shortcomings, lack of privacy is one that hinders its useability significantly. Besides, there exists various types of Blockchain, and depending on their kinds, advantages and disadvantages may differ. The following describes three major Blockchains, public, private and consortium, and their suitability.

1) Public Blockchain (M1-A): A public Blockchain has absolutely no access restrictions. Anyone with an Internet connection can act as a participating node or send transactions. For a public Blockchain to keep operating, the platform provides some form of economic incentive or reward, often in the way of giving away some native currency, but it can be fees too.

A public Blockchain is more trustworthy due to being managed by a large community where no one has particular superiority over others in its governance and decision making. Nevertheless, it is not privacy-friendly due to being always open. This feature allows anyone to read its contents unless encrypted. Public Blockchains are expensive and storing and accessing data on this type of Blockchain can incur huge fees. In general, Blockchains do not come with built-in searching mechanisms, rather applications require developers to implement their own search functionalities. This inefficacy meets with another problem in public Blockchains. Their contents grow very fast, making the search even more difficult.

2) Private Blockchain (M1-B): A private Blockchain is one that a single entity controls. Participating nodes require permission to join a private Blockchain and may have limited privileges. Because of access restrictions, private Blockchains offer some degrees of privacy and they do not grow as fast as public Blockchains. A big advantage of using private Blockchains is that they do not require *real money* to store and access data. However, they are not entirely trustworthy. The entity that controls their governance and operations may retain a superior power for tempering data.

3) Consortium Blockchain (M1-C): A consortium Blockchain can have the best of both public and private Blockchains. It is sometimes referred to as a shared ledger or federated ledger because of multiple approved parties using it within a federated environment. These Blockchains are private Blockchains operated by a group or consortium and usually require permission. However, instead of a single body controlling it, various organisations can share governance. The administrators of a consortium Blockchain may restrict users' reading rights and allow a limited set of trusted nodes to execute the consensus protocol.

The main advantage of consortium Blockchains is they can bring the best of both public and private Blockchains. Because of having access restrictions (as only invited, and approved entities can join the Blockchain), they are more privacy-friendly than a public Blockchain. Besides, unlike a private Blockchain, a single entity may not hold control of the consortium Blockchains, making them more trustworthy. However, consortium Blockchains can still be vulnerable. Their number of controlling authority is likely to be limited, making it possible to group and a launch 51% attack quickly [8].

B. Model M2: Distributed Storage-based Decentralisation

Potential decentralisation strategies using distributed storage include two possible routes. The first is solely based on distributed storage, while the second option uses a combination of distributed storage and Blockchain.

1) Distributed Storage Only (M2-A): Data can be distributed across multiple servers by duplication with anyone wishing to use the desired copy must know its precise location. This approach, however, fails to ensure the integrity of the data as there remains no straightforward way to identify if the data is altered. An improved method could be making the distributed storage to act as a filesystem for storing data with clients keeping copies of hashes of all files locally. Clients can then run the queries with these hashes to retrieve the data (e.g., IPFS). This technique helps to verify the integrity of the data because if the stored data gets altered, there will be a mismatch between the locally stored hash and the hash of the data, tearing apart the connection. In such cases, clients' query does not return the altered data, and in the event of no results, we can assume that either the data got tempered or went missing [20].

2) Distributed Storage and Blockchain (M2-B): Instead of using distributed storage alone, another approach is to incorporate a Blockchain in the management of the data [21]. This use of a distributed storage with Blockchain can help to reduce the cost encountered while using pure Blockchain-based decentralisation. This model makes the decentralisation cost-effective but incorporates guaranteed data integrity. It also enables clients to avoid the need for maintaining the hashes locally; instead, data goes to a distributed storage while hashes and their associated timestamps stay as a trustworthy record on the distributed ledger [23].

C. Model M3: Solid-based Decentralisation

Solid can offer a third rote to decentralisation. Solid pods are decentralised and give users full control of their data. They also ensure privacy as only approved entities can read and access the data. There are two possible ways Solid can be used, standalone or in combination with a Blockchain.

1) Solid-only Decentralisation (M3-A): The use of Solid is sufficient to introduce decentralisation. The ability of users while using Solid to store various types of data, such as personal, financial, educational, health, and so on, in different Solid pods makes way for creating customised privacy control. Users may give certain entities access to their personal and educational data but restrict access to financial and health data while using Solid. A significant shortcoming of Solid-only decentralisation is trust. Because of users having full control over their data, they can modify them anytime. Third parties having to rely on user data can find this model less prudent.

2) Solid and Blockchain (M3-B): The use of a Blockchain with Solid pods is a type of decentralisation where Solid holds the data while a hash of it goes to the Blockchain, ensuring the integrity and trust of the user-controlled stored data. This strategy brings all the benefits that a Solid-only model can offer and solves the trust issues. Because a hash of the data goes to the Blockchain, third parties can quickly check the integrity by hashing the data stored on the pods and matching it with its Blockchain counterpart [22].

V. PROPOSED EDUCATIONAL LANDSCAPE

In decentralising the educational landscape, we propose a four-layer architecture where Blockchain forms the first layer from the bottom. The design embraces three other layers on top of the Blockchain layer, namely data layer, verification layer and support layer – Figure 3, shows the architecture and the arrangement of the layers in the design.

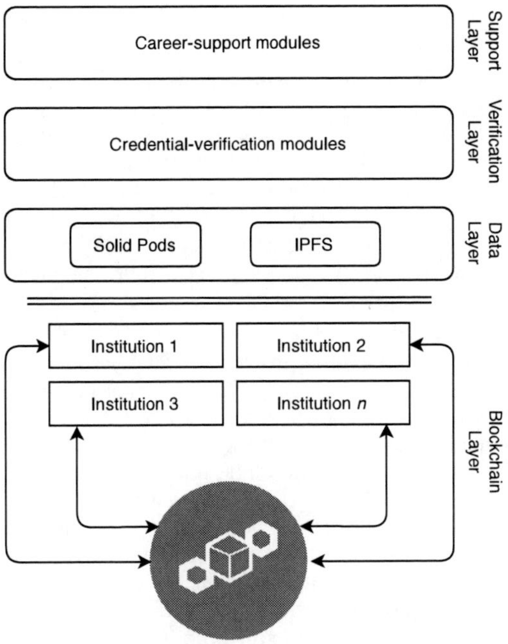

Figure 3. The layered architecture of the Blockchain-based proposed decentralised educational landscape

Three problems, P1, P2 and P3, that we identified in Section 2 represent three broad areas of the educational landscape and form the top three layers in our design. P1 represents data management and governance and creates the data layer, P2 focuses on the credential verifications and forms verification layer, and finally, P3 states the continued career support for the students and produces the support layer.

A. Blockchain Layer

The Blockchain layer forms the foundation of our proposed architecture. We recommend using a consortium Blockchain due to its ability to mimic the best of both private and public ledgers. In our architecture, participating institutions will join and govern this consortium Blockchain. The remaining three layers will operate over the Blockchain and will have the ability to access it directly or through other layers.

B. Data Layer

The second layer in our architecture is the data layer responsible for data governance. It manages students data in a decentralised style. Institutions generally maintain a central database to hold all kinds of data, including students records and information. Data layer disintegrate this database and distribute its contents to various stakeholders, such as students, teachers and administrators. Amongst the suitable decentralised models, M1-C, M2-B and M3-B from Section IV look useful for developing this layer. However, due to lack of privacy, M1-C does not fit for sensitive data like personal information, students record and results; therefore, we prefer M2-B and M3-B, which means storing data on either IPFS or Solid with their hashes on the Blockchain. Between these two models, Solid offers added benefits in the form of advanced access control; hence, we use Solid while describing the remaining architecture.

The data layer consists of Solid pods managed by students, teachers and administrators. Students will have their personal information on their pod that they grant access to only their institutions. Administrators of the institutions can have some student data on their pods too, such as results and qualifications. In this case, they grant at least read access to students so that they can be aware of what data institutions hold on their behalf. This access may be time-dependent; for instance, results data will be made visible to students only when the results are announced. Teachers can have their pods to store and share students marks and initial results. They may only grant access to this data to administrators before the results are finalised. Institutions should have specific policies tailored to their practice concerning when to share data and how.

In a decentralised architecture, multiple sources can hold the data making it difficult to run queries using traditional methods. Linked Data and federated query can help to solve this problem. It works as follows: Each and every entity in a Solid pod are represented in the form of URIs. If the data stored in the Solid pods are expressed in RDF format, it can be queried using SPARQL, which is a query language for accessing linked data [11]. SPARQL can also be used to query data from multiple Solid pods as long as the query engine is granted access to the Solid pods [20].

The data layer solves P1. It gives students control over their data and allows them to see what their educational institution holds on their behalf. By employing Blockchain, data layer also ensures the integrity of the information contained by students and administrators.

C. Verification Layer

The verification layer is responsible for verifying credentials. This layer helps students and lifelong learners to get their qualifications checked for potential employers and other educational institutions. All institutions that confer degrees or award micro-credentials must give students a badge or similar object that students keep in their Solid pods. Later at the time of applying for courses in other institutions or jobs in companies, they show the badge as a representative of their qualification certificate.

Badges are digital objects that students can temper. Therefore, to ensure the integrity of the data, issuing authorities insert hash of the issued badge to the consortium Blockchain. They also keep a record of the credentials to their Solid pods with students having access to it. An entity wishing to verify a particular credential does not have to go to the issuing authority. Again, Linked Data and federated query help us achieve this. The verifier can be a web application which seeks access to a Solid pod stored qualification badge, which then hashed by the web application. The badge hash is compared with the hash stored on the Blockchain which was previously uploaded by the badge issuer. If it matches, then the employer knows that the student badge is valid [24].

The verification layer solves P2. By making verification automated, it allows students to get their credentials verified at the expense of a few mouse clicks. It reduces time and saves money for both students and parties who check their credentials.

D. Support Layer

The support layer paves the path for both educational and non-educational institutions to participate in providing career support to students and lifelong learners. These supports can come in various ways, including suggesting jobs, courses and preparing automated CVs.

Our architecture already showed how data are made accessible for approved entities through Linked Data and federated query engines. Educational institutions can run federated searches on the available job and qualifications of their graduates to pinpoint suitable employment for them. Potential employers can also benefit from this decentralised architecture as they can shortlist potential candidates on their own through verified qualification matching. Educational institutions can further suggest courses to students based on the qualifications they do not have but would help them land their preferred jobs. Institutions and commercial companies providing HR support can also use the data to offer students smart resumes where verified credentials and job information will be appended automatically.

The support layer solves P3 by opening data to approved parties. In a centralised and isolated system, educational institutions cannot see what qualification students have in addition to theirs. In this proposed architecture, institutions do so; hence can come up with job and course suggestions more precisely.

VI. CONCLUSION

Educational institutions behave like islands – isolated and remote. Their reluctance in sharing teaching and credentials create sufferings for the students. In this paper, we try to find a trade-off proposing a decentralised educational landscape where institutions do not have to lose their individuality but can still participate in collaborations. Using existing technologies, we showed how record-keeping, credential verifications and continued career support could be provided in a decentralised atmosphere.

REFERENCES

[1] M. Chiappetta, "Historiography and Roman Education", History of Education Journal 4, no. 4, pp. 149-156.

[2] A. J. Coulson, "Market Education: The Unknown History", ed. 1, Transaction Publishers, 1999.

[3] F. Cordasco, "A Brief History of Education: Handbook of Information on Greek, Roman, Medieval, Renaissance and Modern Educational Practice", Revised ed., Rowman & Littlefield Publishers, 1976.

[4] Opinion, "Looking after number one", Nature, Volume 419, Issue 6909, October 2002.

[5] S. Cassidy, "Imperial College and UCL in merger talks to create 'the world's number one university'", The Independent, 15 October, 2002.

[6] D. MacLeod, "Opposition ends Imperial and UCL merger dream", The Guardian, 18 November, 2002.

[7] S. Nakamoto, "Bitcoin: A Peer-to-Peer Electronic Cash System", Bitcoin.org, Last Access 29 February 2020.

[8] P. Franco, "Understanding Bitcoin", ed 1, Wiley, 2015

[9] N. Chowdhury, "Inside Blockchain, Bitcoin, and Cryptocurrencies", ed 1, Taylor and Francis, 2019

[10] D. Wood, M. Zaidman, L. Ruth, and M. Hausenblas, "Linked Data", Manning Publications, ed. 1, 2014.

[11] M. Schmidt, M. Meier and G. Lausen "Foundations of SPARQL query optimization", in Proceedings of the 13th International Conference on Database Theory, pp. 4–33, Lausanne, Switzerland, March 2010.

[12] T. Berners-Lee, "Linked Data: Design Issues", w3.org, 2006, URL: www.w3.org/DesignIssues/LinkedData.html, Last Access 29 February 2020

[13] H. Huang, J. Lin, B. Zheng, Z. Zheng, and J. Bian, "When Blockchain Meets Distributed File Systems: An Overview, Challenges, and Open Issues", IEEE Access, 2020

[14] J. Benet, "IPFS - Content Addressed, Versioned, P2P File System", arXiv.org, Last Access 29 February 2020.

[15] J. H. Hartman, I. Murdock and T. Spalink, "The Swarm scalable storage system", in proceedings of the 19th IEEE International Conference on Distributed Computing Systems, Austin, TX, USA, June 1999.

[16] J. Benet and N. Greco, "Filecoin: A decentralized storage network", Technical Report, Protoc. Labs, 2018.

[17] T. Berners-Lee, "Weaving the Web: The Past, Present and Future of the World Wide Web by its Inventor", HarperCollins, 1999.

[18] A. Sambra et al. "Solid: A Platform for Decentralized Social Applications Based on Linked Data", Technical Report, MIT CSAIL & Qatar Computing Research Institute

[19] E. Mansour et al. "A Demonstration of the Solid Platform for Social Web Applications", in proceedings of the 25th International Conference Companion on World Wide Web, pp. 223–226, Montreal, Canada, April 2016.

[20] A. Third and J. Domingue, "LinkChains: Exploring the space of decentralised trustworthy Linked Data", in proceedings of Decentralising the Semantic Web, Vienna, Austria, July 2017.

[21] A. Third and J. Domingue, "Linked Data Indexing of Distributed Ledgers. in proceedings of the 1st International Workshop on Linked Data and Distributed Ledgers", Perth, Australia, April 2017.

[22] Third, A. and Domingue, J., LinkChains: Trusted Personal Linked Data, in proceedings of BlockSW, Auckland, New Zealand, October 2019.

[23] J. Domingue, A. Third, and M. Ramachandran, "The FAIR TRADE Framework for Assessing Decentralised Data Solutions", in proceedings of World Wide Web Conference, pp. 866—882, San Francisco, USA, May 2019.

[24] A. Mikroyannidis, A. Third, and J. Domingue, "Decentralising online education using blockchain technology", in proceedings of the Online, Open and Flexible Higher Education Conference, Madrid, October 2019

Digital Transformation of Education Credential Processes and Life Cycles – A Structured Overview on Main Challenges and Research Questions

Ingo R. Keck
Scientific Data Management
TIB Leibniz Information Centre
for Science and Technology
Hannover, Germany
Email: Ingo.Keck@tib.eu

Maria-Esther Vidal
Scientific Data Management
TIB Leibniz Information Centre
for Science and Technology
Hannover, Germany
Email: Maria.Vidal@tib.eu

Lambert Heller
Open Science Lab
TIB Leibniz Information Centre
for Science and Technology
Hannover, Germany
Email: Lambert.Heller@tib.eu

***Abstract*—In this article, we look at the challenges that arise in the use and management of education credentials, and from the switch from analogue, paper-based education credentials to digital education credentials. We propose a general methodology to capture qualitative descriptions and measurable quantitative results that allow to estimate the effectiveness of a digital credential management system in solving these challenges. This methodology is applied to the EU H2020 project QualiChain use case, where five pilots have been selected to study a broad field of digital credential workflows and credential management.**

Keywords–Credentials; Education credentials; Digitisation; Challenges in digitisation.

I. INTRODUCTION

Education credentials are an important part of our modern life. Pupils exit schools with a set of marks certified on their final school report, then, based on these results, they are able to apply for acceptance at higher education institutes or for apprenticeship. Students and employees continue to collect credentials at university, at work or via other ways of education. Even today, when digitisation has entered into almost every part of our lives, these education credentials often still are printed and written on paper. These paper-based credentials present several problems in practice. For example, managing of these credentials applying for a job position is tiresome for the applicant and even more so for the company that offers the position. Indeed, most companies nowadays require scans of the paper credentials and will only check the validity of the originals once the candidate for the position has been selected, to avoid the manual labour involved. Additionally, surveys show that lying about education and employment credentials is a common problem. According to a survey by CareerBuilder [1], 58% of employers have caught a lie on a resume. Similar findings arise from another recent survey by StatisticBrain [2], which reports that over half of resumes and job applications (53%) contain falsifications and over three quarters (78%) are misleading. Digitisation of education credentials has the potential to make credential handling both easier and more secure. Nevertheless, it is important to ask the correct questions to be able to investigate how well a solution performs in the implementation and management of digital education credentials.

The main contribution in this work in progress article is to present the main challenges encountered in education credential management and usage, and in the changes from analogue to digital credential workflows. We propose specific questions that will allow an qualitative and quantitative assessment of the performance of a credential management system and infrastructure in regard of these challenges (given in Table I). Finally, we introduce the use case of the EU Horizon 2020 project QualiChain [3], where these research questions will be evaluated with the help of the participants in the project's pilots.

The article is organised as follows: In Section II, we elaborate the different challenges we encountered while analysing the reports and questionnaires provided by the QualiChain pilots. In Section III, we propose a set of questions for every challenge presented in the previous section. In Section IV, we present the use case of QualiChain. The article closes with Section V where our conclusions and future work are outlined.

II. CHALLENGES IN EDUCATION CREDENTIAL MANAGEMENT

How can the performance of a solution offering the issuing, management and verification of digital education credentials be evaluated? Based on the results acquired in [4], we propose to segment the questions of interest into three subtopics, that follow the process of changing from an analogue to a digital setting:

A. *Challenges of paper-based credentials*;
B. *Challenges of transition to digital credentials*; and
C. *Challenges of digital credentials.*

In the following sections, we present these experienced difficulties and propose ways how to measure the performance of a presented solution for the implementation and management of digital education credentials.

A. Challenges of Paper-Based Credentials

Paper-based credentials are the state of the art and have a history dating back to medieval times. Their use over centuries makes it obvious that, before digitisation, they were widely seen as the best solution. However, the developments in the last decades and the move to digital workflows increased the pressure on analogue, paper-based credentials and lead to increasing problems, especially in the field of fraud prevention.

1) Fraud and Verification: Advances in digital printing make it continuously more difficult to protect paper-based credentials against fraud. As already mentioned, a survey by CareerBuilder [1] reports that 58% of employers have caught a lie on a resume and 33% of them have seen an increase in resume embellishments and fabrications like embellished skill sets (57%), embellished responsibilities (55%), dates of employment (42%), job titles (34%), academic degrees (33%), companies worked for (26%) and awards (18%). A different survey [2] states that over half of resumes and job applications (53%) contain falsifications and over three quarters (78%) are misleading. Most issuers do not have the capabilities to use advanced falsification protection in their paper credentials, compared to what is done, for example, for paper-based money. Without a general standard, it would also be impossible for a non-expert to decide if the credential in front of him/her has the correct characteristics, as there are over 3000 higher education establishments in the European Union alone [5]. Instead, institutions and states commonly register important credentials and allow interested individuals to inquire on the validity of a presented credential. The UK, for example, offers the Higher Education Datacheck service [6]. The use of this service is chargeable, and the process can take up to seven days [7]. The process is also highly manual and time consuming.

2) Dependence on Issuer: The problems with fraud make it difficult for other than official education establishments to issue education credentials. This leads to the problem that learners will be unable to furnish sufficient and incontestable proof over several types of qualifications gained outside this established system. In the job market, written recommendation statements (also easy to falsify) or contact persons of reference are used to compensate for this. These methods are also manual and time costing for the people involved. The challenge to correctly identify the issuer of such as statements is related to this problem. Additionally, this can be the reason why direct access to reference persons often is preferred, as in this case the authenticity of the reference person can be checked by other means, like contact over official phone numbers or email addresses.

3) Handling: Paper-based credentials are easy to handle and store for the bearer, but in situations where many credentials have to be collected, screened and analysed, the high manual handling costs make their use expensive. This leads to a time consuming and costly recruitment process. For staffing private and especially public sector organisations it can be challenging to efficiently handle competency management in large organisational structures, as was reported in our questionnaire collection at the QualiChain pilots.

4) Data Security: Using high-quality acid free paper and storage in low humidity and at room temperature in pest free environments, paper has successfully been archived over many decades. Additionally, data protection can be enforced by physical access restrictions that are commonly available. However, most users of paper-based credentials outside of official archives and libraries lack the means of long-term storage, which makes paper-based credentials vulnerable to loss and damage. This is made more severe by the impossibility to create identical copies of paper-based credentials.

B. Challenges of Transition to Digital Credentials

Any solution that asks users to move from a well-established analogue paper-based workflow to a digital workflow, will face challenges in this transition. In the following points we present the issues we encountered in our data collection.

1) Digitisation of Existing Credentials: Analogue credentials are put into existence using written text, images, drawings and security characteristics in various forms. To retain all this information in digital form is difficult, and to efficiently work with the content of the credential, it is necessary to convert the unstructured text, for example gained by a scan of the document, into structured data, that has been semantically enriched.

2) Interaction Between Analogue and Digital Workflows: While workflows for both digital and analogue paper-based credentials exist, it is desirable to cater for both types, if technically feasible and sensible. Often this will mean making manual adjustments possible in a digital workflow or to temporarily create digital twins of paper-based credentials to incorporate them into pure digital workflows. This can also mean that digital credentials are printed out, to be included in paper-based credential workflows.

C. Challenges of Digital Credentials

Digital representations of credentials have their own challenges, that may be quite different from the paper-based ones.

1) Private Data Protection: Digital data can easily be copied, and creating identical copies of digital data is part of the normal workflow in IT. If, for example, a digital credential is sent from the issuer over a secure channel to the credential holder, its actual data is copied multiple times in the process: The credential is copied from the data storage at the issuer to the network stack of the issuers system, then copied into a transport format, copied over various relays in the communication system till it is copied once more into the network stack of the receiver, unpacked and finally copied into the receiving application's memory. However, this characteristic of digital data makes it also easy to leak private data in the process. Where in paper-based credentials simple physical access control often is enough, for digital credentials, access control has also to be secured digitally.

2) Data Security: Digital data is stored in physical storage and this storage will degenerate over time. It is, therefore, important to be able to copy the digital credential to new physical storage and to continuously monitor the quality of the storage before the degradation leads to damaged data. In libraries the "lots of copies keep stuff safe" (LOCKS) model has been successfully implemented for electronic publications, based on the idea that independent copies of the same data in physical and geographical independent data stores ensure high data security and availability [8].

3) Data Management: Unlike their paper-based siblings, digital credentials can only be perceived by the user if their content or metadata is rendered in a perceivable form (usually visual). Management systems need to ensure that users know what is stored and what is transmitted if requested.

TABLE I. PROPOSED RESEARCH QUESTIONS TO EVALUATE THE PERFORMANCE OF A DIGITAL EDUCATION CREDENTIAL MANAGEMENT SYSTEM IN SOLVING THE CHALLENGES EXPERIENCED BY THE USER.

Challenge	Question	Units
Fraud protection and verification	How is the system protected against fraud?	qualitative
	What are the costs of a successful attack against the fraud protection?	time, money
Issuer dependence	What are the requirements for an issuer of digital credentials?	qualitative
	How much does issuing a credential cost?	time, money
Handling	Describe the workflow of a credential in the system.	qualitative
	How much does handling of a credential in the workflow cost?	time, money
Data security	How is the credential stored in the system?	quantitative
	Is the credential data format public and open?	yes/no
	How many independent copies of the credential are stored in the system at any time?	number
	How is the credential secured against accidental loss or data change?	quantitative
	How is the credential secured against unauthorised, but intentional, loss or change of data?	quantitative
Digitisation of existing credentials	How can existing analogue credentials be included into the digital workflow?	quantitative
	Is the content of the analogue credential converted to structured data to the same level of detail as digital credentials?	yes/no
Interaction between analogue and digital workflows	How can the system interact at the same time with digital and analogue credentials	quantitative
	How much increases the effort in the workflow, if digital and analogue credentials are mixed?	time, money
Private data protection	How is the private data stored in the system protected against unauthorised access?	quantitative
	What are the costs of a successful attack against the private data protection?	time, money
Data management	How is the data managed from the user perspective?	quantitative
	Can the user tell at any time of the workflow, what data exactly he/she is working with?	yes/no
	Can the user tell at any time of the workflow, who is able to access the data in question?	yes/no
Data sovereignty	How is data sovereignty enforced in the system?	quantitative
	Can the holder of the credential decide at any time of the workflow, who is able to access the data in question?	yes/no
	How much does it cost the user to store the data under his/her exclusive physical access?	time, money
	What are the costs of a successful attack against the access protection (access, denial of service, data change)?	time, money
	If there are other possibilities of storage, how convenient are they to the user?	time money
	What are the costs of a successful attack against these other storage possibilities (access, denial of service, data change)?	time, money

4) Data Sovereignty: The ease of copying of digital data allows for the storage of digital credentials physically far from the users, for example, on the cloud. However, this also means that the actual data then is outside the physical oversight of the user. The term "data sovereignty" [9] has been coined in recent years to describe "the idea that users, being citizens or companies, have control over their data" [10].

III. PROPOSED RESEARCH QUESTIONS

In this section, we collect the questions whose answers will be utilised to validate the effectiveness of a system devised to achieve the challenges presented in the previous Section II. Each presented topic translates into a set of questions. We start each topic with a question asking for a qualitative description of how the proposed solution approaches the relevant challenge and then, by adding quantitative questions that should enable us to measure the effect that the proposed solution has on each challenge in a given use case. Using this mixed qualitative and quantitative approach, it should be possible to compare a digital credential solution to the status quo of non-digital workflows.

In Table I, our research questions are presented; they are grouped according to the challenges presented in Section II. The challenge *data security* affects both digital and paper-based credentials in very similar ways, so we were able to combine all relevant questions into one field.

IV. USE CASE

The EU Horizon 2020 research and innovation action QualiChain "targets the creation, piloting and evaluation of a decentralised platform for storing, sharing and verifying education and employment qualifications and focuses on the assessment of the potential of blockchain technology, algorithmic techniques and computational intelligence for disrupting the domain of public education, as well as its interfaces with private education, the labour market, public sector administrative procedures and the wider socio-economic developments."[11] The fundamental idea of the project is to build an open source, distributed platform supporting the storage, sharing and verification of education credentials. This platform will allow for the implementation of additional services which will fulfil the needs of the participating actors, such as data analytics and decision support systems. QualiChain hosts five pilot projects distributed over Europe (for details please see [12]), where the system is tested in four real-world scenarios:

- Lifelong learning;
- Smart curriculum design;
- Staffing the public sector; and
- Providing HR consultancy and competency management services

We provided online questionnaires to support the participants in the pilots in the definition of the use cases, challenges and possible research questions, as well as to define key performance indicators. These questionnaires were filled in and discussed with the people involved in the pilots in early 2019. The process is discussed in detail in [4] and not repeated here for the sake of brevity.

V. Conclusion and Future Work

The intention of this article is to discuss the main challenges in education credential management and to present a methodology to both qualitative and quantitative measure a system's effectiveness in addressing them. Additionally, we aim at gathering feedback from the scientific community regarding these measurements and their adequacy. We apply this methodology to the use cases of the Horizon 2020 EU Project QualiChain, that cover a wide area of applications of education credentials. This will allow us an in deep evaluation of the project's performance. Based on the experience we will gather in this process, we plan to extend this work in the future to a full framework for the evaluation of the performance of education credential management solutions. This framework should be able to capture the whole life cycle of education credentials from creation and issuing over storage, management and access control, towards credential expiring or retraction.

Acknowledgement

This work has received funding from the European Union's Horizon 2020 research and innovation programme under grant agreement No 822404 (QualiChain).

References

[1] *Fifty-eight percent of employers have caught a lie on a resume, according to a new careerbuilder survey.* [Online]. Available: https://www.careerbuilder.com/share/aboutus/pressreleasesdetail.aspx?sd=8%2F7%2F2014&id=pr837&ed=12%2F31%2F2014 (visited on 2020-02-24).

[2] *Statisticbrain - resume falsification statistics.* [Online]. Available: https://www.statisticbrain.com/resume-falsification-statistics/ (visited on 2020-02-24).

[3] *QualiChain – decentralised qualifications' verification and management for learner empowerment, education reengineering and public sector transformation.* [Online]. Available: https://qualichain-project.eu (visited on 2020-02-24).

[4] I. Keck *et al.*, "D7.1 – qualichain pilots preparation handbook", Tech. Rep., 2019. [Online]. Available: https://alfresco.epu.ntua.gr/share/s/AQjQwquNRwOl-CtaHFDBLQ (visited on 2020-02-24).

[5] European Commission, *The role of universities in the europe of knowledge*, 2003. [Online]. Available: https://eur-lex.europa.eu/legal-content/EN/TXT/?uri=LEGISSUM:c11067 (visited on 2020-02-24).

[6] HECSU, *Prospects hedd verification + authentication.* [Online]. Available: https://hedd.ac.uk/ (visited on 2020-02-24).

[7] D. Matthews, "What blockchain technology could mean for universities", *Times Higher Education*, Aug. 2017. [Online]. Available: https://www.timeshighereducation.com/news/what-blockchain-technology-could-mean-for-universities (visited on 2020-02-24).

[8] V. A. Reich, "Lots of copies keep stuff safe as a cooperative archiving solution for e-journals", *Issues in Science and Technology Librarianship*, 2002. [Online]. Available: http://doi.org/10.5062/F47P8WCW (visited on 2020-02-06).

[9] R. Posch, "Digital sovereignty and it-security for a prosperous society", in *Informatics in the Future*, H. Werthner and F. van Harmelen, Eds., Cham: Springer International Publishing, 2017, pp. 77–86, ISBN: 978-3-319-55735-9.

[10] S. Amaro, *Europe's dream to claim its 'digital sovereignty' could be the next big challenge for us tech giants*, Nov. 2019. [Online]. Available: https://www.cnbc.com/2019/11/20/us-tech-could-face-new-hurdles-as-europe-considers-digital-sovereignty.html (visited on 2020-02-24).

[11] *QualiChain – decentralised qualifications' verification and management for learner empowerment, education reengineering and public sector transformation*, Nov. 2018. [Online]. Available: https://cordis.europa.eu/project/rcn/218758_en.html (visited on 2020-02-24).

[12] C. Agostinho *et al.*, "D2.2 – qualichain stakeholders' requirements and use cases", Tech. Rep., 2019. [Online]. Available: https://alfresco.epu.ntua.gr/share/s/EflUU9mbTESnrZo74WAZHg (visited on 2020-02-24).

Fingers and Toes: A Hidden BioMetric Story

Rachel M. Stange
Lord Fairfax Community College
Middletown, VA, USA
Email: rms25145@email.vccs.edu

***Abstract*— The work presented in this paper has two main objectives. The first objective was to determine if fully related siblings have similar fingerprints due to genetics. The data showed that only one sibling set had less than 40% similarity. The right index finger of all sets had a median of 40%, even within one set of siblings that had only a 20% match on the right thumb. The mode for the left index fingers was 40% with twelve of the fifteen sibling sets being at that level. The majority of the sets were at 33% or higher, yet two sets had no matching major classifications and the mode for ridge classifications was 80%. Arches were the least found major classification and loops were the most popular major classification. The hypothesis was that fully related siblings would have similar fingerprints. The results support the hypothesis even though the fingerprints may have slight differences within some classifications, all sibling sets having at least an 80% similarity. The second objective was to determine if fully related siblings have similar toeprints. The data from toeprint collections showed that most of the sibling sets ridge classifications being 80% similar and three of them 90% similar. While the similarity of the ridge classifications did not vary much, the similarity of the major classifications varied.**

Keywords- Fingerprints; Toeprints; Biometrics; Security; Science.

I. Introduction

Fingerprints are a biometric mark of everything a human has touched and where they have been. Fingerprint tracking has been documented from the Chinese Qin Dynasty to modern society. There currently is no common fingerprint point requirement between countries, but the more point matches, the stronger the match. Fingerprints have basic patterns and more detailed patterns that allow for good evidence of a match. Just as fingerprints are unique to a person, so are toeprints. There are three basic patterns of fingerprints known as arches, loops, and whorls [5]. The more detailed items of fingerprints are forks, double forks, triple forks, delta, dot, bridge, hook, eye, short ridge, and ending ridge [8]. It can be inferred that toeprints are classified using the same classifications as fingerprints because they have similar characteristics [3]. Trying to classify toeprints and footprints to identify crime victims and to help catch criminals is not new. Moorthy and Sulaiman [18] attempted to help solve crime in Malaysia by collecting footprints of over 400 adults and found various features of the toes. When they compared them against findings of those in Indians, they found that the morphological length of toes were different due to nationality and genetic makeup [18].

In Section 2, a brief history of fingerprints and toeprints and background for understanding fingerprints and toeprints is given. In Section 3, the data for the fingerprint and toeprint research is presented and explained. In Section 4, a summary of research and possibilities of future research are given.

II. History

Before Christ (BC) the Chinese Qin Dynasty recorded details of using handprints as a way to find burglars and Han Dynasty records show clay seals showing fingerprint ridge impressions [24]. Von Minden also indicates evidence of fingerprinting in the 14th century Persian book *Jaamehol-Tawarikh* by Khajeh Rashiduddin Fazlollah Hamadani, that there is evidence of the Dr. Nehemiah Grew publishing details of friction ridge skin observations in the *Royal Society of London* paper in 1684, Govard Bidloo writing a book in 1685 about papillary ridges, and Marcello Malpighi at the University of Bologna's work with ridge, spirals, and loops in 1686 [24]. French criminologist Alphonse Bertillon created an eleven point measurement system known as anthropometrics [11]. The anthropometry system failed when two people were found to have the same eleven measurements in the Will and William West Leavenworth Prison case [11]. This sparked several scientists to start looking for improved ways to identify people by their fingerprints. The following timeline shows the movement from the judicial failure of anthropometrics to modern fingerprinting [9][11]-[13][23]-[24]:

- 1893-Scotland Yard adds fingerprints to Bertillon
- 1901-Fingerprints replace anthropometrics ID
- 1902-New York, USA fingerprints used for work ID
- 1905-U.S. Military starts using fingerprints
- 1918- Locard confirmed 12 point differences
- 1971-Federal Bureau of Investigation (FBI) has over 200 million fingerprints stored
- 1974-United Kingdom created a fingerprint society
- 1977-Certified Latent Print Examiners test created
- 2012-Interpol's repository includes 190 countries
- 2014-U.S. Automated Fingerprint Identification System (AFIS) systems has over 120 million fingerprint records
- 2014-Unique Identification Authority of India (UIAI) has over 560 million biometrics stored

The classification system that is used today evolved from

a method developed by Sir Edward Henry who was in collaboration with Sir Francis Galton, Sir William Hershel, and Dr. Henry Faulds [11].

Fingerprints contain DNA and substances that are on the finger. Recently, researchers have been working on the best way to obtain and analyze DNA from latent fingerprints with the goal of provide another source of gathering DNA samples for criminal investigations [6]. Also, other researchers are looking at the traces of non-DNA substances left in fingerprints to find more information that may be used in criminal investigations [1]. Most of the research on non-DNA substances in fingerprints is focused on drug testing [1].

In history, toeprints have served a significant purpose. There was an article in the *Fingerprint and Identification Magazine* from March 1953 titled The Case of the Great Toe Print. The police found a toeprint on a safe that was stolen during a robbery and the guilty verdict was based on the toeprint alone [21]. In 2010, police identified Colton Harris-Moore as the barefoot bandit through his toeprints [20]. Additionally, another example would be when coroners in Japan decided to use footprints to identify the deceased of an earthquake [2]. Beall also reported that this method could be used to identify patients with dementia [2]. Despite the advantages of using toeprints for identification purposes, it should be noted that a ghost image or shadow may appear two-dimensional within latent prints [4]. This phenomenon has implications for the collection and interpretation and thus for the comparison made between unknown and known footprints in the criminal justice system [4].

A. Patterns

Fingerprints have several characteristics which are categorized into two main categories. The first category focuses on basic patterns and the second category focuses on the more detailed items within the basic patterns. There are three basic patterns known as (1) arches, (2) loops, and (3) whorls. Arches are the least common of the basic patterns [5]. The pattern of an arch can be identified because the ridges enter on one side and exit on the other side. About 5% of people have arch type fingerprints [17]. Loops are the most common type of print [5] and in this pattern some of the ridges enter and exit on the same side of the finger. "Approximately 65% of all fingerprints are loops" [17]. Whorls are the third pattern and these ridges create a circular pattern. According to the Education Bureau of Hong Kong, approximately 34% of people exhibit this as their basic fingerprint pattern [8].

The more detailed items are forks, double forks, triple forks, delta, dot, bridge, hook, eye, short ridge, and ending ridge [8]. As explained by the Education Bureau of Hong Kong, a fork is similar to when one is driving and comes to a dead end in the road that forces one to make a decision about going left or right [8]. A double fork is when the fingerprint line branches off to the left or right and then immediately makes another left or right branch. A triple fork is when someone's fingerprint comes to the intersection, but instead of just turning right or left, the line can also go straight [8]. The delta is also known as bifurcation and sometimes people have two deltas which is known as a double bifurcation [5]. A dot characteristic allows a person to have a single dot or multiple dots anywhere in their fingerprint [8]. A small ridge connecting two large ridges is known as a fingerprint bridge. Spurs known as hooks, look like a crochet hook and the hook varies in different depths [5]. An eye is also known as an enclosure or a lake and is basically the same as an eyeball. Short ridges are also known as islands, because the ridge lines are small and do not connect to any other ridge [5]. The last detail is the ending ridge, which is where the print ridge lines end and do not make a full ridge [8]. The same fingerprint patterns also apply to toeprints.

B. Types

The four types of fingerprinting methods are plastic, visible, latent, and inked. According to Gaensslen et al. [11], plastic fingerprints are generally "three-dimensional and found in soft material", while visible fingerprints are generally left in fluids, such as paint or blood, and latent fingerprints are invisible to the human eye, but are made visible by dusting or spraying chemicals on the print. Ink fingerprints are the older style, where fingers are rolled in ink and printed on a paper card. An example of a plastic fingerprint would be your print left in putty and an example of a visible fingerprint would be when you stick your hand on wet paint and leave your hand print on the wall. Another example of a visible fingerprint is when someone puts their hand on a non-fogged window, the next morning fog shows the persons handprint.

There are two primary ways to obtain latent prints: (1) powered-dusting and (2) chemical spray [11]. The multi-colored powders are cheaper and commonly used in conjunction with lifting tape and specially designed brushes. The most common chemicals used are iodine fuming, silver nitrate, ninhydrin, and super glue [11]. Lipid components and porous surfaces respond well to using iodine, while ninhydrin reacts with amino acids and also works well on porous surfaces [11]. "Silver nitrate has been an established agent for the detection of latent fingerprints for some 120 years, and it was one of the few reagents suitable for use on porous surfaces until ninhydrin was introduced in forensics. The method is based on the reaction of silver ions with chlorides in the fingerprints, which are visualized in brown, violet or black" [15]. By heating the super glue, an interaction occurs on the print residue displaying a visible fingerprint impression [11]. The same fingerprint types also apply to toeprints.

C. Analyzing

One way to compare and analyze fingerprints is to follow the five steps below [8]:

1. Identify the basic patterns (loop, arch, whorls) of a fingerprint
2. Identify ridgeline details
3. Compare fingerprint measurements point by point to another fingerprint
4. Determine if capture print matches prior stored print

5. Obtain second person or software program to confirm findings

Using a computer software program to analyze fingerprints is much faster and easier as manual fingerprint comparison generally requires the use of a magnifying glass. During the comparison, the examiner must record their findings, generally in a digital database that can be searched later. These stored analyses are helpful in biometric security, identifying amnesia victims, criminal identification, and identifying unknown deceased [19]. As the USA National Forensic Science Technology Center and Bureau of Justice Assistance points out, most criminal justice cases use computerized systems to conduct the analysis for matches. The match is determined by a programed algorithm. Certified print examiners then manually review the listed matches and make the final determination [19]. "Fingerprint examiners use a method called ACE-V. That stands for analysis, comparison, evaluation, and verification. Below is an explanation of each section of ACE-V" [19].

Analysis is the process of determining if the print is good enough to use for a comparison. If the print is found not to be suitable for comparison, it is because it was not of good quality or did not have enough visual features; at this point, the print is reported as not suitable. If the print passes inspection, the print tolerance level (the amount of variation that will be accepted) is determined [19]. "The analysis may also uncover physical features such as recurves, deltas, creases, and scars that help indicate where to begin the comparison" [19]. Comparisons occur when prints from known persons and people of interest are looked at side-by-side comparing minutiae characteristics and locations to determine if they match. "Known prints are often collected from persons of interest, victims, others present at the scene or through a search of one or more fingerprint databases such as the FBI's Integrated Automated Fingerprint Identification System" [19]. "Evaluation is where the examiner ultimately decides if the prints are from the same source (identification or individualization), different sources (exclusion) or is inconclusive. Inconclusive results may be due to poor quality samples, lack of comparable areas, or insufficient number of corresponding or dissimilar features to be certain" [19]. Verification is when someone else does the analysis, compares, and evaluates the prints themselves to either support or disagree with the conclusions of the first fingerprint examiner. The second examiner might additionally verify the suitability of determinations made by the first examiner in the analysis phase [19].

According to the USA National Forensic Science Technology Center and Bureau of Justice Assistance, there are four possible results of fingerprint analysis. These results are "(1) the fingerprint was made by (identified) a known source (suspect, victim, etc.), (2) the fingerprint was not made by a known source, (3) the fingerprint cannot be identified or excluded to a known source, (4) the fingerprint is of no value to compare to a known source" [19].

D. Measurements

Fingerprints are measured by points. A system has been created that uses different spots on the fingerprint to compare the similarities. The different spots are called points. There are approximately fifty points per fingerprint. The minimum requirement is different for every country. The United States has no minimum requirement of points that you must have to match a print, however the more you have the better in a court of law. The United Kingdom requires that you to have a minimum of sixteen points to be a match [10]. Australia requires you to have at least a minimum of twelve points to be a match [10]. Just like Australia, Germany requires a minimum of twelve points for it to be a match [7]. France requires you to have a minimum of seventeen points for it to be a match [7]. The US court system and the government does not require you to have a certain amount to have a case, but they prefer that you have at least a minimum of nine points that are a match. At the time of this research, there are no requirements for toes, unless used as finger replacements.

E. Heredity

A person's fingerprints are formed approximately during the seventh month of fetus development, and the finger ridges do not change unless a person gets a bruise, cut, or scar on the fingertip [14]. According to Bhangu [3], the pressure on the toes from the amniotic fluid and the fetus' movement in the womb affects the resulting toeprints at birth. There are prior studies that show a correlation of ridge count, width, separation, and depth among identical twins, while others show that some parent fingerprint traits are shared with their children [14]. While fingerprinting children under the age of two can be difficult, research has shown there are similarities between family members [22]. "There is an inheritable quality to fingerprints. Pattern types are often genetically inherited, but the individual details that make a fingerprint unique are not" [16].

III. Research

A. Fingerprint Analysis

For this part of the research, there were fifteen sibling sets, or thirty participants, who were fingerprinted. The participants' fingerprints were analyzed for the major classifications and five specific ridge classifications. Then, fingerprints of siblings were compared and similarities determined.

The data for this part of the research showed that when comparing all three of the major classes and the five ridge classes on the four fingers tested, all the sibling sets had at least 80% similarity, as seen in Figure 1.

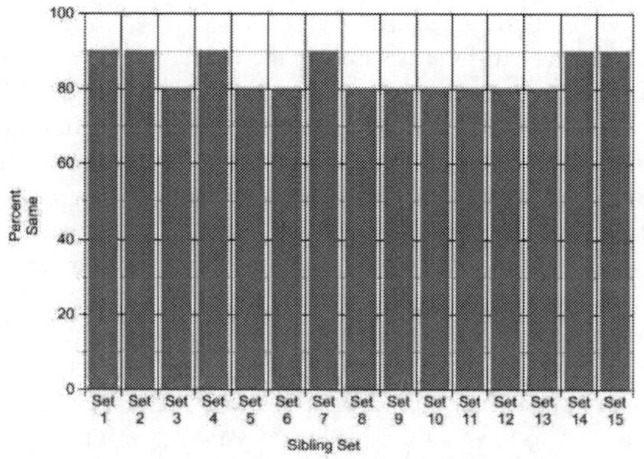

Figure 1. Overall Similarity of Fully Related Siblings Fingerprints

The majority of siblings had at least 33% similarity in the major classes, as seen in Figure 2.

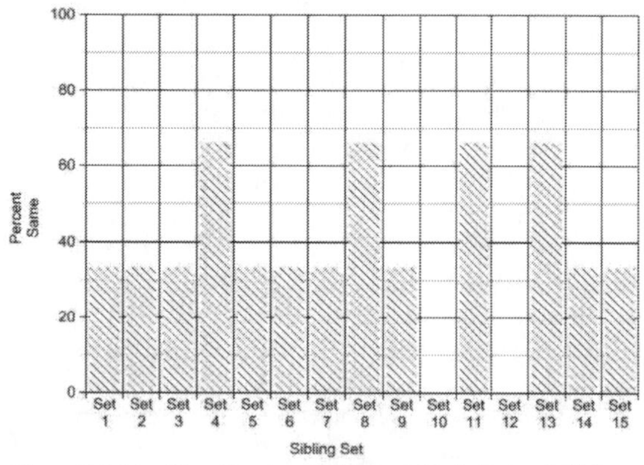

Figure 2. Major Classification Similarity of Fully Related Siblings Fingerprints

Also, the data showed that the right index finger of all sets had a median of 40%, even with Set 7 that had only a 20% match. The right thumb of all sets had a median of 60%, even with Set 8 that had only a 20% match. The left thumb for all sets had a mode of 40%, even with five sets having a 20% match and one set having no similarity in the left thumb. The left index finger for all sets had a mode of 40% with ten of the fifteen sibling sets being at that level.

The individual finger similarities were calculated by taking all found major and ridge classifications and dividing them by all eight possible classifications. The overall percentage of similarity was determined by adding all found matched classifications divided by all possible classifications for all fingers. Major class similarities were further evaluated by looking for similarities of whorls, arches, and loops on matching fingers. The majority of the sets were at 33% or higher, yet two sets had no matching major classifications. This percentage was determined by taking the number of found matches divided by the total possible classifications. When looking at total ridge similarities, the mode was 80%.

The data showed the left thumb was less of a match then the right thumb of siblings. The same was shown to be true on the right and left index fingers. When looking at individual classifications the data showed five sets did not have forks, four sets had double forks, and only one set had a triple fork. There were ten sets that did not have matching short ridges and fourteen sets did not have matching ending ridges. The matches were determined by each sibling within a set having the classification, most sets had at least one sibling who had some type of ridge. Arches were the least found major classification and loops were the most popular major classification. One set of siblings was compared to another because that set consisted of a male parent and a male uncle. The findings were supportive of the prior research showing genetic effects on fingerprints, in that there was an 85% similarity with the parent and a 70% similarity with the uncle. Two sets of siblings also had one female grandparent within another sibling set. When the sibling sets were compared with their grandparent's prints, they found to have a 74% match.

Upon evaluating the quality of the fingerprint cards, it could be seen that the sibling sets that included participants between the ages of two and five years were not as clear which made it harder to determine classification. The participants over the age of 45 also presented issues because they contained more fingerprint damage, such as scars and burn spots. One sibling set had a participant that had a fresh cut which caused a thick solid line to appear across the fingerprint. The younger participant's prints were darker due to the struggle between researcher and participant to roll the finger properly in ink and on the card. The older participants were found to have the lightest prints most likely from the researcher being more concerned about hurting them during the fingerprinting process in comparison to other participants.

B. Toeprint Analysis

Confounding variables in this portion of the research were

- Cuts, scrapes, and/or callus on toes
- Lotions and/or oils used on feet prior to printing
- Flexibility of research participants
- Length of participant's toes
- Medical conditions of participants

For this part of the research, there were ten sibling sets, or twenty participants, who were toeprinted. The participants' toeprints were analyzed for the major classifications and five specific ridge classifications. Then, toeprints of siblings were compared and similarities determined.

The average ridge classification similarity was 83%. The average right big toe similarity was 88%. The average left big toe similarity was 78%. The right big toe similarity is the number of ridge classifications similar on the siblings right big toe. The left big toe similarity is the number of ridge classifications similar on the siblings left big toes. The average major classification similarity was 55%.

One set of siblings was compared to another because that set consisted of a female parent and a female aunt. While the researcher was unable to find prior research on the genetic effect of toeprints, the data of this research shows that genetics do play a role in toeprint formation. This is similar to the findings of prior research showing genetic effects on fingerprints [16]. This research showed that there was an 85% similarity with the parent and a 70% similarity with the aunt. Two sets of siblings also had one female grandparent within another sibling set. When the sibling sets were compared with their grandparent's prints, there was a 74% match.

The similarity of ridge classifications, major classifications, the right big toe, and the left big toe in related siblings is graphed in Figure 3.

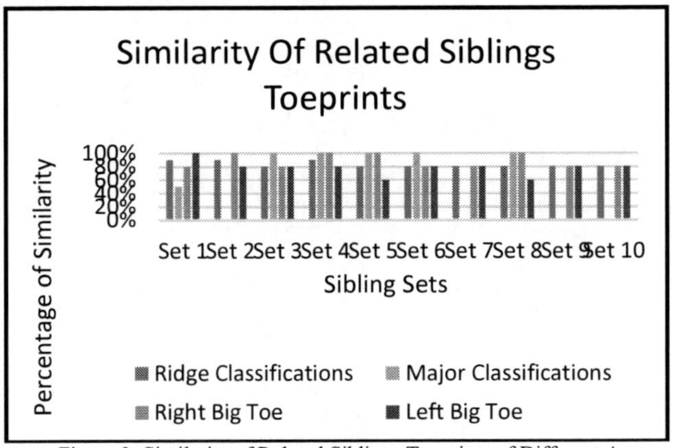

Figure 3. Similarity of Related Siblings Toeprints of Different Ages and Ethnic Backgrounds

IV. CONCLUSION

Based on the findings of this research, the hypothesis that fingerprints of siblings are similar overall even though they may have slight differences within some classifications with all sibling sets having at least an 80% match. This supports the prior research findings from Jain et al. [14] which states that while everyone has a unique fingerprint, siblings do have similarities based on genetics during fetus development. One set of siblings had a participant who was conceived using in-vitro fertilization and one who was not. The fingerprint results may have shown different results if all five fingers were evaluated instead of just the thumbs and index fingers. This was not done due to time restrictions placed on the researcher by the project due date and when the research received Institutional Review Board (IRB) approval. The researcher also learned how hard it was to actually find full siblings; it appeared that a large majority of siblings around the researcher were actually step or half siblings. It was interesting to the researcher to also see the high interest level of the participants to understand more about fingerprints and the reading process. The researcher now understands why the criminal justice system is unable to set a specific number of matches to confirm a print obtained during a crime. Future fingerprint research is to evaluate all five fingers on each hand for each sibling, to use a digital inking device, and to allow more time for evaluation, fingerprinting all the parents of the siblings, and looking at other biometric prints such as the ear. This additional data may lead to more details of the human biometric system.

The data from the toeprint portion of this research showed that when comparing the three major classes that five sibling sets had a 100% similarity and four sibling sets had absolutely no similarity. Three sibling sets had an overall ridge classification similarity of 90%, which was 10% higher than all other sibling sets. There was no correlation between major class similarity level and the ridge classification similarity level. All sibling sets had at least an 80% or higher similarity for ridge classification on the right big toe. This varied from the left big toe ridge classification comparison, which showed two sibling sets had only a 60% match. Additionally, only one 100% match was found on the left big toe, but four 100% matches were found on the right big toe. The most common percentage was 80% for both the right and left big toes. Major class similarities were further evaluated by looking for similarities of whorls, arches, and loops on matching toes. Half of the sets were at or below 50% and the other half were perfectly matched at 100%. This percentage was determined by taking the number of found matches divided by the total possible classifications. When looking at total ridge classification similarities, the mode was 80%. The data showed the left toe was less of a match than the right toe of siblings. When looking at individual ridge classifications the data showed that both participants in the set had forks, seven sets had double forks, and no set had a triple fork. All ten sets had ending ridges and only two sets had both participants having short ridges. The matches were determined by each sibling within a set having the classification; most sets had at least one sibling who had some type of ridge. Whorls were the least found major classification and loops were the most popular major classification.

Comparing the manual and computer analysis there is a slight to major difference. The cause of the difference is that manual analysis considered only certain classifications (three major and five ridge classifications) and the computer looked at all possible major and ridge classifications for fingerprints. The five ridge details in the manual analysis were forks, double forks, triple forks, short ridge, and ending ridge. The ridge details looked at in the computer analysis are fork, double fork, triple fork, delta, dot, bifurcation, double bifurcation, opposed bifurcation, lake, short ridge, and ending ridge. Upon evaluating the quality of the toeprint cards, it could be seen that the sibling sets that included participants under the age of twelve were not as clear, which made it harder to determine classification. The participants over the age of 45 also presented issues because they contained more toeprint damage, such as scars and calluses. Younger participant's prints were darker and older participant's prints were lighter.

In conclusion, the toeprint findings show that the hypothesis that toeprints of siblings are similar overall even though they may have slight differences within some classifications with all sibling sets having at least an 80%

match in the ridge classifications. This supports the prior research findings for fingerprints done by Langenburg [16], which stated that while everyone has a unique print, siblings do have similarities based on genetics and differences from fetus development. Future research in the area of toeprints include creating a toeprint database and looking at toeprints as an indicator of medical conditions.

ACKNOWLEDGMENT

I would like to thank Mrs. Barbara Agregaard for her support during the fingerprint portion of the research project and Dr. Melissa Stange for her support during the toeprint portion of the research. To my participants, thank you for being willing to participate and hope you enjoyed learning more about your family biometrics.

REFERENCES

[1] M. Bailey, "The Hidden Data in Your Fingerprints," Scientific American, 2018. Retrieved November 2020 from https://www.scientificamerican.com/article/the-hidden-data-in-your-fingerprints/.

[2] A. Beall, "Forget fingerprints, FOOTPRINTS can help identify bodies: Experts reveal everyone has unique ridges and grooves on their feet," MailOnline, 2016. Retrieved November 2020 from http://www.dailymail.co.uk/sciencetech/article-3496636/Forget- fingerprints-FOOTPRINTS- help- identify-bodies- Scans-reveal- unique-ridges- grooves-feet.html.

[3] A. Bhangu, "Are the prints on our toes identical to our fingerprints," 2012. Retrieved November 2020 from https://www.howitworksdaily.com/are-the-prints-on-our-toes-identical-to-our-fingerprints/.

[4] J. G. Burrow, "Ghosting of Images in Barefoot Exemplar Prints Collection: Issues for Analyses," Journal of Forensic Identification, vol. 65, no. 5, pp. 884-900, 2015.

[5] Center for Technology in Teaching and Learning Rice University, "CSI: Web Adventures," Forensics, 2014. Retreived November 2020 from http://forensics.rice.edu.

[6] T. Dawson Cruz, M. E. Hytinen, A. M. McClain, A. M. Miller, and A.D. Solomon, "An Optimized DNA Analysis Workflow for the Sampling, Extraction, and Concentration of DNA obtained from Archived Latent Fingerprints," Journal of Forensic Sciences, vol. 63, pp. 47-57, 2018, doi: 10.1111/1556-4029.13504.

[7] Department of Justice and Federal Bureau of Investigation, "Fingerprint Identification," 2010. Retrieved November 2020 from http://www.slideshare.net/guest8cbcb02/fingerprint-identification.

[8] Education Bureau of Hong Kong, "Forensic Science," 2010. Retrieved November 2020 from http://resources.edb.gov.hk/gifted/ForensicSci/Files/L2/4_Lesson2_worksheets.doc.

[9] "The Fingerprint Society," Fingerprint Society Website, 2013. Retrieved November 2020 from www.fingerprintsociety.com.

[10] Fun Trivia, "Fun Trivia: F: Forensic Science," 2013. Retrieved November 2020 from http://www.funtrivia.com/en/subtopics/Fingerprints-170308.html.

[11] R. E. Gaensslen, H. Howard, and H. Lee, "Introduction to Forensic Science and Criminalistics," New York: McGraw-Hill, 2017.

[12] International Association for Identification, "International Association for Identification," 2014. Retrieved November 2020 from http://www.theiai.org/.

[13] Interpol, "Forensics," 2008. Retrieved November 2020 from http://www.interpol.int/INTERPOL-expertise/Forensics.

[14] A. K. Jain, S. Prabhakar, and S. Pankanti, "On the similarity of identical twin fingerprints," The Journal of Pattern Recognition, vol. 35, pp. 2653-2663, 2002, doi:10.1016/S0031-3203(01)00218-7.

[15] A. Kriminol, "Detection of latent fingerprints by the use of silver nitrate," PubMed, vol. 227, pp. 111-123, 2011. Retrieved November 2020 from http://www.ncbi.nlm.nih.gov/pubmed/21661253.

[16] G. Langenburg, "Are one's fingerprints similar to those of his or her parents in any discernable way?," Scientific American, 2005. Retrieved November 2020 from http://www.scientificamerican.com/article/are-ones-fingerprints-sim/.

[17] J. S. McCann, "A Family Fingerprint Project," Identification News, pp. 7-10, 1975. Retrieved November 2020 from http://onin.com/fp/family_fingerprints.pdf.

[18] T. N. Moorthy and S. F. B. Sulaiman, "Individualizing characteristics of footprints in Malaysian Malays for person identification from a forensic perspective," Egyptian Journal of Forensic Sciences, vol. 5, no. 1, pp. 13-22, 2015.

[19] National Forensic Science Technology Center and Bureau of Justice Assistance, "A Simplified Guide To Fingerprint Analysis," n.d. Retreived November 2020 from http://www.crime-scene-investigator.net/SimplifiedGuideFingerprints.pdf.

[20] B. Palmer, "And This Little Piggy Went to Jail," Slate, 2010. Retrieved November 2020 from http://www.slate.com/articles/news_and_politics/explainer/2010/07/and_this_little_piggy_went_to_jail.html.

[21] C. Parker, "The Case of the Great Toe Print," 2008. Retrieved November 2020 from http://clpex.com/phpBB/viewtopic.php?f=2&t=878.

[22] G. Shahan, "Heredity in Fingerprints," Identification News, vol. XX, no. 4, pp. 9-25, 1970. Retrieved November 2020 from http://onin.com/fp/fp_heredity.pdf.

[23] Unique Identification Authority of India, "Fingerprints," 2014. Retrieved November 2020 from http://uidai.gov.in/.

[24] D. L. von Minden, "The History of Fingerprints," 2014. Retrieved November 2020 from http://onin.com/fp/fphistory.html.

Exploitation of Radio Frequency Technologies Through the use of Microcontrollers

Daniel J. Joachim Jr.
Lord Fairfax Community College
Middletown, Virginia, United States of America
email: djj2985@email.vccs.edu

***Abstract*—Radio Frequency Identification (RFID) uses a simple principle of signal broadcast by a transmission station. The signal is broadcasted to the open air and intercepted by a metallic object whose molecular structure reflects the wave being broadcasted back to the transmission station. The transmitting station can then evaluate the signal to determine the identity of the object. RFID has been around since World War I, but due to cost, research was limited. It was not until militarization during World War II that RFID research was cost effective. The RFID technology is used within offices buildings, airports, grocery stores, and academic institutions for access control. This paper is a study in which the evolution of RFID was reviewed and an attempt was made to exploit the encryption of a German Schoko Ticket and District of Columbia (D.C.) Metro MiFare card RFID signals, by using publicly available devices. The devices used were Arduino micro-controller board and an MFRC522 RFID reader. The research showed that both of the RFID cards included in the student were actually from the MiFare DESfire family and that there is a security threat to these cards that users need to be aware of.**

Keywords- RFID; cybersecurity; Microcontroller; Arduino.

I. INTRODUCTION

After the conclusion of World War I, military forces turned their attention towards technologies that would provide clairvoyance, in reference to future attacks. Research on radio technologies up to this point was expensive to facilitate an had little rate of success. This held true until a discovery by the United States Research Laboratory (NRL)[3]. The NRL had successfully broadcasted a signal towards a secondary location across the Potomac river, which was refracted by a naval vessel upon its transmission.

RFID is a technology that is used for access control purposes by people and objects. This is widely used by academic institutions and corporate business offices where tapping of the personal RFID chip based card on the tag reader will grant employees access to secure areas to aid in security of data. Similar technologies are used in keeping track of inventory at the local grocery stores and to gain access to public transportation systems. RFID helps the world meet various organizational needs and in most situations is a cost effective process.

The Pre-Pottery Neolithic Era was the first to create large scale storage facilities to store food that had been left over from their gathering season [1]. People living during this time chose a location that was remote to their villa, ensuring that their precious food was easily accessible. Their existence depended on access to food, marking the creation of the first theorized security. As mankind traversed from stone to bronze, securities shifted to follow the progression. Once mankind had established a way to produce food, they realized the need to protect their food source from danger – resulting in the erection of walls around the town villa. The concept of securing critical possessions has followed us into the world that we live in today. We have locks on the front doors of our homes, armed military guards around the white house, and access cards to control our entry to our place of work. The physical dangers of having a neighboring tribe raiding the village and stealing the village's food have been translated into the digital danger of using a weak password to protect monetary funds from cyber criminals. As civilization progresses through the Technological Age, it has created a commodity; the security of digital data. Business, organizations, governments, educational institutes and municipalities all rely on the confidentiality, availability and integrity of data to ensure continuity in their respective field of practice. The identification of this commodity has opened a wide range of opportunities for both offensive and defensive members of the Information Technology (IT) taskforce. With each defender's innovation, a challenge is posed to the offender. This affinity has been identified as *Red Team versus Blue Team* [2].

This paper is a study about RFID technology to understand its security threats and use of the German Schoko Ticket and District of Columbia (D.C.) USA Metro MiFare card for transportation systems. Cards are used to ride on public buses and trains and record the passenger travel on the system. Each time the card is swiped for entry at bus or train stations, data is transmitted that someone may intercept. The study concluded with a Red Team [2] approach to exploit, extract information contained on RIFD technologies and provide a structured understanding of inner workings of Access Control (AC) Systems. Section II provides a brief history of security technologies, while Section III provides a brief background of access control technologies. In Section IV, Microcontrollers and RFID cards will be discussed. Section V will present the exploratory research and the conclusions from the findings of the research from Section V, will be discussed in Section VI.

II. History

A. Primitive Technologies

The origins of Radio Wave Technologies can be traced back to Scottish physicist James Clerk Maxwell. Maxwell theorized the first correlation between magnetism, electricity, and light. His discoveries can be summarized into three primary concepts:

- Electricity may penetrate most metallic objects because of movement of electrons within the atom. When electrons move, they create a magnetic field [3].
- Electromagnetic devices may be combined into one device. Fluctuating magnetic waves produce an electric current [3].
- Radio Waves share the same characteristics as light waves, but with varying frequencies [4].

These discoveries supplied the groundwork for scientists and engineers to fabricate technologies utilizing wireless communication. "His work was later adopted by German physicist, Heinrich Hertz, refracted a 66cm radio wave off dielectric and metallic objects " [5]. Six-teen years later, the first patent for a ship navigation device utilizing his technology was issued to German engineer, Christian Hansmeyer, who received acceptance for his patent from multiple countries [5]. Despite being awarded his patents, the complexity of the invention prevented it from becoming a tool that could be commonly utilized until its adoption by the military for approximately another 20 years.

B. Radar

Monopulse radar, which NRL developed in 1943, is the basis for all modern tracking and missile control radars in the United States [1].

III. Access Control

Resources are critical to the development of private infrastructures, government agencies and organizations alike. To ensure the continuity, integrity, and authenticity of an organization's resources, i.e. data,, certain preventative access measures are put in to place. Access control is referenced as any mechanism used within an information system for granting or denying approval to used specific resources [6]. This may be accomplished through external perimeter defenses, internal physical access security, and physical device security.

A. Types of Physical Access Control

There are many thigs that have been used for physical access controls, such as barriers, cages, barricades, bollards, motion detection systems, security personnel, keyed door locks, deadbolt locks, and cipher locks.

B. Types of Electronic Access Control

This study focuses primarily on the components used to read and write information located within an RF identifiable object. This study will refer to that object as a tag, card or fob interchangeably. This work focuses primarily on the components used to read and write information located within an RFID identifiable object. The words: "tag", "card", "token" and "fob" may be used as an interchangeable reference to the device that holds the data activated by the RFID reader. RFID tags consist of four primary components that allow their data to be accessed by the RFID reader: transponder, rectifier circuit, controller and memory.

The RFID reader consists of three primary components: signal generator, Microcontroller and receiver. The signal generator and receiver are sub-derivatives of the analog circuit block, which is responsible for driving the radio signal and receiving the radio signal's modulated voltage. This analog data is then covered by an Analog-Digital-Converter and passed to the Microcontroller to enumerate the cryptographic functions that have been performed by the tag, as seen in Figure 1 below [8].

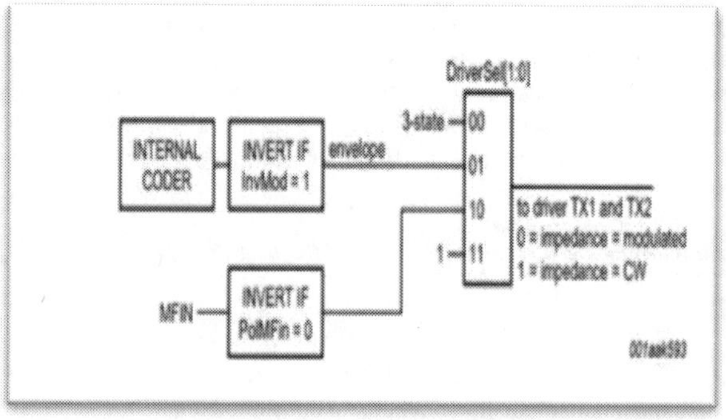

Figure 1. Serial Data Switch for p-driver Tx1 & Tx2 [8].

C. RFID

The three frequencies that tags normally operate at are Low (LF), High (HF), and Ultra High (UHF) [18][19]. Figure 2 shows the common bands that RFID operates within.

Band	Frequency	Distance	Usage
Low Freq. (LF)	125-150 kHz	< 2 m	Animal ID
High Freq. (HF)	13.56 kHz	< 20 cm	Access & Security
Ultra-High Freq. (UHF)	433-868 MHz 865-928 MHz	< 100 m < 2 m	Logistics
Ultra Wide Band (UWB)	2.45-5.8 GHz	< 1 m	Vehicle toll

Figure 2. Common RFID Operating Bands [22].

RFID is popular because it offers improved security in access control to reduce theft, allows for tag linking, automated identification, location tracking, reduction of human interaction, improved data integrity, and range reading capability and high data transfer rate [20]. There are many applications where RFID is used, as seen in Figure 3 below.

Figure 3. RFID Applications [21].

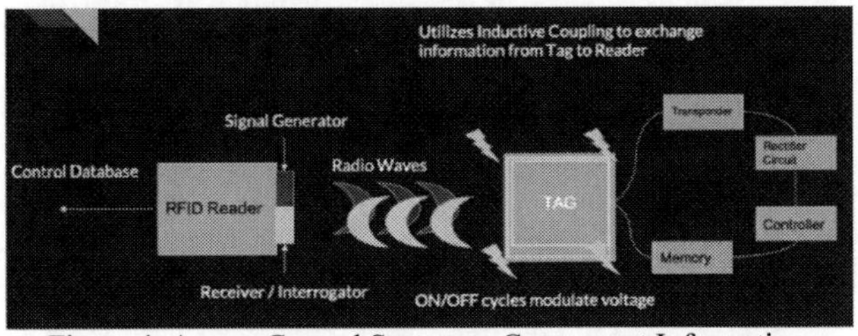

Figure 4. Access Control Systems - Component Information.

The component information for this study is found in Figure 4 above. These components consist of a database, RFID Reader, signal generator, Interrogator, and a tag.

IV. MICROCONTROLLERS & CARDS

For the sake of this study, the terms "Microcontroller", "microprocessor" and "chip" will be used interchangeably. Microcontrollers are chips or microcomputers manufactured through Very-Large-Scale Integration (VLSI), a process where thousands of transistors are combined into a single chip. This chip may be used as an embedded component of a Real Time Operating System (RTOS). The advantages of this technology over prior semiconductor technologies are its ability to produce a chip that is smaller, less expensive, faster, requires less power and contains more logic gates than preceding chips [9]. The word "Microcontroller" is used as a misnomer for the word "Microcontroller Board", which references the Printed Circuit Board (PCB) holding the Microcontroller, the integrated Random Access Memory (RAM) on the chip and the peripheral Input / Output (I/O) circuits that are attached to the PCB. Common Microcontroller applications include: robotics, smart home automation, car engines, computer peripherals, mobile phones, washing machines, cameras and security alarms [10].

A. Microcontrollers

The primary function of a Microcontroller is to process binary data. This is accomplished by passing electrical pulses representing data through a series of registers and transistors called logic gates to perform the desired binary arithmetic. Two common applications of computational instruction sets are Complex Instruction Set Computer (CISC) and Reduced Instruction Set (RIS). A RIS Computer (RISC) accepts only one operand per instruction cycle whereas a CISC compacts operand arguments into one instruction. CISC require more physical logic gates within the processor to execute the commands stored within the processor's registers, therefore making this technology more expensive. RISC technologies are still used as they provide backwards compatibility to processors that have not been designed and/or capable of accepting CIS commands [9]. Common examples of Reduced Instruction Set opt codes for binary arithmetic include: ADD, AND, OR, XOR, and NOT. The density of the binary data that is being transmitted every clock cycle should be known as a "word length". This number is often referenced by the word "bit" after the respective word size. The maximum amount of data that a Microcontroller can process is determined by the width of the registers contained within the controllers Arithmetic Logic Unit (ALU). A 8-bit Microcontroller is capable of transmitting 0x00 – 0xFF (0 – 255) per clock cycle, while a 16-bit bit processor is capable of performing arithmetic with a range of 0x000 – 0xFFFF (0-65535) per clock cycle [11].

Microcontroller families may be identified by one of the following characteristics: bit depth, memory architecture, simple / complex instruction or memory devices [11]. Microcontroller boards are simply small form factor Printed Circuit Boards (PCB) that are designed to handle a single operation or program. They operate in the same way that the computer's PCB is being used to view this journal. Microcontroller boards or, single-board Microcontrollers, are comprised of a Microcontroller that is implanted or imbedded on to a PCB. These boards have low power draw, are small formfactor and contain I/O systems that enable the use of multiple sensory devices. They are inexpensive -- currently as of March 2019, the Arduino Uno REV3 costs $22.00 excluding tax and shipping [12]. Controller boards are manufactured by a wide range of vendors [9]. some such as Arduino and Raspberry Pi, provide open source documentation to the controller board, as well as source code for projects of any application [10].

Microcontroller boards share some of the same characteristics as Microcontrollers but are to be considered the component that hosts the embedded Microcontroller rather than the component being embedded into the Real Time Operating System. Microcontroller boards share the following characteristics:

- They must contain a way to preform binary arithmetic via a processing unit. These Microcontrollers may be embedded or modular.

- They must have a means to load a program into memory. This is typically done through a Easily Programmable Read Only Memory (EPROM) chip, or Electrically Erasable Programable Read-Only Memory E2PROM chip that is stored on the Microcontroller board.

B. *Arduino*

Arduino is an easy to use, open source, project-oriented Microcontroller board developed by Interaction Design Institute Ivera in Ivera, Italy [8]. Its sources can be traced back to Hernando Barragán, who laid the schematic foundation of the Arduino project [8]. Missimo Banzi and David Cuartielles sought to build from Hernando's work, creating user friendly programmable device geared towards design and interactive art [8]. David Mellis thereafter joined the development team, created the Arduino Independent Development Environment that was designed paralleled with the board's schematics. Gianluca Martino and Tom Igoe were the last two members to join the Arduino project [8]. These five members are known to be the original creators of Arduino [8]. The purpose of Arduino's creation was to provide an inexpensive, easy-to-use tool that allowed designers interoperability between hardware components. This resulted in the Atmel AVR 8-bit processor (Atmega8) to be selected during the board's prototyping phase [17].

C. *MiFare Card*

The Mifare RFID card was used in this study has an internal memory of 1 kB. This memory is divided into sixteen sections, each section composed of four blocks of sixteen bytes, see Figure 5 below.

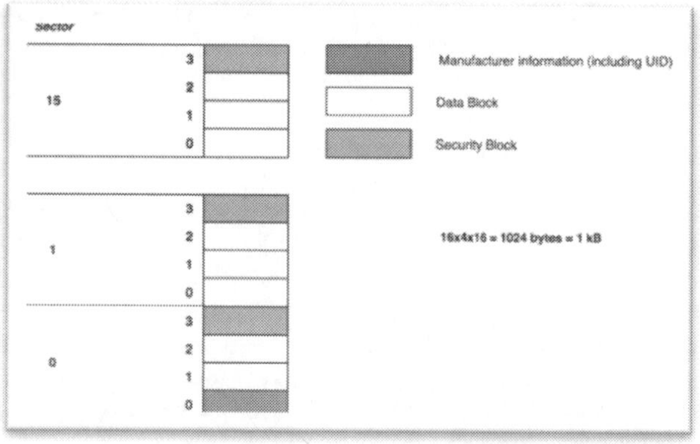

Figure 5. Details of the memory organization of the Mifare RFID [9].

The first block of the first section includes the card Unique IDentifier (UID) and the rest of the blocks are reserved for application data that can be read and written by the user, e.g. usually user-related information [22].

V. Exploitation Research

In October 2008, the Netherland educational institute, Radboud Universität Nijmegen, announced its intentions to publish the complete reverse engineering of the CRYPTO-1 algorithm used by NPX Semiconductor's MiFARE Classic cards. NPX Semiconductor is an American Dutch semiconductor manufacturer who responded by placing the publication under judicial process in hopes to prevent it from being published, eventually being overruled by legislature under constitutional freedom of speech [23]. Libraries may be built around to aid the exploitation of the ~3.5 billion MiFARE cards are in circulation around the world [24]. Shortly after, security research company "Nethemba" published "MFOC", a package for nested offline attacks on MiFARE Classic cards. Andrei Costin, an assistant professor at University of Jyvaskyla in Finland, also received a great benefit from the research conducted was the development of the MiFare Classic Universal Toolkit now known as "MFCUK" [25]. These tools allow for the complete enumeration and replication of cards that implement the CRYPT0-1 encryption algorithm aided by Microcontrollers with RFID reader-writers. These software libraries, among others, have been combined to form the first multi-platform low level RFID Application Programing Interface known as Near-Field Communications (NFC) tools provides functionally between a multitude of RFID reader-writers. NFC-Tools is integrated by default with downloading the latest platform of Kali Linux and is considered the de-facto library for cracking MiFARE Classic cards.

In this study, cloning to a blank and re-writable RFID card is a relatively inexpensive and easy approach to execute two main types of attacks known as card skimming and unauthorized use. RFID card skimming captures the data without the card owner's knowledge and then the attacker uses the data to clone a new card to impersonate the legitimate user's authentication systems. RFID card unauthorized use is when a card is replicated to give the attacker authenticated access to specific services such as ability to ride a Metro train or bus.

With these vulnerabilities in mind, a model attack was setup with a clone RFID card. The writing block is composed of an Arduino RC522 RFID reader. To complete this cloning process, the test cards were written to blank tags. Then the card information is directly obtained from the application layer and must be inserted manually on the Arduino sketch. The Arduino UNO was coded in Arduino C using the MFRC522 open source library [26] to interact with the rC522 RFID reader.

VI. Conclusions and Future Work

There are several known vulnerabilities associated with the use of RFID technology that have major impact on card owners, who become victims. The use of RFID-based cards in the context of Public Transportation Systems, such as Metro, presents several vulnerabilities that compromise their effective use for authentication and balance tracking. Current use of the tested cards provides an opportunity for attackers to easily and successfully carry out card cloning attacks.

This research was paired with an attempt to break the encryption of the German "Schoko Ticket" and District of Columbia "Metro" MiFARE cards. The Arduino Uno Rev3 was the Microcontroller board that was supplied paired with the RFID-RC522 RFID reader-writer to conduct tag enumeration and reading/writing. The MFRC522 was the Arduino library used to control the RC522 reader. The results showed that by using low-cost commercial-off-the-shelf hardware and open-source source software, it is easy and simple for cyber criminals to perform attacks. These vulnerabilities allowed for cloning of any RFID card within the testing RFID reader range. This means that if an attacker can get close enough to any Metro RFID card with a RFID reader, the card maybe cloned and then used to ride for free on the public transportation system.

Methods of reducing these types of attacks include changing the authentication from the default, applying cryptographic algorithms on transmitted data to hide information, employ encrypted access tokens on data blocks to identify the RFID owner, add a privacy bit controlled, or employ random numbers to identify the card.

Future research may be using the RFID device around campus to see if able to obtain and clone fob data that faculty, maintenance staff, and security use to enter into restricted areas.

ACKNOWLEDGMENT

The author would like to thank Dr. Melissa Stange for providing the Arduino Kit. I also want to thank Lord Fairfax Community College and Dr. Melissa Stange for their support with this work.

REFERENCES

[1] CompTIA. Are You Red Team or Blue Team? How Your Skills Fit into a Cybersecurity Career. [Online]. Retrieved November, 2020 from https://certification.comptia.org/it-career-news/post/view/2018/09/28/cybersecurity-red-team-or-blue-team, 2018.

[2] I. Kuijt & B. Finlayson. Evidence for food storage and predomestication granaries 11,000 years ago in the Jordan Valley . PNAS,07-Jul-2009. [Online]. Retrieved November, 2020 from https://www.pnas.org/content/106/27/1096

[3] J.C. Maxwell. Discoveries - James Clerk Maxwell - Science Hall of Fame - National Library of Scotland. Retrieved November, 2020 from https://digital.nls.uk/scientists/biographies/james-clerk-maxwell/discoveries.html#electro, 2019.

[4] P. Higgs. Electromagnetic Theory. Electromagnetic Theory. [Online]. Retrieved November, 2020 from http://www.clerkmaxwellfoundation.org/html/electromagnetic_theory.html, 2020.

[5] M.I. Skolnik. Radar. Encyclopedia Britannica, Encyclopedia Britannica, Inc., [Online]. Retrieved November, 2020 from www.britannica.com/technology/radar/History-of-radarI. 2020.

[6] M. D. Ciampa. 9-2a External Perimeter Defenses, 6th ed, 2018.

[7] Bosnianbill. Kaba Simplex Door Combination Lock Defeated w/Sparrows MAGNETO. YouTube. Retrieved November, 2020 from https://www.youtube.com/watch?v=2KSoPIeN9wY, 2015.

[8] NXP Semiconductors. Retrieved November, 2020 from https://investors.nxp.com/news-releases/news-release-details/nxp-semiconductors-reports-fourth-quarter-and-full-year-2017.

[9] MFRC522 Microchip Technology Inc. [Online] Retrieved Novemer, 2020 from "http://ww1.microchip.com/downloads/en/DeviceDoc/Microchip 8bit mcu AVR ATmega8A data sheet 40001974A.pdf, 2017.

[10] J. M. Hughes. Arduino: A Technical Reference, O'Reilly. [Online]. Retrieved November, 2020 from https://www.oreilly.com/library/view/arduino-a-technical/9781491934319/ch01.html, 2016.

[11] VLSI. Development and Basic Principles of IC Fabrication, Electronics For You, [Online]. Retrieved Novemer 2020 from https://electronicsforu.com/resources/learn-electronics/vlsi-developments-ic-fabrication, 2017.

[12] Types and Applications of Microcontrollers, Engineering Institute of Technology. [Online]. Retrieved November, 2020 from https://www.eit.edu.au/cms/resources/technical-resourses/types-and-applications-of-Microcontrollers

[13] S. D. Burd. Chapter 6 System Integration and Performance in Systems Architecture, 7e ed., Boston, MI: Cengage, pp. 120–121, 2015.

[14] Microcontrollers, Introduction Microcontrollers Types and Applications, ElProCus. [Online]. Retrieved November 2020 from: https://www.elprocus.com/Microcontrollers-types-and-applications/, 2018.

[15] What is a Raspberry Pi?," Opensource.com. [Online]. Retrieved November 2020 from https://opensource.com/resources/raspberry-pi, 2020.

[16] Microchip, ATmega8A - 8-bit AVR Microcontrollers. [Online]. Retriveved Novemer 2020 from https://www.microchip.com/wwwproducts/en/ATmega

[17] S. Jacoband C.P. Bean. Fine particles, thin films and exchange anisotropy in Magnetism, vol. III, G.T. Rado and H. Suhl, Eds. New York: Academic, pp. 271-350, 1963.

[18] A. Hagl and K. Aslanidis. RFID: Fundamentals and applications, RFID Security, pp. 3-26, 2008.

[19] R.K. Mota. Role of Cryptographic Welch-Gong (WG-5) Stream Cipher in RFID Security, 2012.

[20] Y.Z. Mehrjerdi, "RFID enabled healthcare systems: risk□ benefit analysis", International Journal of Pharmaceutical and Healthcare Marketing, 2010

[21] RFIDHY Technology. [Online]. Retrieved November 2020 from https://www.rfidhy.com/how-is-rfid-used-in-real-world-applications/, 2019.

[22] H. Pereira, R. Carreira, P. Pinto and S. I. Lopes, "Hacking the RFID-based Authentication System of a University Campus on a Budget," 2020 15th Iberian Conference on Information Systems and Technologies (CISTI), Sevilla, Spain, pp. 1-5, doi: 10.23919/CISTI49556.2020.914094, 2020.

[23] E. Mills. Dutch chipmaker sues to silence security researchers. [Online]. Retrieved Novemer, 2020 from https://www.cnet.com/news/dutch-chipmaker-sues-to-silence-security-researchers, 2008.

[24] M. Almeida. Hacking Mifare Classic Cards. [Online]. Retrieved November, 2020 from https://www.blackhat.com/docs/sp-14/materials/arsenal/sp-14-Almeida-Hacking-MIFARE-Classic-Cards-Slides.pdf, 2014.

[25] A. Costin. Firmware.re and Jyu.Fi. [Online]. Retrieved November, 2020 from https://www.blackhat.com/us-18/speakers/Andrei-Costin.html, 2018.

[26] Arduino Library List. [Online]. Retrieved November, 2020 from https://www.arduinolibraries.info/libraries/mfrc522.

Incorporating Cyber Competencies in K-12

Rachel M. Stange
Bethany College
Bethany, WV, USA
Email: rstange@bethanywv.edu

***Abstract*—Over the past several years, the kindergarten through twelfth (K-12) community has been told to include computer science and cybersecurity in all curriculum. However, the K-12 community does not have the proper knowledge to do so. This paper includes a guide on what to teach to meet the requirements, how to teach it in order to engage students, and how to incorporate it into the curriculum. This guide is different from others because it works with new or existing curriculum and it incorporates the entire K-12 community.**

Keywords- Computer Science; Cybersecurity; K-12 Education; K-12 Curriculum.

I. INTRODUCTION

The author's efforts started out to help her peers and have since spiraled into a crusade to improve cyber competencies within K-12. Two other students who were bullied through cyber stalking and classroom discussion boards had an impact on me. During my sixth grade year, a fellow student killed herself after being cyberbullied, and school officials were unaware. Amanda was a 14-year-old girl from my local community who was cyber stalked, abducted, raped, and left for dead, but sadly, local educators talking about these topics did not know of her story. Now, the book [1] telling her story is in school libraries and used in English classes. Amanda and her mother speak to ninth grade health classes in hopes to prevent this from happening to others. Amanda's story has been combined with two other stories to create the movie *Finding Faith* [5].

In 2016, President Barack Obama released the Computer Science (CS) For All initiative. The goal of CS for All is to teach K-12 students about computer science and provide them computational thinking skills [2]. The issue with CS for All is that many K-12 educators are not knowledgeable in computer science and cybersecurity. As many K-12 school systems are trying to add computer science and cybersecurity into the curriculum, they are realizing that they tend to teach cyberbullying, cyber safety, and certifications without providing educators the needed education to fully understand the fundamentals of computer science and cybersecurity. This is often due to administrators and educators themselves not understanding what cyber competencies are actually needed due to constantly changing fields. At the same time, K-12 continues to teach the Generation Y (Millennials) way. Studies show that social engineering, hacking and defending, cyber awareness, and personal connections have more impact on Generation Z and Generation Alpha students [14].

To many people's surprise, Generation Z is more similar to older generations than Generation Y which means that most of the educational changes put into place for Generation Y needs to be reversed. Generation Y, or Millennials in the United States, do have a few differences from Generation Z, in part because of the majority of the group's parents being Generation X. Due to lower attention span, Generation Z want 'snackable' content meaning that one communicates in bite-sized messages [14]. To reach Generation Z, content must become visually based with text being left as a witty caption, headline, or replaced by an emoji. A large portion of Generation Z have a digital footprint, but they do not know what it is, how it is affected, or that googling themselves actually puts their information into Google's repository to have their information appear higher in the results [14] Generation Z is truly a 'digital first generation' and has a very high trust level which is why it is important to ensure they are taught by cyber competent educators.

Currently, K-12 students are getting the impression from educators that computer science and cybersecurity is just programming. This is seen in many school systems when looking at the curriculum and standardized testing. For example, there is a new high school in Virginia, USA that is supposed to focus on computer science and cybersecurity education, but when you look at the curriculum, they are just teaching coding and different coding concepts. For those educators who are trying to teach more than programming they are struggling as they are using canned lessons to teach students. Canned lessons are lessons that have been made by qualified educators, educators who know the material, for educators that do not know the material to use. The issue with canned lessons is that the educators do not know the material, so they are teaching how to use the system or program and not the concept behind the system or program.

The traditional way of fighting cyberbullying is giving the definition and examples students cannot relate to. The traditional way of fighting cyberbullying is ineffective with Generation Z and beyond because they have heard the same thing for so long, so they are no longer listening. The best way to address cyberbullying is to educate on the issues that lead to cyberbullying by using cyber competencies.

In Section 2, the four main cyber competencies are described and examples of how to present to students are given. In Section 3, the additional cyber competencies are described and examples of what to present to students are given. In Section 4, the solution model for including cyber competencies in K-12 is presented. In Section 5, the success of using this model and this model's development is given.

II. MAIN CYBER COMPETENCIES

The four main cyber competencies are digital footprints, social media, security, and cyber laws. The components of the four cyber competencies are shown below in Figure 1.

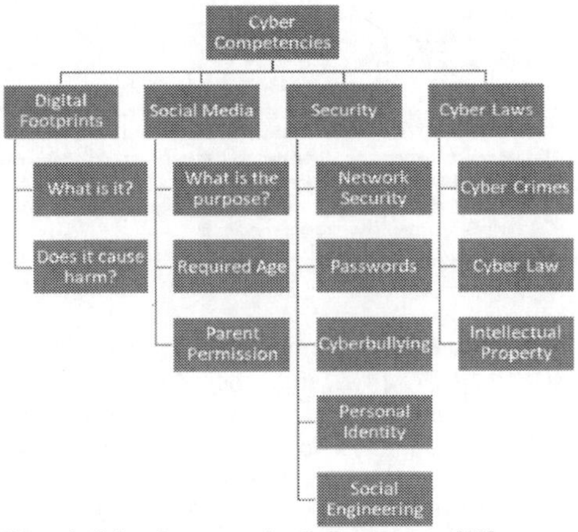

Figure 1. Cyber Competencies & Components [12].

For the digital footprint competency, one must explain what they are, how they help sites and stalkers track one, and how privacy is being given up. Students need to understand all the information online posted by them or by those with access to their social media sites. The goal of the digital footprint competency is to stress to students that people learn about them from their actions on the Internet of Things (IoT). People learning about one online use what one searches, where one searches, what one posts, and what others post about one or in response to one. The easiest way to teach this competency is by using nine phrases, shown below in Figure 2.

1. Don't be a DIGITAL DUMMY: Get real! The Web is **public** and **permanent**
2. Don't be a DIGITAL GOSSIP: Talking about others negatively, makes you look shallow
3. Don't be DIGITAL WEAK SAUCE: Don't let friends influence your better judgement
4. Don't be a DIGITAL DIVA/DIVO: Inappropriate Screen names/pictures & legal issues
5. Don't be a DIGITAL DAREDEVIL: Be careful about sites & friends
6. Don't be a DIGITAL CREEPER: Be careful about what you download, look at, even for a laugh
7. Don't be a DIGITAL MEAN KID: Don't hide behind your computer
8. Don't be a DIGITAL DORK: Information about you is impossible to remove 100%
9. Don't be a DIGITAL PRIVACY KIDDIE: There are always ways to get around privacy settings

Figure 2. Digital Footprint Competency Phrases [14].

When giving examples, educators should be able to connect them to the phrases and make sure they are able to be related to by the students. An example for phrase three is if someone posts something that you view as inappropriate, do not join the conversation unless it is in an attempt to encourage mature and responsible comments. For phrase seven, have students think about what their digital posts will say about them as a person to others. A phrase eight example would be, just like a tattoo on your thigh, an embarrassing post or tweet can last a lifetime.

For the social media competency, explain the purpose of social media sites, why there is required age limits, and the legal consequences of lying about your age to create an account. For example, you are supposed to be sixteen-years-old to use SnapChat, but many educators encourage SnapChat use in their classrooms for students under that age. SnapChat is a mobile application that allows pictures, messages, and short videos to be sent to others with them only being available for a limited amount of time. Generation Z and Alpha students have heard several times that they have to be a certain age and the purpose of social media, so keep this part of the lesson short. The social media competency is mainly taught to students with examples that allow educators to point out good and bad pieces of the situation. Two examples of cyber issues related to social media that can be real life examples used when teaching this competency is Jojo Siwa and the *Blue Whale Challenge*.

JoJo Siwa is a 16-year-old from Nebraska, who became famous after being on *Dance Moms*, *Abby's Ultimate Dance Competition*, and her upbeat songs. During a TV interview she said that she turned the commenting feature on her Instagram off after someone posted a bad comment. However, commenting is still on for Instagram and she never considered changing her settings on YouTube. During another TV interview, she encouraged children ages four to thirteen to follow her on Instagram and YouTube. Talking point one is that Instagram requires you to be 13 years of age to create an account, but even at that age parent approval is still needed. Talking point two is children ages 4-13 should not be creating accounts on YouTube to follow because they should be using YouTube Kids, which has more security protocols as they expect younger members of society to be using it. Talking point three is parent approval should be obtained before creating an account on any social media sites. Talking point four is that famous people and friends should not influence whether you have social media.

The *Blue Whale Challenge* is a challenge that exists on YouTube. The challenge is linked to human trafficking and forced suicide. Teenagers appear to be drawn into online forums where suicide was being discussed. In those forums, blue whale memes where being shared. But the idea of a sinister game, one that slowly roped in vulnerable teens and led them down an increasingly tortured path to suicide, seems th be a simplistic explanation for a complex problem. Participants of the *Blue Whale Challenge* have a whale drawn on their wrist. The last challenge is to either run away into human trafficking or to kill yourself. Talking point one is if you ever find yourself in this situation or know someone in this situation, then you need to tell a trusted adult immediately, even if told or asked not to. Talking point two is that misuse of YouTube needs to be reported.

For security competency, talk about network security, passwords, personal identity, social engineering, and cyberbullying with how they are all interconnected. For example, the social engineering discussion should include geotagging, background of pictures, and the amount of information shared online. The network security discussion should be about the differences in public and secure wi-fi and when it is safe to connect to public wi-fi.

For the cyber law competency, explain the categories of cybercrime, intellectual property, the categories intellectual property is broken into within cyber laws, and the new cyber laws being put into effect. Intellectual theft is stealing or using without permission of someone else's intellectual property. Intellectual property is protected by patent for inventions and copyrights in creative pursuits such as music, photos, and poems. Cyber law is any law that applies to the Internet and Internet related technologies. The categories of cybercrime, which should be discussed with students are people, property, and government. Cybercrimes against people include cyber harassment and stalking, distrubtion of child pornography, spoofing, credit card fraud, human trafficking, identity theft, and online related libel or slander [14]. A real life example of a cybercrime against people is in 2017 journalist Juan Thompson was sentenced to five years for stalking former girlfriend Francesca Rossi. Cybercrimes against property include Distributed Denial of Service (DDOS) attacks, hacking, virus transmission, cyber squatting, computer vandalism, copyright infringement, and Intellectual Property Rights (IPR) violations [14]. A real life example of cybercrime against property is the Wanna Cry ransomware attack of 2017 which targeted computers running the Microsoft Windows operating system by encrypting data and demanding ransom payments in the Bitcoin currency. Cybercrimes against government include hacking, accessing confidential information, cyber warfare, cyber terrorism, and pirated software [14]. An example of a cybercrime against government is the 2016 election intrusion.

III. Additional Cyber Competencies

For the high schools that offer computer science and cybersecurity courses there are two additional cyber competencies that are to be taught to students in those courses. The two additional cyber competencies are computer science and cybersecurity. The components of these two competencies are shown below in Figure 3.

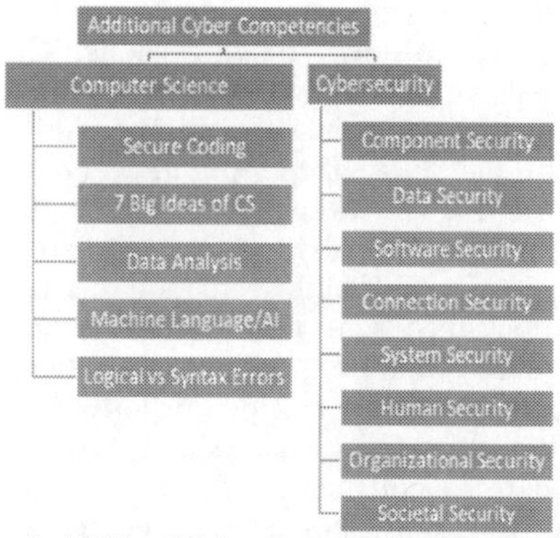

Figure 3. Additional Cyber Competencies & Components.

The computer science competency aligns with CSTransfer2017 [7] so that it allows for better flow from K-12 to college. CSTranfer2017 created by the Association of Computing Machinery (ACM) Committee for Computing Education in Community Colleges (CCECC) is a computer science curriculum guide for Associate Degree transfer programs [7]. For the computer science competency, teach secure coding, the seven big ideas of computer science, data analysis, machine language and Artificial Intelligence (AI), and logical vs syntax errors. The seven big ideas of computer science that should be taught are shown below in Figure 4.

1. Computing is a creative human activity that engenders innovation and promotes exploration
2. Abstraction educes the information and detail to focus on concepts relevant to understanding and solving problems
3. Data and information facilitate the creation of knowledge
4. Algorithms are tools for developing and expressing solutions to computational problems
5. Programming is a creative process that produces computational artifacts
6. Digital devices, systems, and the networks that interconnect them enable and foster computational approaches to solving problems
7. Computing enables innovation in other fields including science, social science, humanities, arts, medicine, engineering, and business

Figure 4. Seven Big Ideas of Computer Science [14].

The cybersecurity competency aligns with Cyber2y2020 [6], CSEC2017 [4], and the Accreditation Board for Engineering and Technology (ABET) so that it allows for a better flow from K-12 to college. Cyber2y2020 created by the ACM CCECC is a cybersecurity curriculum guide for Associate Degree programs [6]. CSEC2017 created by an Association for Computing Machinery (ACM), Institute of Electrical and Electronics Engineers Computer Society (IEEE-CS), Association for Information Systems Special Interest Group on Information Security and Privacy (AIS SIGSEC), and International Federation for Information Processing Technical Committee on Information Security Education (IFIP WG 11.8) joint taskforce is a cybersecurity curriculum guide for post-secondary degree programs [4]. The cybersecurity competency aligns with ABET's program accreditation criteria for Associate Degree programs.

For component security, teach the security aspects of the design, procurement, testing, analysis, and maintenance of components integrated into large systems. For data security, teach the protection of data at rest, during processing, and transmit. For software security, teach the development and use of software that reliably preserves the security properties of the protected information and systems. For connection security, teach the security of the connections between components, both physical and logical. For system security, teach security aspects of systems that use software and are composed of components and connections. For human security, study the human behavior in the context of data protection, privacy, and threat mitigation. For organizational security, teach how to protect organizations from cybersecurity threats and managing risk to support successful accomplishment of the organizations' missions. For social security, teach the aspects of cybersecurity that broadly influence society as a whole.

IV. Solution

The solution to the problem has four steps, as shown below in Figure 5. This solution model has had a positive impact in reducing the amount of K-12 cyber distress for the many school districts using it.

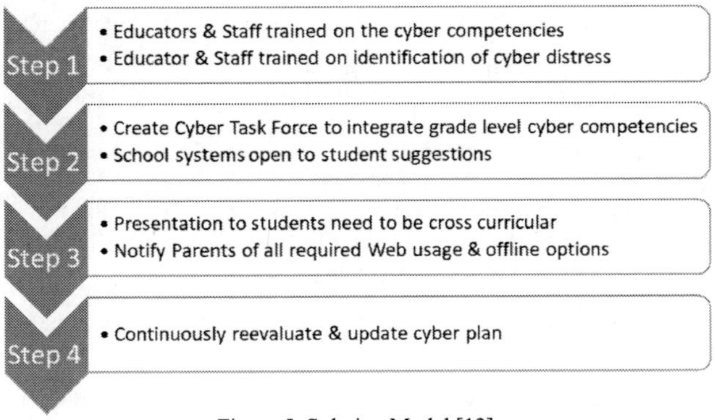

Figure 5. Solution Model [12].

Step one is the most time consuming and difficult as it involves training and convincing educators and staff to change the way they think about cyberbullying and being open minded. For example, do not share students' personal information with third party vendors for classroom tools. Educators and staff need to be trained on the cyber competencies, how to apply the cyber competencies, and actions that should be taken when dealing with students in cyber distress. An example of a good training program is the First Bytes Academy that Lord Fairfax Community College in Virginia has. In First Bytes Academy, educators and staff learn the four main competencies through classroom lectures and hands on activities. During the academy, educators and staff work with students so that they can practice different techniques for teaching the cyber competencies to their students. The First Bytes Academy teaches the two additional cyber competencies to those educators and staff who are at schools that would need them. Also, the First Bytes Academy has professionals come and train the educators and staff on how to properly handle cases of cyber distress.

Step two requires support from administration and collaboration between school system IT staff, educators, and students. The cyber taskforce should actively be sharing cyber competency resources with all members of the K-12 community. By sharing the cyber competencies with the entire K-12 community there will be more people aware of the different causes of cyber distress so they will be more active in protecting their information and more aware if the signs of cyber distress. The cyber taskforce is comprised of administrators, educators, staff, and students from the school district. The cyber taskforce is to work together and integrate the cyber competencies into the already existing curriculum for each grade level. This process will seem time consuming, but once you figure out how to integrate it at one grade level you can replicate it at another just with either a higher or lower degree of difficulty.

Step three is presentations have to be relevant and relatable at a local level. For example, have a local cyber victim speak or have a student panel allowing students to express their concerns. The in school presentations should be one of two ways. The first way is bringing in a professional from the area who has a personal experience with cyber distress and someone the students can relate to. The second way is to have student panels where students can share their experiences with cyber distress and share with the school how they think they could help those in cyber distress. The out of school presentations involve partnering with organizations such as the Girl Scouts, the Boy Scouts, the Moose, and the Elks. The school partners with these organizations and hosts events or presentations for them in which the students at the school teach the cyber competencies to the community. This allows school administration to ensure students are understanding the cyber competencies and students are teaching their peers which Generation Z and Alpha are more willing to learn from. Also, during this step school administration needs to be actively informing parents about all of the web usage that their child is being required to do for school. The parents also need to be informed of the offline options for the web usage in case the parents do not feel that it is safe for their child to be using certain tools online.

Step four is important to ensure that cyber education at the K-12 level is successful. The cyber plan needs to continuously be reevaluated and updated to stay current with modern technology and generational times. For example, many school systems are still focusing on what Generation Y needed instead of Generation Z and Alpha demands. The cyber taskforce should constantly be collecting feedback from educators, staff, administrators, parents, and students about the integration of the cyber competencies into the curriculum. If a component of the cyber competencies is not being perceived well, then the cyber plan needs to be reevaluated to have that component incorporated in a different way.

Many organizations are trying to aid in the effort of educating through the cyber competencies. Some of the organizations that are the most active in educating through the cyber competencies are the Safe Surfin' Foundation [15], Bikers Against Child Abuse [3], National CyberWatch Center [9], Internet Safety 101 Organization [8], and StopBullying [16].

Incorporation of cross-curricular cyber problems leads to students that are actively engaged in solving the problems. Educators and staff are more competent in the CIA (Confidentiality, Integrity, Accountability) Triad and can encourage student learning beyond a canned lesson plan to produce better mastery of and interest in computer science and cybersecurity. This method focuses on the outcome of increasing the number of computer science and cybersecurity professionals while keeping students involved and providing a solution that they can have a voice in. Educators are held accountable for understanding the risks involved with using free tools just because they are cool. Finally, this method is a source of open communication and partnership between K-12 school systems, higher education institutions, computer science organizations, and cybersecurity organizations.

V. Conclusion

Frederick County Public School System in Virginia, USA and Texas Public School System in USA have found a decrease in K-12 cyber distress and an increased interest in computer science and cybersecurity courses as a result of using this model. To ensure that K-12 and higher education expectations are in line, community college professors should serve on K-12 program advisory boards and K-12 representatives should serve on the community college curriculum advisory committee. Community colleges that take this approach have found that it has allowed for open discussions on how to better connect K-12 computer science and cybersecurity courses to community college computer science and cybersecurity courses.

In conclusion, my efforts to improve K-12 cyber education and increase cyber enrollment has evolved through national organizations, such as Safe Surfin' Foundation by providing speakers at schools and educational materials. Early parts of this model have been vetted by inclusion in the National CyberWatch's 2017 [11], 2018 [10], and 2019 [13] Innovations in Cybersecurity Education. Also, parts of this model have been vetted through the National Center for Women & Information Technology (NCWIT) AspireIT Grants and Aspirations in Computing (AiC) awards and Girls Scouts USA Gold Award. Other parts of this model have been supported by research presented at the 2019 Federal Partners in Bullying Prevention (FPBP) Summit on Cyberbullying Prevention. This solution was initially presented at the 2019 Association for Computing Machinery (ACM) Special Interest Group on Computer Science Education (SIGCSE) [10] and updated model presented at the 2019 Community College Cyber Summit (3CS) [11]. This solution continues to evolve into a duplicable K-12 to higher education cyber curriculum model that engages students in cyber at the elementary school level to high school seniors, so that they will want to continue in the field.

References

[1] V. Johnson, "A Lifetime Promise: The Amanda Straubs Story," 2014.

[2] About CSForAll. Retrieved August 2, 2020, from CSForAll: https://www.csforall.org/about/.

[3] Bickers Against Child Abuse. Retrieved November 14, 2020 from: https://bacaworld.org/.

[4] M. Bishop, S. Buck, D. Burley, J. Ekstrom, L. Futcher, D. Gibson, E. Hawthorne, S. Kaza, Y. Levy, H. Mattord, and A. Parrish "CSEC2017," ACM, IEEE-CS, AIS SIGSEC, & IFIP WG, 2017. DOI: 10.1145/3184594. Retrieved November 1, 2020 from: https://www.acm.org/binaries/content/assets/education/curricula-recommendations/csec2017.pdf.

[5] Finding Faith. 2013. Retrieved November 14, 2020, from IMDb: https://www.imdb.com/title/tt2201760/.

[6] M. Geissler, C. Servin, M. Stange, C. Tang, and C. Tucker, "Cyber2yr2020," Association of Computing Machinery (ACM) Committee for Computing Education in Communty Colleges (CCECC), 2020. United States. DOI: 10.1145/3381686. Retrieved November 1, 2020 from: http://ccecc.acm.org/files/publications/Cyber2yr2020.pdf.

[7] E. Hawthorne, T. Moore, C. Servin, C. Tang, and C. Tucker, "CSTransfer2017," Association of Computing Machinery (ACM) Committee for Computing Education in Community Colleges (CCECC), 2017. United States. DOI: 10.1145/3108241. Retrieved November 1, 2020 from: https://ccecc.acm.org/files/publications/CSTransfer2017.pdf.

[8] Internet Safety 101 Organization. Retrieved November 14, 2020 from: https://internetsafety101.org/.

[9] National CyberWatch Center. Retrieved November 14, 2020 from: https://www.nationalcyberwatch.org/.

[10] R. Stange, "Cyber Tween," National CyberWatch 2018 Innovations in Cybersecurity Education, p. 61, 2018.

[11] R. Stange, "A High School Sophomore and CSTA Cyber Teacher Leads Her Peers In Day of Cyber," National CyberWatch 2017 Innovations in Cybersecurity Eductaion, p. 42, 2017.

[12] R. Stange, "Increase K-12 Cyber Competency to Prevent Cyberbullying," Association of Computing Machinery (ACM) SIGSCE, 2019.

[13] R. Stange, "Increase K-12 Cybersecurity Competencies to Increase Cybersecurity Enrollment," National CyberWatch 2019 Innovations in Cybersecurity Education, p. 59, 2019.

[14] R. Stange, M. Stange, and H. Coffman, "Increasing K-12 Educator Knowledge to Prevent Cyberbullying & Enhance K-12 Cybersecurity Courses," Community College Cyber Summit (3CS), 2019.

[15] Safe Surfin' Foundation. Retrieved November 14, 2020 from: https://safesurfin.org/.

[16] StopBullying. Retrieved November 14, 2020 from: https://www.stopbullying.gov/.

Mobile Application for University Courses of Journalism and Research

Claudia A. Lerma-Noriega
Media and Digital Culture
Tecnologico de Monterrey
Monterrey, México
e-mail: clerma@tec.mx

Maria Leticia Flores-Palacios
Media and Digital Culture
Tecnologico de Monterrey
Monterrey, México
e-mail: lflores@tec.mx

Genaro Rebolledo-Mendez
Writing Lab, TecLabs
Tecnologico de Monterrey
Monterrey, México
e-mail: g.rebolledo@tec.mx

***Abstract*—One of the most common activities of university students in the areas of journalism and communication is to write news or research articles for their classes. To do this, students apply the concepts they studied in their courses to do fieldwork, conduct research, and to write the news. To facilitate this academic activity, we developed the InContext mobile application (app), which contains preloaded templates to guide the student through the process of news writing and research reporting. This application allows a student to add audio, video files, photos and link this to the information. The first stage of our research was for diagnostic purposes. It consisted of a review of the reports and textual articles prepared by students to identify the necessary characteristics that should be considered for the templates we were designing. The second stage consisted of the development of the application and its testing to get feedback and make necessary adjustments to the app. The results so far indicate that, with the teacher's guidance, students follow the required structure of the template, but elements of formatting that could be predicted with the use of the app escape them. Ideally, the app will allow the student to focus on the quality of the content. The future evolution of the app envisages redesigning it to include activities that promote the development of cognitive skills through the use of the app.**

Keywords - higher education; educational research; mobile applications; journalism; educational innovation.

I. INTRODUCTION

Educational institutions are responsible for providing their students with the tools and skills that give them the competencies they need to be future professionals in journalism and communication [1]. The students have to be able to work with state-of-art technology, inform society, and know how to request and obtain information. Similarly, professionals in creative industries must be able to respond to media outlet demands. Changes in how information is received and disseminated have created a new need: universities must update the courses offered to students in curricula where communication is an integral part of their studies. The variations in training are a result of different trends in how people read and consume information. Nowadays, the use of portable devices such as tablets, mobile phones, and laptops allows access to online journals and magazines. In Mexico, there are 79.1 million Internet users, and 89% of the connections are through mobile phones [2]. The use of social media is very high (89%), and there is a high percentage of users (82%) searching for information online [2]. This is why the technology provided by the cell phone can be incorporated into teaching, as young Mexican students use it daily. To bring about change, teachers, when doing course design, must focus their attention on learning experiences in which technology can be integrated into them [3].

This paper presents the results of our study. The work is structured as follows. In section II, we present the theoretical background. Section III provides a description of the methodology employed. Section IV presents the research results, and Section V presents the conclusion of this work.

II. THEORETICAL BACKGROUND

Heutagogy is self-determined learning, focused on the development of capabilities and capacity of the student. Heutagogy is appropriate to the needs of learners in this century [4].

The theoretical-conceptual perspective of heutagogy recognizes the need to be flexible in learning, in the use of resources, and in the facilitation or guidance that a teacher provides to students. Heutagogy is defined by the idea that the student can design and negotiate his/her own learning. The student determines what is most essential and subsequently arranges his/her reading and evaluation assignments [4].

As an example, the journalism schools of the Auckland University of Technology (AUT) in New Zealand use heutagogy as a teaching method in their social media courses in journalism. This method prepares students through a new style of educating that incorporates dealing with the vast amount of information available on the Internet. In this case, a heutagogic framework provides the flexibility for students to perform their course work using existing technological tools familiar to them [5].

Along these lines, this work proposes the hypothesis that the use of mobile applications is useful in academics to enhance critical thinking [6]. There is evidence in this regard: Reen and Ramnarayan's research with medical students at Manipal University, India, is an example [7]. The authors asked medical students to use social media to work on their projects. They concluded that the heutagogic method allowed their students to generate learning products and develop critical thinking, so the union of this learning methodology with technology can be considered a key to learning for 21st-century youth [7].

According to Crittenden et al. [8], it is crucial that university students know how to use digital technology such as artificial intelligence, augmented reality, drones, the Internet of Things, robots, virtual reality, and 3D printing, among others. Technology applied in the classroom to theory helps students develop critical thinking and creativity, so they can generate value in the professional arena. The authors add that one of the criticisms of technology has been that it can be distracting; however, distraction is also present in traditional teaching [8].

Today's world is characterized by an abundance of data, shortened decision times, and the elimination of geographical boundaries brought about by information technologies [9]. Foreseeably, communication technologies will remain a permanent part of the continuous connectivity in people's work. [10][11]. For these reasons, educators must guide the creators of future content toward the skills of communication and precision. To that end, we developed a mobile application called *InContext,* which specifically targets those competencies. With *InContext*, students have many features now like standard templates, guides, focus group formats, and the key questions and components needed to write journalistic articles or editorials, among others.

Educators have the advantage of being able to leverage student engagement in the classroom through the use of technology. Making the students co-responsible for learning the topics in class leads to their greater involvement. In our research, we see that this involvement occurs when the student, as a user of our app, can add photographs, audio, and video files to content with a smartphone or tablet at the time of the event. These tools, like Google Drive, facilitate the collection of information.

The objective of this study was to design this mobile app with interactive formats that assist the beginning of the writing process or the beginning of social research. *InContext* lets the student use one of the pre-loaded, interactive multimedia templates that correspond to the different journalistic genres and research designs to generate content suitable for journalism or social research. The target users were students of journalism and communication at Tecnologico de Monterrey, Mexico, during the winter 2018 and spring 2019 semesters.

III. METHODOLOGY

A. *Participants*

The students who participated in the first two stages were men and women between 18 and 25 years old, with 21 being the average age. They were enrolled in various curricula such as Journalism, Communication, International Relations, Advertising, Political Science, and Psychology. All were taking the courses in research and journalism between the second and fifth semesters of their professional curricula on the Monterrey campus of Tecnologico de Monterrey. The risks associated with this experiment were minimal because no personal or sensitive information was requested from them during the study.

In the first stage, developed in the winter 2018 semester, 161 written articles prepared by 305 students enrolled in five courses were taken as a reference for analysis. The classes were Quantitative Methods for Social Research, Research Journalism, Digital Journalism, Qualitative Methods Research, Advertising and Comprehensive Marketing. The second stage, in the spring 2019 semester, entailed the design of the application and its use by some of the students (n=141).

The *InContext* mobile application has 4 templates for research courses and 16 templates for journalism courses. It allows the students to enter and format their report information, including surveys, interviews, content analyses, and various things relating to news reports, like chronicles, stories, semblances, etc.

B. *Procedure*

Three stages were established for this investigation. The first was developed during September to December 2018 and aimed to identify the essential characteristics that an investigative report or a journalistic article should have. To do this, we reviewed works written by the students before using the technology. The second stage occurred from February to May 2019, in which different students tested the application and made adjustments, and the results of this stage are reported in this paper. The third stage will use control and experimental groups to check whether the use of the tool by the students promotes autonomous learning and develops the critical thinking in students to focus on the content of the reports and not just their forms or structures.

C. *Tools*

InContext is an application of specialized software containing custom-made templates for the primary genres of journalism and the elemental procedures of research methodology. The app guides the student to supply the relevant information for each of the points of the templates. The student adds the required multimedia material and sends the content via email or uploads it to the cloud. The use of the app directs the student to the bare minimum inputs necessary to start writing creative or informative text, and it allows the student to explore new ways to deliver content. Also, the app facilitates flexible learning because users can go at their own pace as they practice journalistic writing and conduct academic research.

Although *InContext* is a mobile-device application made explicitly for university students, future versions could be integrated as a suite in the Tec de Monterrey moodle-based learning platform.

This application is based on Laravel, bootstrap, html5, and progressive application techniques. It can be viewed on

Android, Apple, and Windows mobile devices. The app allows the student to access the summary of their contribution (frontend). The teacher can easily design templates, automatic reviews, assessments, and grading scales (backend).

Students access the app at app.incontext.mx/login, register, and then select the preloaded formats. Journalism students find specified templates (various formats for news, report, chronicle, review, semblance, conference, press conference, etc.). Research students find other templates (surveys, interviews, etc.).

Students follow the template, inserting title, author, date, sources, questions and answers, photographs, etc. Upon completion of the template, students generate a PDF file that can be downloaded.

Students enrolled in one of these courses have access to the tool and they select the format needed from 20 options.

Figure 1 shows the *InContext* screen to illustrate how students access the app. Figure 2 shows the dashboard where the students can select the specific template to use, and Figure 3 shows the screens with the survey form as an example. In that form, they find the elements that must be written, such as title and objective, theoretical background, and bibliography, etc. The student can attach photos, videos, audios, and links to the text documents they are preparing, and they can proceed at their own pace. *InContext* allows them to generate a PDF report that can be delivered in print or electronic form to the teacher or anyone.

IV. RESULTS

This initial review carried out was qualitative. We compared the research reports and the news stories that students prepared before using the application with the work they did after using it and considered some possible improvements in the tasks. In the case of research reports, better results were observed in two specific respects (Table I), namely, the manifest presence of the research objective and the demographic data of the study participants.

Figure 1. Access screen to the app.

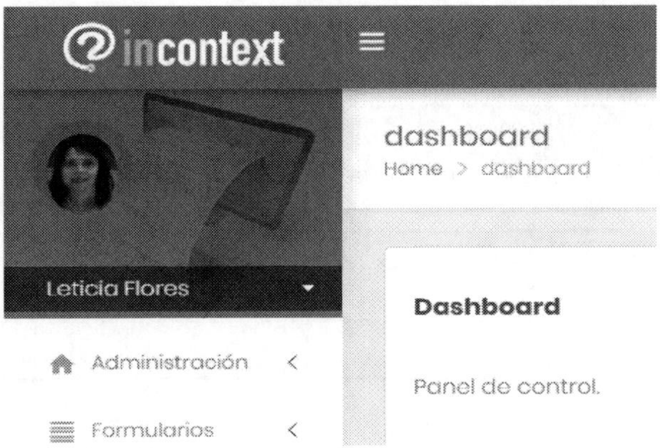

Figure 2. Student access to the dashboard and selection of forms.

In the same way, when reviewing the work of the journalism courses, it was possible to identify improvements with the use of the app (Table II), specifically in the presence of information sources, the news writer credits, and the inclusion of photographs. The application displays the items to be completed in the format, and, therefore, it is difficult to forget or omit their inclusion.

Table I shows the results of the exploratory study using a convenience sample. Please note the low number of students using the app was due to reduced attendance during the days of the study.

V. CONCLUSIONS

In the first two stages, the need to design the templates carefully was evident, as well as the usability of the application on both cell phones and computers. However, the most important thing was to identify whether the use of this technology not only facilitates the learning of formats, but also leads to reflection and analysis of the written content. These aspects will be reviewed in the future stage of this investigation.

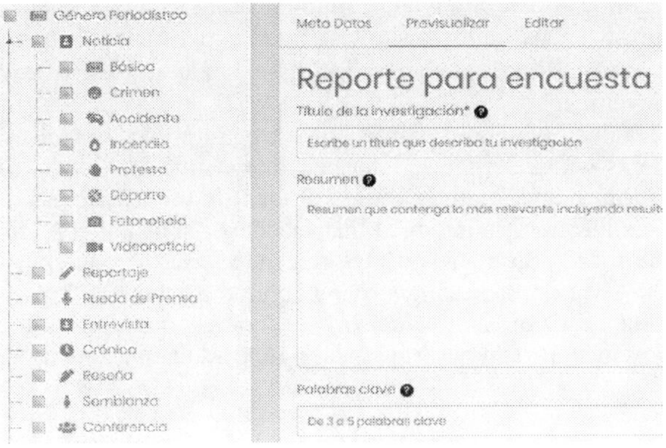

Figure 3. Example of a template that starts the work.

TABLE I. HITS FOUND IN THE RESEARCH WORK WITHOUT APPLICATION AND USING IT

Research work	Without app	Using app
States the research objective	20/54	5/6
Specifies the demographics of the sample data	26/54	6/6
Total work reviewed:	54	6

TABLE II. HITS FOUND IN THE JOURNALISM EXERCISES WITHOUT APPLICATION AND USING IT

Journalism exercises	Without app	Using app
States the news sources	34/41	37/40
Includes photographs	34/41	36/40
Indicates the writer credit	32/41	40/40
Total work reviewed:	41	40

The results presented in this paper seem to align with those shown by Reen & Ramnarayan [7]; *InContext* facilitates student work by offering them a flexible environment where they can learn better. The results presented in this paper also supports the idea presented by Crittenden et al. [8] that technology is not always a distractor and can be used, instead, as a tool to increase concentration [8]. The results of this paper are encouraging. The research indicates that technology can help students focus; in this project, it offers them the elements to guide the development of writing and communicating using templates. Future work will allow us to test, in an experimental setting, how much these elements facilitate students' work and achievements.

Ideally, with the continuous repetition of exercises, students will incorporate into their knowledge the details of the formats and, on their own, will identify the usefulness of this application. It is hoped that teachers using the app can spend more time reviewing the relevance and the content of student work rather than worrying about the details of form.

The use of this type of technology highlights the importance of continuously updating the education for future managers. The universities have to offer new educational strategies so that students participate more while they increase their self-efficacy [4]. The future communicators are today's students; therefore, universities have to offer the instructional strategies that are relevant to their future needs.

ACKNOWLEDGMENT

The authors would like to acknowledge the financial and technical support of Writing Lab, TecLabs, Tecnologico de Monterrey, Mexico, in the production of this work.

REFERENCES

[1] Clasesdeperiodismo.com. "Jeff Jarvis: The journalism recognizes that the public knows more," *Clases de periodismo*, 2017, July 16.

[2] Asociación de Internet. "14 Study about habits of Internet users in Mexico 2018," *Asociación de Internet,* Mexico City, 2018.

[3] C. Marcelo, C. Yot, and C. Mayor, "University teaching with digital technologies," Comunicar, vol. XXIII, no. 45, pp. 117-124, 2015.

[4] S. Hase and C. Kenyon, "From andragogy to heutagogy," National Library of Australia, 2004. [Online]. Available from:https://webarchive.nla.gov.au/awa/20040812230501/http://pandora.nla.gov.au/pan/10088/20010816/ultibase.rmit.edu.au/Articles/dec00/hase2.htm

[5] D. Mulrennan, "Mobile social media and the news: where heutagogy enables journalism education," Journalism and Mass Communication Educator, vol. 73, no. 3, pp. 322-333, 2018.

[6] M. Deuze, "About the media and the entrepreneur as a way of being in the world," in Global education of journalism in the XXI century. Challenges and innovations. Austin, Knight Center for Journalism in the Americas, 2018, pp. 310-327.

[7] R. Reen and K. Ramnarayan, "Heutagogic approach to developing capable learners," Medical Teacher, vol. 39, no. 3, pp. 295-299., 2017.

[8] W. Crittenden, I. Biel, and W. Lovely, "Embracing digitalization: student learning and new technologies," Journal of Marketing Education, vol. 41, no. 1, pp. 5-14, 2019.

[9] L. Lugo-Ortiz, "The academy, the media, and the ideal professional: a generalist-multimedia journalist," Comunicación y Sociedad, vol 29, no. 4, pp.271-287, 2016.

[10] X. López-García, A-I. Rodríguez-Vázquez and X. Pereira-Fariña. "Technological skills and new professional profiles: present challenges for journalism," Comunicar, vol. 25, no. 5, pp. 81-90, 2017. doi:10.3916/c53-2017-08.

[11] X. López-García, A. Silva-Rodríguez, Á-A. Vizoso-García, O. Westlund, and J. Canavilhas, "Mobile journalism: systematic literature review," Comunicar, vol. 27, no. 59, pp. 9-18, 2019. doi:10.3916/c59-2019-01.

New Learning Method for Structural Understanding in Architecture Based on Gamification

Perla R. Santa Ana Lozada
Architecture, Art and Design School
Tecnologico de Monterrey
Mexico City, Mexico
Email: psantana@tec.mx

Aleksandra Krstikj
Architecture, Art and Design School / Writing Lab
Tecnologico de Monterrey
Mexico City, Mexico
Email: sandra.krstik@tec.mx

***Abstract*—One of the challenges architecture students face is understanding static structural and mathematical procedures as part of the structural design concepts they need to apply in their work. This research hypothesizes that gamification and smartphone apps with games using topics of structural design applied to architecture could improve the results in architectural education. Based on gamification and e-learning software, a new learning method was created consisting of six strategies: understanding the target audience, definition of learning objectives, designing the experience, identifying resources, application of gamification elements and recap of the process; the method's importance was found in being the first in its kind at the architecture undergraduate level. To assess the effects of this method, a comparison between two classes (with and without the method) was made. The results obtained were promising: most students gained motivation, engagement, and higher final scores in their structural analysis and design courses.**

Keywords - educational innovation; higher education; gamification; architecture; structural design.

I. Introduction

In the field of architecture, physical and mathematical concepts are integral to the structural design process. However, considering the abstract nature of these concepts, architectural students often find it challenging to understand the mathematical simplifications for solving the behavior of structural elements, such as frames, bearing walls, slabs, columns, and many other built-in structures. In the School of Architecture at Tecnologico de Monterrey, Campus Ciudad de México, e-learning is encouraged as a tool for facilitating course objectives. Thus, in the courses of structural design, we first implemented an existing smartphone app, designed by the principal author of this paper exclusively for practicing physical-structural concepts in architectural design [1]. This app is a game-based learning method built on the potential of video games to improve understanding of structural design concepts such as stresses (tension and compression) and flexural moment and their effect over buildings and other structures, such as bridges, following the game elements of mechanics, story, aesthetics, and technology.

The software is designed as a virtual laboratory with practices to help students review the main concepts by a step-by-step guide to win each game. In the first semester, students were invited to play with this app as an additional learning tool. From a total of 22 students in the two groups of a structural design course, only 13 downloaded the app and played the games, while the others only followed the lab practice to win each level and comply with the assigned task. Even though the content of the application was part of the course syllabus, the students were not analyzing the concepts and were not engaging with the subject.

Therefore, the need for a different learning method to improve student engagement in the structural design course in architecture became clear. We hypothesized that gamification, as a learning method that occurs in a non-game context and focus on students´ engagement and challenge [2], could potentially provide better results in the understanding of structural design for architects. Even though recently, gamification has been gaining momentum in education [3], very few studies measure the impact of the teaching process in the educational context and explore methods for improving the program by gamifying the course literature and material from teachers' point of view [4]. Moreover, no studies have been found by the authors that explore the gamification method in the field of architectural education; this is due to most architecture schools' lack of knowledge on gamification and the existence of free applications that can be used in education.

This research aimed to design and measure the impact of a new learning method based on gamification to improve the structural understanding of architectural education from the teachers´ point of view. The purpose was to facilitate the learning of abstract physical and mathematical concepts related to structural design for architectural students and improve the overall quality of their architectural proposals. The benefits of such a method can bring in improving architectural education are multiple: from better structurally designed buildings to increasing students' satisfaction and self-confidence.

The work done for the research is based on a specific successful educational experience, but the methodology described could be adapted to other areas using mathematics and physics, such as civil engineering.

In order to understand the development and results of the proposed gamification method and its application, Section II of this paper presents the steps used to create the proposed method; in Section III, the working method and class experience are presented, while Section IV presents the assessment of the learning method results. Students' feedback and conclusions/future work are presented in Sections V and VI, respectively.

II. Creating the Method for Structural Understanding in Architecture

Following the six steps proposed by Hsin et al. [3] for gamification at the Management School at the University of Toronto, we designed a new learning method for structural design understanding in architecture with the following six strategies:

A. Understanding the target audience and the context

Within the architecture undergraduate program, the Steel Structural Design course is the last of four courses regarding Structural Analysis and Design. In theory, that implies that the students should have already mastered the structural analysis concepts in previous classes, and the students should be capable of immediately applying structural analysis in the course of Structural Design. The first strategy revolves around verifying students' abilities in structural analysis and setting the app tool and course dynamics.

- Strategy:

Architecture students arrive at this course with different levels of understanding of the basic concepts about structural analysis. To accomplish equal student's understanding, the following actions are considered: explaining different kinds of structural solutions, analyzing iconic architectural buildings, and downloading the smartphone app for the course. Most of the students at Tecnologico de Monterrey have a smartphone at hand, so the downloading and checking the app´s function is done relatively fast.

B. Defining learning objectives

Architecture students go through Structural Analysis courses without understanding their real application in designing buildings´ structural elements. The second strategy is aimed at defining the learning objectives of the Structural Design course in applying structural analysis concepts to propose correct, new, and/or sustainable architectonical solutions.

- Strategy:

Explaining general structural concepts and consequences of using them in architectonical solutions.

C. Structuring the experience

Students need to understand every stage of the structural design process. The third strategy deals with structuring the students' experience hierarchically, from solving smaller to more significant tasks, in order to gradually achieve the course objectives. If students do not understand every stage of the structural design, they will lose interest in the subject.

- Strategy:

Assigning starting exercises focused on smaller tasks to review the main concepts of the pre-courses and gradually increase the difficulty of the tasks to achieve the final solution of the structural design. As an example, we start in class solving a problem where the relation between the tension stress, the tension load, and the cross-section area of a steel cable are related in order to design a staircase suspended with cables from the ceiling.

D. Identifying resources

The course followed "Problem Based Learning" (PBL) [5] strategy before introducing gamification. To have a smooth course transition and become acquainted with this new strategy, at the end of every topic, a PBL challenge was introduced as part of an everyday exercise in the classroom.

- Strategy:

Activities from the gamification process were introduced as part of everyday work in the classroom; the first exercise of each theme was developed by writing down each step used to get the right answer. The following tasks are from the app, where scenarios are more real and displayed with the same topics. The students practiced one game per week.

E. Applying gamification elements

The fifth strategy builds upon the previous experiences in using the app and introduces more complex challenges to deepen the students' understanding of structural design problems. By using the gamification elements introduced in this strategy, the students have an opportunity to conceptualize better structural solutions and improve their course evaluation grade.

- Strategy:

The app selected must include one of the topics of the course and the professor should know how the app works to solve the problem, in order to help students to get the right answer, play the app and win each game.

The student has to solve problems with different levels of complexity and win the game at each level in order to move on to the next level. Every completed practice brings points when finished successfully, and these points were calculated as additional points in the monthly evaluation. Since not all students have the same capacity for solving mathematical problems fast, extra time was assigned to specific individuals to complete the task.

Figure 1. Application use in class 1 for steel design.

They would take the app practice as homework, getting an extended timeframe to finish the task. The course teacher followed up with those students after class by WhatsApp to answer any doubts. We concluded that it is quite important to allow students to work in teams since teamwork discussions encouraged students´ confidence in solving problems.

In Figure 1, the app scenario for a compression problem using a parabolic biarticulated arch is presented; the objective is to understand how the structural design is applied over an architectural project as this bridge.

F. Recap

Previous strategies were tested within the real course focus groups, adapting the strategies to calibrate and improve the method.

- Strategy:

Adapt the method´s strategies to the group´s needs and capabilities in order to get the best results in the learning process.

III. LEARNING EXPERIENCE AT THE CLASSROOM LEVEL

The above-described learning method was applied to three different groups of Structural Design courses in the last three semesters. The courses where the method was applied were "Design of Reinforced Concrete Structures" and "Design of Steel Structures." The main topic of both courses was the structural design of steel or concrete bearing elements, through theoretical explanation of structural behavior and application of building codes equations.

The classes were held twice a week and follow the PBL strategy. The first weekly class was dedicated to an explanation of a theoretical structural analysis approach and a presentation of structural element design on the blackboard with the participation of the students. Since the class time was limited, we focused on solving small problems concerning structural element design.

The second weekly class was dedicated to problem-solving assignments. To evaluate the students' performance, a scenario of a structural problem was presented for students to solve using the concepts learned in class. Since the problems tackled in the class were focused on stand-alone structural elements, students´ found it hard to understand the relationship between that single element and the complete structural system. The PBL strategy was found particularly helpful in establishing the relation between theory and real examples with a constructive problem.

To incorporate the gamification method in the first-weekly class concerning the theory of structural analysis, numerical exercises were designed to be solved together with the students on the blackboard. The exercises were based on small real cases of buildings with the same structural solution so that the students can understand the numeric results over real elements; different structural solutions were analyzed as well.

In the second weekly class, the previous exercise was recalled, and the steps to solve the problem were written on the blackboard. Working in teams, the students used the e-learning app to solve the class assignment. The students were instructed first to read and analyze the problem, and after that, to start proposing solutions. Each virtual practice (e-learning software) contained two or three problems, with the level of complexity increasing as students fulfill each task (adaptive strategy); while using the virtual practice, students must choose an Avatar as part of the game mood. The Avatar is important for game-based learning and gamification in order to allow students to feel part of the game, get a new identity that, in some cases, could be more fierce and challenging.

Students were also allowed to work alone; however, the formation of teams with 2 to 4 students was encouraged for better results. At the beginning of the class, the teacher verified that every student in the class understood the problem correctly and helped them to confirm the steps needed to solve the virtual practice.

As each student finished all the tasks (quest) included in the e-learning software, they got two prizes: game points and a virtual tour of the case study structure using augmented reality. The game points could be exchanged for additional monthly grade points (0.25 additional points for each task finished, so at the end of each month, they could get one extra point on their grade). Since some students needed more time to understand and finish the game quest, they could ask for additional time, with a week being the maximum time allowed to finish the task and earn the same amount of points as the other students. The students showed low interest in the virtual tour of the building, where information about the architect and the project was displayed. Students were already acquainted with this kind of virtual experience as they have played games with more sophisticated imagery (i.e., Nintendo or X-Box), so students have not considered the augmented reality as a grand prize.

After the quests were completed, each team presented their conclusions about: i) the game; ii) the theory involved; iii) the architectural project used for the practice. This part was as important as the game itself because it allowed students to process all the information and understand the relationships between theory and practice. As the experience sank in, the students were able to comprehend the process of application of theoretical analysis and design in the real world and to realize the implications structural design has on the quality of the architectural project.

As teachers, we know that the synthesis of learning and acknowledgment is very important for students thus, when a student archived all the learning goals in the one-course theme, he/she was entitled to a badge: structure expert. This badge made students feel recognized and more engaged with the topic. If a student acquired three badges, he/she was eligible for an exemption from the final exam.

The exams for the structural design courses were also designed using a PBL strategy. The new learning method based on gamification helped the students to a) analyze complex scenario problems with a step-by-step approach; b) improve the design thinking process to solve the problem in stages; and c) gain confidence in their work, therefore leading to better results in the exam evaluations.

IV. ASSESSMENT OF THE LEARNING METHOD RESULTS

Even though the introduction of the new learning method based on gamification has been challenging for us as teachers, the students' performance in the class improved. The improvement was observed in the better final evaluation grades that were mostly due to the better exam performance, as well as to the extra grade points acquired during the class activities.

To confirm the effects of the new gamification method on students learning, we compared partial and final grades from a selected previous group that did not use the method (defined by the authors as control group using just PBL) and a group where the gamification method was used during the same course with the same length and number of students (defined by the authors as experimental group using PBL and gamification).

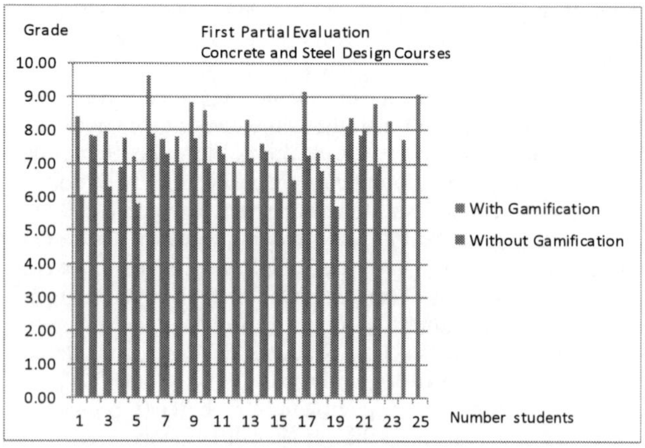

Figure 2. Comparison of group first partial evaluation.

At Tecnologico de Monterrey, the grade evaluation range is from zero to ten, where ten is the highest score, and grade below seven is considered a fail.

In Figure 2, the first partial grades of 52 students were presented. Red lines correspond to students that took the courses without the gamification method, and blue lines are the grades of students that took the same courses with the gamification method. As can be seen from the graph, the grades were relatively higher in the courses with the gamification method. More importantly, there were no grades below seven in the gamification courses. These results are essential for the class, as dropping out from the course is diminished.

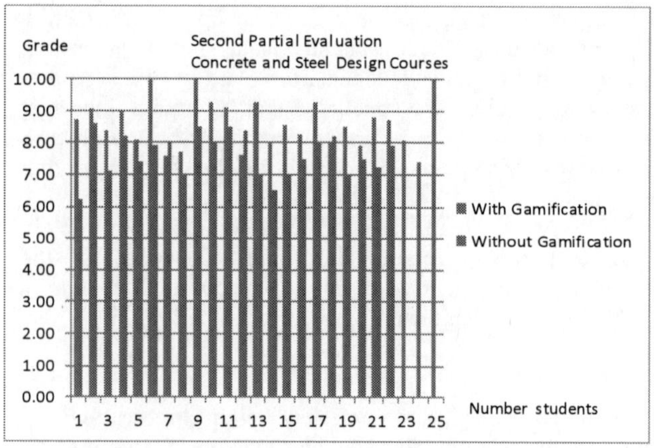

Figure 3. Comparison of group second partial evaluation.

In the second partial evaluation (Figure 3), the students from both courses, with and without the gamification method, had higher grades compared to the first partial evaluation. This behavior could be explained by the fact that as students progress through the course, they get better acquainted and more confident with structural design topics.

In Figure 4, we compared the final exam grades in courses with and without the gamification method. We found a considerable improvement of the average final grade in the courses with the gamification method (average of 8.0), compared to the average grade in the courses using just PBL without gamification (average of 6.8). The increment in the course grades means that students got a better understanding of each topic and its application in real-life problems, like the ones solved in the mobile app.

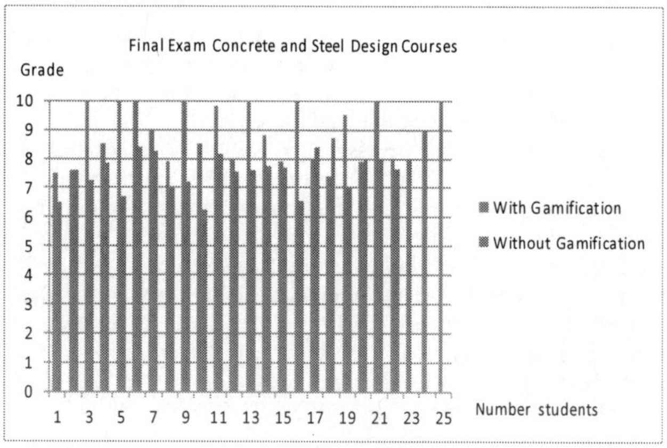

Figure 4. Comparison of final exam grades between courses.

V. STUDENTS FEEDBACK REGARDING THE NEW METHOD

We designed and conducted a questionnaire to analyze students´ feedback regarding the effectiveness of the new learning method based on gamification in the experimental groups. The purpose was to quantitatively assess student personal achievement using the Likert scale [6], ranging from 1 = not at all characteristic of me, to 5 = very characteristic of me. To understand the results in the context of previous courses without the gamification or control group, we conducted the same questionnaire to those groups as well. The mode (statistic) is presented as the evaluation result for each subject.

As presented in Table I, students in the experimental groups were more engaged during the class, asking more questions, and putting more effort into completing the tasks assigned. The experimental groups were also more inclined to using the e-learning software app after class.

TABLE I. EVALUATION OF STUDENTS COURSE ENGAGEMENT QUESTIONNAIRE (SCEQ)

No.	Evaluation		
	Behavior, thoughts, and feelings	***Control group***	***Experimental group***
1	Participating in class	3	4
2.	Asking the instructor questions for a better understanding	3	5
3.	Asking the instructor questions to get the application game done	0	3
4	Playing the application game after class	0	3
5.	Putting forth effort	3	4
6.	Desire to learn the material using the application game	1	3
7	Playing the application in teams	0	4
8	Explaining the solution to solve the app quest between companions	0	4

Looking at the answers for questions 7 and 8, and watching their behavior in class, we discovered that teamwork is one of the necessary conditions for better student engagement. The students felt that within a team, they could quickly clarify misunderstandings from the theoretical aspect and achieve faster and better solutions. The teamwork also positively affected the feeling of confidence while working.

We also evaluated the students´ satisfaction with the courses based on the new learning method. The scores were again based on a Likert scale in five-point grade, five being the best score (Table II). It was assessed that the students´ experience with the course using gamification was overall positive; students were motivated by the prizes and considered the application fun to use, which led to a better understanding of the theory.

TABLE II. EVALUATION OF STUDENTS METHOD PERFORMANCE

No.	Evaluation	
	Phrases	***Evaluation***
1	Performance of the course	4
2.	The application game helps to understand structural behavior	4
3.	Playing the application in the classroom was challenging but fun	4
4	The application clarifies the theory applied to real cases	4
5.	Getting badges and points is adequate	4

Finally, students were asked to evaluate the course teaching approach of mixing the new learning method for class activities in 70% of the course with a more traditional lecture style for the theoretical part in the rest 30%. To our surprise, students considered interesting the combination of strategies during the course that provided time for playing with the app and standard lecture time. Moreover, most of the students were grateful for the extra time allowed for finishing the tasks, as they could try out different answers while playing that led to a better understanding of the theory.

VI. CONCLUSIONS AND FUTURE WORK

By analyzing the grade results and students´ feedback, we concluded that the students´ understanding of structural design was enhanced in the courses that applied the new learning method based on gamification. 90% of students finished all the games assigned in the semester, and 60% got the badge ¨structure expert¨, which implies significant improvement in students´ engagement compared to previous courses that did not utilize the gamification method. Since the first courses using the new method also included 30% of more traditional lectures, we assume that students´ performance could improve even more if the new method is applied more consistently.

One of the most interesting observations was that millennial students do not consider competition as an incentive; they prefer to work at their own pace without pressure and in teams. The preference for teamwork was found in the opportunity to collaborate with more skillful or well-informed students. In fact, students confirmed that giving level awards made them feel uncomfortable, thus in the future, we will only focus on awarding one type of badge to all who complete the game quest.

Time was found to be an important factor in the success of the learning method since less skillful students needed extra time to accomplish their tasks at their own pace. Avatars were found to be slightly significant while playing with the e-software app, however extra points that students acquired for the class activities were found to be incentivizing. Immediate feedback was also appreciated, as students could quickly adjust their work and search for better solutions without wasting time.

The gamification method proposed is more than game points; it is a strategy where the professor gets more acquainted with the student, giving confidence while learning how to solve real-life problems using today's technology; the virtual environment experimentation to solve real-world challenges offers the students a better understanding about the mathematical solution and its application over real architectural projects. In the real world context where stakes are high and human lives at risk, better-prepared architects with a deeper understanding of structural problems are the goal of education.

With the game-based learning app used, made especially for this courses, students knew immediately when they were making a mistake, and that instant feedback allowed them to progress faster, ultimately providing them with a better understanding of structural design. In Mexico, the gamification method has not been developed; there is a world of free apps that can be used for teaching, but a method is needed in order to achieve each course objective.

Teachers may find the following difficulties using the method proposed for other courses: a) finding the best app for each subject; it should get the results needed to get the students understanding and engagement; b) the app must exist for IOS and Android system so every student can use it; c) time should be programmed in order to give the student the theory, its application and solving the problem while playing with the app.

However, there is still more work to be done to improve the method, mainly to increase students′ participation and engagement further. The level of challenges has to be reconsidered carefully since time management is crucial for the success of the method — professors using apps in class need to know how they work and the theoretical concepts they follow in order to choose the one that fits for the subject of each class and guide the student learning with a specific purpose. Finally, further studies are necessary to enrich the students′ educational experience and find ways for better access to teachers' feedback.

ACKNOWLEDGMENT

The authors would like to acknowledge the financial and the technical support of Writing Lab, TecLabs, Tecnologico de Monterrey, Mexico, in the production of this work.

REFERENCES

[1] P. Santa Ana and L. Santa Ana, "Apprendestructo: Learning app joining together structural analysis with architecture project," [Apprendestructo: Aplicación que integra el conocimiento estructural dentro del proyecto arquitectónico], Repentina, UNAM, México, pp 23-25, September 2017.

[2] S. Snezana, Z. Nada, and M. Tripo, "Gamification in higher education learning –state of the art, challenges and opportunities," Proc. The Sixth International Conference on e-Learning, (eLearning 2015), pp 128-134, September 2015.

[3] W. Hsin, H. Yuan, and D. Soman, "A practitioner's Guide to Gamification of Education," Economic School, University of Toronto, 2013.

[4] G. Barata, J. Gama, and D. Goncalves, "Engaging engineering students with gamification," Proc. 5th International Conference Games and Virtual Worlds for Serious Applications (VS-GAMES), pp 1-8, September 2013.

[5] E. Christiansen, M. Leena, and B. Lindstrom, "Problem-based learning for the 21st Century," Aalborg Universitet, Denmark, 2013.

[6] M. Handelsman, W. Briggs, N. Sullivan, and A. Towler, "A measure of college student course engagement," The Journal of Educational Research, Vol. 98, No. 3, pp. 184-192, 2005.

Addressing Prerequisites for STEM Classes Using an Example of Linear Algebra for a Course in Machine Learning

Genady Grabarnik
Department of Math & CS
St. John's University
Queens, NY, USA
email: grabarng@stjohns.edu

Luiza Kim-Tyan
Department of Mathematics
NUST MISIS
Moscow, Russia
email: kimtyanlr@gmail.com

Serge Yaskolko
AD&D
College Board
Pittsburgh, PA, USA
email: syaskolko@collegeboard.com

***Abstract*—While teaching Science, Technology, Engineering, and Mathematics (STEM) subjects, we frequently encounter situations where we have several prerequisites for a particular course. We anticipate that students will have different levels of knowledge in these prerequisites. A prerequisite (Linear algebra for Machine Learning course) was implemented as an interactive online course using Jupyter Notebooks and nbgrader. A preliminary survey shows a preference by students and instructors for this interactive implementation.**

Keywords- prerequisites; machine learning; linear algebra; interactive self-study course; Jupyter Notebooks.

I. INTRODUCTION

While teaching STEM subjects, we frequently encounter situations where we have several prerequisites for a particular course. We expect these students will have different levels of knowledge regarding these prerequisites. In most cases, a conceptual understanding and an ability to apply the prerequisite material are sufficient for most students. Students are not expected to know details, such as proofs, etc.

We encountered one such situation while teaching a Machine Learning (ML) course to first-year graduate students. An ML course relies on knowledge of linear algebra, multi-dimensional calculus and probability. The standard approach is to provide material for student self-study in addition to refresher material, so called crash course material given during the course. The advantage here is that students get at least the minimum amount of the required material, with an option for additional self-learning if desired.

We also encounter multiple disadvantages, however, with such an approach. For one, time needed for the main subject is spent on prerequisites. Review time for prerequisites should be limited as it is very challenging to cover necessary material at a sufficiently high level. While students have the option to self-study, learning with an instructor is significantly more effective and efficient. Another disadvantage: neither students nor instructors could verify whether the necessary level of understanding and application of prerequisite material had been achieved. This may be remedied with quizzes or tests, which in turn require additional precious instruction time.

To address these issues, we decided to use an available teaching technology: we would organize prerequisite material in the form of interactive online self-study. We used Jupyter Notebook [1] - based technology flexible enough to create an interactive course with proper mathematical typesetting as well as programming support (Python) in case we had to do modifications which we assumed should allow us to address these issues.

Thus, instead of providing generic self-study materials for prerequisites in the form of a book or pdf, we provided a concise Interactive Online self-study course that covers prerequisites and offers Concept Inventory (IOCI) based short tests, which evaluate students' understanding of the main concepts and their ability to apply the material. Hence, we precisely target the goals of the course prerequisites.

We implemented the course using iPython Notebook [2] software with additional course management support provided by the nbgrader plugin [16]. The course was developed on Amazon's c9 cloud and was available to students online. The course works in an automated or semi-automated way, allowing the instructor to see test results by topic or intervene and comment on student answers.

In our specific case, we started with linear algebra (LA) prerequisite material for the ML graduate course. We developed prerequisite self-study course material with CI-based tests. Students can return to topics already studied, advance upon completion of an appropriate test, or skip tests altogether and concentrate on study material alone.

Our course offers a two-part novelty: making prerequisite material in the form of interactive online course; incorporating quizzes and homework in the form of Concept Inventory (CI), which addresses only required for prerequisite understanding of concepts and notions and ability to apply the material in the main course context. To the best of our knowledge, such combinations were not used before. The course was also translated into Russian and deployed at two universities: St John's University (New York) and the National University of Science and Technology, MISIS (Moscow). It covered two experimental groups with a total of 30-plus students. According to the preliminary survey, both students and instructors prefer the interactive Jupyter Notebook-based study approach to the standard prerequisite classes.

This paper proceeds as follows. In Section II, we describe existing CIs and state-of-the-art Interactive Online Systems. In Section III, we proceed to a description of LA as a prerequisite material to the Machine Learning course. We show how CI addresses the requirement of the specific prerequisite material. In Section IV, we describe the cloud system used for the initial implementation of the course as well as hardware requirements for running a test experiment of about 200 software simulated test students. In Section V, we provide a preliminary (proof of concept) evaluation of our approach. We end our paper with a conclusion and discussion of future work.

II. STATE OF THE ART

The purpose of a prerequisite class differs from a "normal" class. It prepares a student for another class, not directly for a future career. Hence, it is often perceived as something less necessary. As observed in [10][13], students often see prerequisites as a waste of time and avoidable. If handled appropriately, a prerequisite course would solve motivational issues. One way to minimize time and resources spent is to make it self-paced so that a student goes through it at a comfortable pace and when time is available.

The first part of the outlined program – teaching only the material actually needed - is course-specific and should be addressed on case-by-case basis.

The second part about level and form of material taught, however, can be answered in general, at least for STEM classes.

A. Notion of Concept Inventory

While teaching STEM classes, as we observed in most cases, a conceptual understanding and an ability to apply the prerequisite material are sufficient. Students are not expected to know details, such as proofs, etc. The CI is the best existing approach to assessing conceptual understanding rather than memorization of a set of facts. CI as a form of an assessment is based on checking if a student understands basic concepts of a given subject as opposed to reciting a number of subject specific facts, equations, etc. As David Hestenes states in his paper, *Force Concept Inventory*, [17] CI Assessment is "not a test of intelligence" but rather, "it is a probe of belief systems".

An immediate advantage of CI is that it can be used for any student. That is, it does not matter, what the subject specific background of the student is, since, as stated above, CIs do not test formal knowledge but rather understanding of basic concepts. For example, as was demonstrated in [11], there is no significant difference observed between the test results even if the class time, class readiness, or type of class are different. That includes even classes that lack traditional lectures, such as Matematica-based classes. Typically, CIs are created and delivered as multiple-choice tests. However, as opposed to standard tests CIs are not comparison tests but norm-referenced tests.

The main goal of CIs, as stated above, is to test the students understanding of basic concepts. However, a typical CI test also checks for typical misconceptions.

There are two typical types of misconceptions: general scientific misconceptions and misconceptions introduced during the teaching process – so-called didaskalogenic misconceptions. The tool CIs use for testing misconceptions is known as distractors. Basically, distractors are the answer choices, which are specifically designed to imitate typical misconceptions. Summarizing, a CI test is a multiple-choice test consisting of problems with "distractors" as incorrect options that represent typical misconceptions. Typical multiple-choice problems of this type would be:

The following are temperatures for a week in August: 94, 93, 98, 101, 98, 96, and 93.
By how much could the highest temperature increase without changing the median?
A. Increase by 8°
B. Increase by 2°
C. It can increase by any amount
D. It cannot increase without changing the median.

To answer this question, a student needs nothing more than to understand the concept of median. Yet, at the same time, the problem does check for typical misconceptions, providing possible answers that conform to concepts of midrange or mean. Indeed, option D would be true if the question would be about midrange or mean, not about median and is, therefore, a typical example of a "distractor."

The first CI was developed and published by David Hestenes in 1992 [17]. It is known now as the Force Concept Inventory (FCI) and covers Newtonian Mechanics concepts. It had immediate success and was recognized and accepted by thousands of educators. Hestenes coined the term "modeling" to describe the conceptual approach to teaching – as opposed to the traditional factual approach. By now "modeling" approach covers well over 100,000 students each year. As a result of CI's popularity, the American Modeling Teachers Association (AMTA) was created and grew into a nationwide community. Moreover, CIs began in various fields of engineering, science and mathematics.

CI assessment in introductory and prerequisite classes was studied, in particular in [8][9][12][20][22]. With CI the subject specific background of a given student is not significant as stated above because CIs do not test formal knowledge, but rather test the student's understanding of related concepts, which is the student's working knowledge.

An understanding of related concepts is exactly what is needed in prerequisite classes. Mastering prerequisite material at a working knowledge level in order to apply it to the upcoming class.

Another advantage of using Cis in that they are already developed for a wide variety of the subjects including, but not limited to:

1) Natural Sciences:
   a) Physics
      i) Force and Motion
      ii) Electricity and Magnetism
      iii) Statics
   b) Chemistry
   c) Geoscience

2) Engineering
   a) Material Sciences
   b) Fluid Mechanics

3) Life Sciences:
   a) Basic Biology
   b) Natural Selection
   c) Genetics

4) Mathematics & Statistics:
   a) Calculus
   b) Statistics

Therefore, there already exist large depositories of test problems for many subjects in case a need to create a prerequisite class for one of such subjects.

The last aspect – the interactive, self-paced form of the class – can be addressed only through the use of technology.

B. Existing Interactive Online Systems

By now numerous Interactive Online Systems exist, including ALEKS [24], Cengage WebAssign [25], Knewton [26], Pearson MyMathLab Study Plan [27], Acrobatiq [28], Adapt [29], etc. All these systems offer self-paced automatically graded classes for various subjects. Typically, each such class offers an Initial Assessment and then, based on the output each student gets, activities and learning material to work on with regular re-assessments to check on progress. Such re-assessment outputs, in turn, are again used to adjust the assigned activities and learning material.

For instance, ALEKS provides the following self-description: "ALEKS uses adaptive questioning to quickly and accurately determine exactly what a student knows and doesn't know in a course. ALEKS then instructs the student on the topics she is most ready to learn. As a student works through a course, ALEKS periodically reassesses the student to ensure that topics learned are also retained. ALEKS courses are very complete in their topic coverage and ALEKS avoids multiple-choice questions. A student who shows a high level of mastery of an ALEKS course will be successful in the actual course she is taking."

According to [18], "When asked if there are pieces of the traditional classroom setting that are lost in an online course, the overwhelming response by all recipients was the lack of professor to student and student to student interaction and communication."

However, the classes based on such systems have several advantages over traditional classes. Such advantages include flexibility, adjustability to a student's knowledge base, pace, availability of various learning tools, timely feedback, etc. And as stated in [18], "All respondents unanimously answered that they would take an online course in the future, regardless of the challenges that they may have experienced."

The largest summary of online vs. classroom comparison research [19] concludes that "students in online conditions performed modestly better, on average, than those learning the same material through traditional face-to-face instruction. Learning outcomes for students who engaged in online learning exceeded those of students receiving face-to-face instruction, with an average effect size of +0.20 favoring online conditions."

At the same time, the same source states that "instruction combining online and face-to-face elements had a larger advantage relative to purely face-to-face instruction than did purely online instruction. The mean effect size in studies comparing blended with face-to-face instruction was +0.35, $p < .001$." The existing systems, however, all emulate traditional classes in terms of curricula and syllabi. The only difference is the form in which the material and assessment are presented.

On the one hand, it makes the comparison quoted above reliable since there is an objective expected output for each curriculum – and the only difference is the form of presenting the material. Indeed, according to the study itself "analysts examined the characteristics of the studies in the meta-analysis to ascertain whether features of the studies' methodologies could account for obtained effects. Six methodological variables were tested as potential moderators: (a) sample size, (b) type of knowledge tested, (c) strength of study design, (d) unit of assignment to condition, (e) instructor equivalence across conditions, and (f) equivalence of curriculum and instructional approach across conditions. Only equivalence of curriculum and instruction emerged as a significant moderator variable ($Q = 6.85$, $p < .01$)."

On the other hand, simply emulating the existing traditional classes does not allow the online interactive form to use completely its intrinsic advantages. We do believe that prerequisite classes can benefit more from advantages that the online interactive form offers.

While a variety of platforms exist for creating online accessible interactive classes, Jupyter Notebook looks to be one of the best fits here. Jupyter Notebook makes it easy to start, further develop, and support a class. It is also quite easy to create interactive auto-graded assignments using Jupyter Notebook.

As stated in [1], "Project Jupyter is three things: a collection of standards, a community, and a set of software tools. Jupyter Notebook, one part of Jupyter, is software that creates a Jupyter Notebook. A Jupyter Notebook is a document that supports mixing executable code, equations, visualizations, and narrative text. Specifically, Jupyter Notebooks allow the user to bring together data, code, and prose, to tell an interactive, computational story. Whether analyzing a corpus of American Literature, creating music and art, or illustrating the engineering concepts behind Digital Signal Processing, the notebooks can combine explanations traditionally found in textbooks with the interactivity of an application."

To summarize, Jupyter Notebook allows putting together a comprehensive custom-tailored text using both newly written lectures and excerpts from existing textbooks while also supplementing the text with interactive auto-graded assignments.

Putting these three aspects together facilitates the creation of prerequisite classes that cover only the material really needed and taught in a conceptual form, assessed using the CI approach and put in a form of a self-paced interactive online class using Jupyter Notebook, or a similar platform.

III. LINEAR ALGEBRA AS A PREREQUISITE COURSE FOR MACHINE LEARNING

The LA prerequisite class for Machine Learning class is an online interactive self-paced class built on the Jupyter Notebook platform. The lectures are based on "Linear Algebra Review and Reference" by Zico Kolter and consist of four chapters:

1. Basic Concepts and Notation
2. Matrix Multiplication
3. Operations and Properties
4. Matrix Calculus

The material presents basic definitions and concepts of LA necessary for studying Machine Learning. Each chapter is divided into smaller sections. For example, the "Matrix Multiplication" chapter is divided as follows:

2.1 Vector-Vector Products

2.2 Matrix-Vector Products

2.3 Matrix-Matrix Products

Each section is supplemented by an auto-graded assessment based on CI principles.

A typical problem for Basic Concepts would be:

Find the dimensions of the matrix

$$A = \begin{bmatrix} 1 & 2 & 3 \\ 4 & 5 & 6 \end{bmatrix}$$

A. *2x3 (*)*

B. *3x2*

C. *1x6*

D. *6x1*

Option A is a key since the matrix has two rows and three columns.

Option B is a distractor that checks for a misconception that mixes rows with columns.

Option C is a distractor that checks for a misconception that considers a matrix as one long row with six elements.

Option D is a distractor that checks for a misconception that considers a matrix as one long column with six elements.

Another typical example:

Matrix

$$\begin{bmatrix} -1 & 0 \\ 0 & 2 \end{bmatrix}$$

has eigenvalues:

A. *-1 and 0*

B. *-1 and 2 (*)*

C. *0 and 2*

D. *It has no eigenvalues*

Option B is a key since (-1-x)(2-x)-0·0=0 has two roots:

-1 and 2.

Option A is a distractor that checks for a misconception that defines the eigenvalues as the values of the first row elements.

Option C is a distractor that checks for a misconception that defines the eigenvalues as the values of second row elements.

Option D is a distractor that checks for a misconception that defines a characteristics polynomial as -1·2-(0-x) (0-x).

In the final version assessments will be based on a sufficiently large pool of problems and will be randomly generated for each student and for each attempt.

A student is able to take this class any time before taking the Machine Learning class, at the pace that fits her or his schedule and degree of prior knowledge. In addition to the lectures, we include the option of having students ask the instructor questions or discussing any aspect of the class with other classmates. Each assessment is auto graded but also can be graded by the instructor in case a student challenges the grade.

IV. SYSTEM IMPLEMENTATION

The system was initially implemented on Cloud 9 (currently Amazon c9) virtual machines with 20 Gb. hard-drive and 2 Gb RAM running Ubuntu v. 14, with Python 3.6, miniconda and installation of JupyterHub with nbgrader.

Installation was almost straightforward, the only issue being restriction on use of miniconda instead of full anaconda installation. This is due to restriction of the provided hard-drive size. The main benefit of the system was its low cost: VMs are available for free from AWS. We would like to thank Amazon for providing Cloud based virtual hardware. This essentially made our work possible.

While sufficient for development, the system nonetheless had performance issues. Thus, we had a choice either to proceed to paid Cloud based virtual machines or moved to dedicated home hosted hardware. Our choice was to move the developed system to a Lenovo P-520C workstation with Intel Xeon 6 core W-2133 Processor with vPro, 32 Gb. of RAM with dual hard-drive 512 Gb SSD and 2 Tb. HDD and 2 GB Nvidia P2000. This PC configuration proved to be sufficient to run up to 200 test students. We did not try IOCI to stress the system to run for more students.

V. EVALUATION OF THE APPROACH

We evaluated standard and interactive approaches by running parallel classes for over 30 graduate students taking the Machine Learning course. Half of the students studied the LA prerequisite material in the form of provided reading material. Another half used the interactive Jupyter/nbgrader online system, with a built-in auto-graded CI based tests provided for both self and regular assessment. We ran pre- and post- preparation CI-based tests that check the required comprehension of the LA material as well as a one-question survey for both instructors and students. The survey seeks to discover if the student/instructor prefers reading material or an interactive prerequisite course. An outline of the measurements approach may be found in [19]-[21][23].

Both classes offered a sample that shows prerequisite materials used by their counterparts. Both tests and survey showed a statistically significant preference of interactive prerequisite materials for students with 5% significance level.

Tests results analysis is summarized in Table 1 and uses standard t – test with a different standard deviation for testing if one of the means is larger than the other. The value of the test t shows statistical significance with a confidence level of $\alpha = 5\%$. Here the value *df* is degree of freedom, *d* is value of statistics, *t* is value of t-test corresponding values *d* and *df*.

TABLE I. ONE SIDED TWO MEANS T-TEST FOR GRADES IOCI VS READING

	IOCI	Read
N	16	15
mean	88	84
std	6	6.75

df (degree of freedom)	28.05503
d (see formula (1))	1.739542
t	0.046462

Survey preference is analyzed in Table 2 using small samples t-test for population proportion, see [14][15]. A summary of analysis is offered below in the Table 2. Here, the value of *N-2* is the degree of freedom, the value *d* is calculated as [14][15]:

$$d = (ae - bc)\left(\frac{N-2}{N(nac+mbe)}\right)^{\frac{1}{2}} \quad (1)$$

and values of the variables *a, e, b, c, N, n, m* used in the formula are the corresponding ones in the numerical data below.

TABLE II. SMALL SAMPLES T- TEST FOR POPULATION PROPORTIONS COMPARISON

	IOCI Users	Read Users	Total
Prefer IOCI	a = 14	b = 8	s = 22
Prefer Read	c = 2	e = 7	f = 9
Total	m = 16	n = 15	N = 31

N-2	29
d	2.186271331
t	0.018506791

A similar implementation with similar results (translation of the material into Russian) was done at the National University of Science and Technology, MISIS (Moscow).

VI. CONCLUSION AND FUTURE WORK

The issue of prerequisites impacts many STEM courses because many major courses require a deep understanding of Mathematics, Statistics, etc. This may be challenging in situations where graduate students wish to enroll in major courses at the start of their studies. We encountered such a situation with Machine Learning courses, which require knowledge (or at least a conceptual understanding and hands-on ability) of LA, Matrix Calculus, Probability and Statistics. Standard approaches require that students wait a year during which they complete all prerequisites or attack prerequisites as reading material. As the latter approach has several disadvantages, we decided to make prerequisite material more attractive by implementing it using JupyterHub and nbgrader as a self-study interactive course with auto-grading. CIs are used to check how well students understand the material. Students have access to self-check exercises and feedback; instructors can monitor student' success and, if needed, recommend some adjustments. We ran it on an experimental group of students, and both students and instructors prefer this form of study over reading material.

We would like to emphasize that this approach can by no means compare in depth and outcome to regular courses on the topic. As we saw in multiple cases, this approach is used mainly because of students schedule conflicts or a desire to expose students to major courses as soon as possible.

We plan to run the LA prerequisite course by larger numbers of instructors and students and incorporate comments and suggestions from all participants. We further intend to offer the course as open source available to anyone.

REFERENCES

[1] L. A. Barba et al., "Teaching and Learning with Jupyter", https://github.com/jupyter4edu/jupyter-edu-book, retrieved January, 2020

[2] F. Perez and B. E. Granger, "IPython: A System for Interactive Scientific Computing," in Computing in Science & Engineering, vol. 9, no. 3, pp. 21-29, 2007.

[3] F. Perez, B. E. Granger, and J. D. Hunter, "Python: An Ecosystem for Scientific Computing," in Computing in Science & Engineering, vol. 13, no. 2, pp. 13-21, March-April 2011.

[4] K.J. O'Hara, D.S. Blank, and J.B. Marshall, "Computational Notebooks for AI Education", Proceedings of FLAIRS, pp. 263-268, 2015

[5] S. Freeman et al., "Active learning increases student performance in science, engineering, and mathematics." Proceedings of the National Academy of Sciences, 111(23), pp. 8410–8415, 2014.

[6] M. G. Moore, "Three types of interaction", The American Journal of Distance Education 3(2), pp. 1-6, 1989.

[7] J. Libarkin, "Concept inventories in higher education science." BOSE Conf. pp. 1-10, 2008.

[8] G. Ya. Grabarnik, M. Guysinsky, and S. Yaskolko. "An integrated approach to using statistics concept inventories in instruction" Integrated STEM Education Conference (ISEC), 2014 IEEE.

[9] S. Krause, J. C. Decker, and R. Griffin, "Using a materials concept inventory to assess conceptual gain in introductory materials engineering courses", Frontiers in Education, 2003. FIE 2003 33rd Annual, Volume 1, pp 7-11.

[10] B. K. Sato et al., "What's in a Prerequisite? A Mixed-Methods Approach to Identifying the Impact of a Prerequisite Course", CBE Life Sci Educ. 2017 Spring; 16(1): ar16

[11] J. Epstein, The Calculus Concept Inventory — Measurement of the Effect of Teaching Methodology in Mathematics, Notices of the AMS Volume 60, N. 8, 2013, pp 1018-10.

[12] G. Ya. Grabarnik, and S. Yaskolko. "Teaching statistics to non-mathematics majors: Interdisciplinary integration with R and EDA." 2013 IEEE Integrated STEM Education Conference. IEEE, 2013.

[13] G. Ya. Grabarnik, L. Kim-Tyan, S. Yaskolko, "Improving STEM's Calculus education using cross-countries best teaching practices." 2018 IEEE Frontiers in Education Conference (FIE). IEEE, 2018.

[14] R. B. D'Agostino, W. Chase, and A. Belanger, 1988.'The Appropriateness of Some Common Procedures for Testing the Equality of Two Independent Binomial Populations', The American Statistician, August 1988, vol. 42, no. 3, pp. 198-202.

[15] G. J. G. Upton, "A comparison of alternative tests for the 2 times 2 comparative trial." *Journal of the Royal Statistical Society: Series A (General)* 145.1 , 1982, pp. 86-105.

[16] A system for assigning and grading Jupyter Notebooks. https://github.com/jupyter/nbgrader, retrieved Jan. 2020.

[17] D. Hestenes, Force concept inventory. The Physics Teacher, 30(3), 1992, p. 141.

[18] Gilbert, Brittany, Online Learning Revealing the Benefits and Challenges, St. John Fisher College Fisher Digital Publications, http://fisherpub.sjfc.edu/cgi/viewcontent.cgi?article=1304&context=education_ETD_masters, retrieved Jan. 2020.

[19] U.S. Department of Education, Office of Planning, Evaluation, and Policy Development, Evaluation of Evidence-Based Practices in Online Learning: A Meta-Analysis and Review of Online Learning Studies, Washington, D.C., 2010. https://www2.ed.gov/rschstat/eval/tech/evidence-based-practices/finalreport.pdf, retrieved Jan. 2020.

[20] D. Sands, M. Parker, H. Hedgeland, S. Jordan, and R. Galloway, Using concept inventories to measure understanding. *Higher Education Pedagogies*, *3*(1), 173-182. 2018.

[21] C. Evans, K. Howson C, and A. Forsythe, Making sense of learning gain in higher education. Higher Education Pedagogies. 2018 Jan 1;3(1), pp.1-45.

[22] A. Madsen, S.B. McKagan, and E.C. Sayre, Best practices for administering concept inventories. The Physics Teacher. Dec. 2017, 55(9). pp. 530-6.

[23] P. Gossman and S. Powell, Learning Gain: Can It Be Measured?. InEmployability via Higher Education: Sustainability as Scholarship 2019, pp. 37-51. Springer, Cham.

[24] ALEKS, www.aleks.com, accessed Jan. 2020.

[25] WebAssign, WebAssign.net, accessed Jan. 2020.

[26] Knewton, www.knewton.com, accessed Jan. 2020.

[27] MyLab Math, Pearson, www.pearsonmylabandmastering.com, accessed Jan. 2020.

[28] Acrobatiq, acrobatiq.com, accessed Jan. 2020.

[29] Adapt, https://www.adaptlearning.org/, accessed Jan. 2020.

DelphiCare 6.0
A Project-Based Learning Approach

Réne Joaquín Díaz Martínez, Rafaela Villalpando Hernández, Yamilín Aracely Zamora, Enríquez, Juan Francisco Medina Leal, César Eduardo Cuevas Garza
Tecnologico de Monterrey, Campus Laguna
Torreón, México
Emails: {renejdm, rafaela.villalpando}@tec.mx, {A01235198, A01234038, A01235274}@itesm.mx

Abstract- **Sometimes, it is interesting to approach an academic laboratory class from a different perspective. This paper takes on the experience of a group of mechatronic engineering students taking an academic course on laboratory of integral electronics. The students were asked to design a system capable of measuring three vital signs of a patient. To achieve this, they use the knowledge acquired in their career up to that moment to manage other knowledge that was required. In order to carry out the project, a project-based learning methodology was followed. This experience allowed the students involved to solve a real problem with a product that responded to the specifications of cost, portability and information available from a mobile device, as well as meeting the requirements to revalidate their laboratory subject matter.**

Keywords - project-based learning; vital signs; sensors; mobile applications.

I. INTRODUCTION

The realization of projects that introduce students to the solution of real-life problems that are related to a particular subject constitutes a commonly employed method within engineering. Often referred to as the Project Based Learning (PBL) technique, it was defined as a formal method by the end of the XIX century by William Heard Kilpatrick [1]. It was renewed during the decade from 1960s as it became popular again, and continued to be used up to current days. In [2], PBL is defined as a methodology that enables students to obtain the required knowledge and key skills from the XXI century, through the development of projects that address and solve real life problematics. Some of the core features are:

1) The students are capable of becoming the protagonists of their own learning as they develop their autonomy and responsibility, since they are in charge of planning, organizing the work, and elaborating the product that attempts to overcome the established problematic.

2) The teachers change their main role to a support and guidance role.

3) It enables users to obtain relevant and discipline-related skills, some of which are: teamwork, problem solving, responsibility, spoken and written communication, analysis and synthesis of gathered data, experiment development, socializing with external environments to college, among others [3].

Despite this method being defended by multiple authors, researchers and teachers, it is relevant to take into consideration some unfavorable elements that come with it. For instance we can mention the implementation costs, the location where the project will be developed, the communication towards the final users who will be using the product, and finally, the time accessibility regarding the involved students due to the project being developed in parallel with the rest of the college classes. In order to implement this didactic technique, a ten-step methodology (see Table I), was followed.

TABLE I. STEPS TO CARRY OUT PBL

Step	*Short description*
1	Topic selection and guide question definition. What is known already?
2	Group and role assignment.
3	Defining a real product or final challenge. Setting goals and skills to reach and the criteria to evaluate them.
4	Planification. Establishment of the job's schedule, specifying tasks, who is responsible for those tasks, and deadlines.
5	Investigation. Revision of previous concepts, new required concepts and information research.
6	Analysis and synthesis. To share gathered information, to contribute and debate ideas, to formulate hypotheses, to structure information and to decide among team members the best solution.
7	Product elaboration. To apply the learnt design techniques (use its methodologies).
8	Presentation of the product to team members.
9	Collective answering of the initial question. Following the presentation, students must ruminate in order to collectively answer the starting question.
10	Appraisal and self-appraisal. The teacher must evaluate the work in compliance with a defined rubric and propose a self-appraisal activity to the students.

Under the previously described context, this work has as its purpose to show an experience applying PBL. The work has been performed during the period between August and December 2019 for the laboratory of integral electronics class, in the seventh semester of the mechatronic engineering career, Tec de Monterrey, campus Laguna, Mexico. As the class name implies, the course proposes the realization of 8 to 10 laboratory practices in which the students get to apply the acquired knowledge from two subjects from previous semesters: electronics and applied electronics. The student's work culminates with an integrating project. For a few years, this project has been oriented towards the design and construction of a domotic house, where a series of electronic devices and sensors guarantee three basic elements: comfort, security and the saving of non-renewable resources.

In this course, we came with the idea of changing the project's subject to a new one: the construction of a device that allows the measurement of three vital signs from a person. The idea had as its background other similar works developed by this paper's author with students from eighth and ninth semester from the mechatronic engineering career. Some questions arose from this idea: Can a mechatronic engineering student from seventh semester accomplish this task? What knowledge the student does not master, but needs to apply on the design, nonetheless? Is one semester enough time for its execution? The idea was proposed at the beginning of the course to a group of 14 students, from which, 5 students felt motivated and committed to its construction. The goals of the work were defined as shown in Table II.

TABLE II. GENERAL AND SPECIFIC GOALS OF THE WORK

Main goal	To apply the PBL approach in order to solve a real-life problem, within a class from seventh semester of mechatronic engineering.
Specific goals	1. To design, mount and test a mechatronic device that allows a real time measurement of temperature, blood's oxygen and an electrocardiographic signal from a patient while it is displayed on a mobile device. 2. To encourage the obtainment of new knowledge not seen in class. 3. To promote teamwork among the students. 4. Spoken and written presentation of a functional designed prototype.

The paper is structured as follows. Section 2 describes the approach taken to address the proposed project. Section 3 covers the results achieved until the writing of this paper, which are not definitive as it is a work-in-progress. Finally, in Section 4, conclusions are discussed.

II. METHODOLOGY

As it can be appreciated, part of the student's group followed the traditional final project while a group of five students chose to participate in this new experience. With the latter ones, a group was formed whose students were exempt from making the regular laboratory practices, so they could dedicate their whole time and attention to the solution of the established challenge. Taking into consideration the methodology to apply PBL, the following stages were presented:

1) Starting question: Is it possible to design a mechatronic device capable of measuring three vital signs from a person, with the device being portable, low cost, and accessible from a mobile device?

2) Selection of a team leader.

3) Design of the rubrics to evaluate the project and the definition of the required skills:

a) Discipline: To design, build, and test prototypes of innovative mechatronic devices.

TABLE III. WORK PHASES

Phase	***Action***
1	Circuit board: oximeter, temperature
	Finish prototype EGC signal
	Pulse in Arduino programming
	Oximeter Thimble
	Attach the components to the thimbles
	Accommodate and couple the circuits and thimbles to the chassis
	Digital filter programming
	Couple positive and negative voltage supply
2	Arduino-App communication
	Android application
	Design and manufacture new Chassis
3	Research for the integration of new sensors
	Start with the prototypes of the new sensors

b) Transversal: Teamwork, knowledge self-management and spoken and written description of the project.

4) Definition of work schedule (Table III).

5) Analysis of the required knowledge:

a) Previous: Signals analysis, electronic components, sensors, design of mechanical parts, and microcontrollers.

b) Self-studied: Development boards, mobile application development, wireless communication, sensing of oxygen presence in blood and the electrocardiographic signal.

6) This point summarizes the stages 6 and 7 of the PBL methodology, applying the general steps of the Ulrich-Eppinger mechatronic product design methodology [4].

7) At the moment of writing of this paper, phases 8, 9 and 10, from the PBL methodology, were in process.

III. PARTIAL RESULTS

To present the results obtained so far, we refer to stages 3 and 5 of the PBL methodology. In stage 3, it was very important to verify the acquisition of the defined disciplinary and transversal competences. Stage 5 allowed to determine what was the new knowledge that students had to manage independently.

The disciplinary competence proposed the construction, assembly and testing of a prototype enabling to measure three vital human signs: temperature, oxygen concentration in blood and an electrocardiographic signal.

The block diagram in Figure 1 presents the process of the prototype.

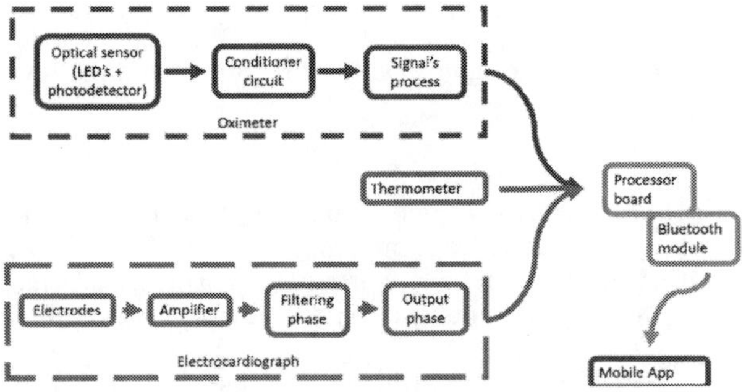

Figure 1 Delphi's block diagram.

Next, a brief explanation is given about the implementation and obtained results, with the help of the block diagram, and gained knowledge.

A. Temperature Measurement

The temperature module of the system consists of the MLX90614 sensor [5], which is an infrared thermometer suitable for measuring temperatures in the necessary range between 20°C and 50 °C, with digital outputs of 17 bits. The sensor provides an output using the I2C protocol for maximum resolution (0.02°C). The sensor has a default range of temperatures between -40 °C and +85 °C. The given temperature value is the average temperature of the object detected by the sensing field from the device. The accuracy of the sensor is of 0.5 °C at room temperature at 25 °C. This sensor is compatible with the analog pins of Arduino.

The temperature data obtained through the device was compared against measurements made with a thermometer, as shown in Table IV. Observe that the collected data in both cases is very similar.

TABLE IV. WORK SCHEDULE

DelphiCare	*Thermometer*
37.48	37.1
37.24	37
36.94	36.8
36.7	36.6
36.52	36.5
36.3	36.2
36.14	36.5

B. Measurement of Oxygen Concentration in Blood

The oxygen sensor was designed from scratch. The SpO2 sensor (oxygen concentration in blood) [6] is based on the principle of pulse oximetry. It generates two beams of light, one of them in the red light spectrum (wavelength: 600nm-750nm) and the other in the infrared spectrum (wavelength: 850nm - 1000nm) and measures the amount of light that is transmitted through the index finger and reaches the photodetector, in this case a photodiode connected to a current/voltage converter made out of operational amplifiers.

The oximeter is composed of three main parts: the optical sensor, the conditioning circuit, and the processing board. Table V shows the readings obtained by the DelphiCare's oxygen sensor, compared against a commercial sensor.

TABLE V. OXYGEN READINGS

Oxygen Saturation (%SpO2)	
DelphiCare	*Commercial Sensor*
98	98
99	98
98	98
98	99
99	99
99	99

C. Electrocardiograph

There is a large number of circuits that measure the electrocardiographic signal. One of the goals of the DelphiCare was to obtain a system that was low cost and had a large portability in comparison with similar systems. Finally, a circuit that obtains a signal from the heart was chosen and built. As it is shown in the block diagram in Figure 1, the signal is obtained through a series of electrodes connected to the chest of the user. After collecting the said signal, it is then subjected to several amplifications and filters, so it becomes easier to be identified and to work with before reaching the analog port of the Arduino board and finally being transferred to the mobile app. The resultant signal is shown in Figure 2.

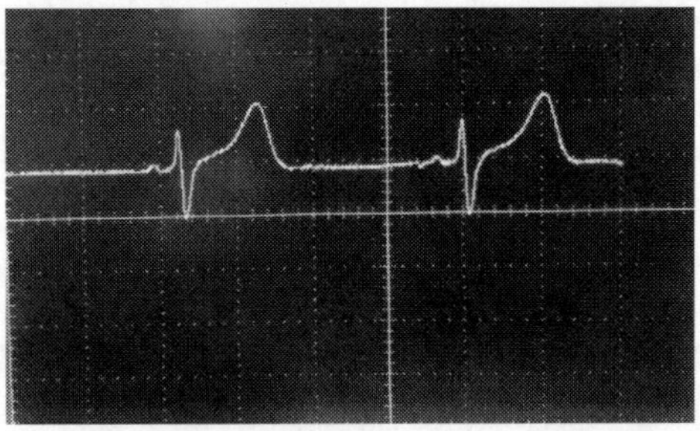

Figure 2. Resultant electrocardiographic signal.

D. Processing Board, BT Module and Mobile Application

The goal of the mobile application is to offer the user an intuitive and reliable way to communicate with the different sensors. The application is planned to perform a synchronization process with a server in order to store the incoming information in a database; the server shall display that data on a Web platform for physicians to analyze. In other words, the objective of the mobile application is to serve as a bridge between the user, the sensor and the server.

The application shows a main menu where the user is prompted to choose a sensor to start a reading (Figure 3).

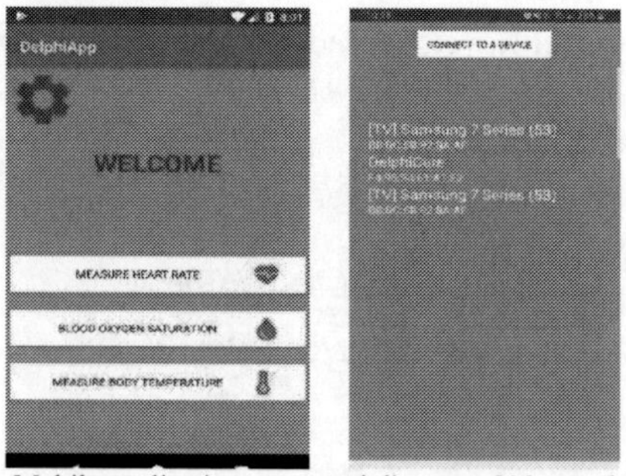

Figure 3. Mobile application menu and discovered bluetooth devices.

Before any reading is performed, the user must connect the mobile device to the DelphiCare device by means of an RFCOMM channel established via bluetooth. The application is capable of starting the connection from within, so the user does not need to minimize the application nor use the phone's built-in configuration app in order to start trading data with the sensor.

The user is able to select a device to establish a connection with, and once done, the buttons to start the measurements with any of the three integrated sensors on the DelphiCare are enabled.

As expected, there are three main use cases: measure heart rate, measure blood oxygen concentration, and measure body temperature. In the first case, the user will be asked to put the electrodes on their chest and press the confirmation button in order to start the reading process. Once the measuring is finished, the user will be shown a graph with the acquired data plotted in order to achieve a proper visualization. In the second and third case, where the user can measure their oxygen saturation and body temperature, the user will be asked to insert their index finger into the corresponding finger grip and wait a couple of seconds before showcasing the results.

Currently, the application is designed to work on Android devices only, as it is still being used as a proof of concept. The Java programming language was selected as the technology for development because it is highly flexible and, contrary to the most recent Android development language released, Kotlin, Java has a huge legacy, and, therefore, the learning curve is very straightforward. Moreover, there is an enormous amount of online resources available for research.

E. New Knowledge Management Required

As expected, this project required to manage the following information:

1) Arduino UNO board. This board was studied and used in order to take advantage of its analog ports, voltage source of 3.3V, the MLX 90614 library (used for infrared thermometers), functions for reading analog inputs, outputting and signal filtering.

2) Oxygen concentration in blood: the use of optoelectronic techniques (visible and infrared light), pulse oximetry, light absorption principle (Beer-Lambert law).

3) Electrocardiographic signal: use of high gain sensors aimed to sense biomedic signals.

4) Wireless communication through a Bluetooth module.

5) Mobile app design using Android Studio and the Java Programming Language.

IV. CONCLUSIONS

In this paper, we reported on the student's progress throughout their experience in designing a system capable of measuring three vital signs of a patient. This project has shown how the students had experimented and accomplished the established goals using the Project Based Learning method. As for the project itself, it is highly interesting to observe how current technology can be integrated into past technology in order to renew it and scale it towards more complex systems. The usage of mobile phones for daily and recurrent services has successfully proven to be easier and cheaper, in this case, there was no difference. This powerful tool will certainly allow for future escalation and spreading of the DelphiCare system.

As noted before, this work was submitted to be considered before completing all the phases from the PBL methodology. However, it is worth mentioning some results and information gained through the process:

1- A prototype from a mechatronic device was implemented, allowing the measurement of three vital signs of a human being, applying the PBL approach. The device is simple, portable and low cost (lower than 3000 MXN pesos).

2- Through the course of the semester, the students showed progress, which was proved by oral and written presentations, partial and final tests, which were received and evaluated with their corresponding rubric form.

3- In order to reach a solution, the students had to apply the gained knowledge.

4- The project covered 80% of the program from the class, from a different didactic approach.

ACKNOWLEDGMENT

The authors would like to acknowledge the financial and the technical support of Writing Lab, TecLabs, Tecnologico de Monterrey in the production of this work.

REFERENCES

[1] W. H Kilpatrick, "The project method". Teachers College Record, 1918, pp. 319-335.

[2] "How to apply project-based learning in 10 steps", *Aulaplaneta.* Retrieved from: https://www.aulaplaneta.com/2015/02/04/recursos-tic/como-aplicar-el-aprendizaje-basado-en-proyectos-en-diez-pasos/ [retrieved: February, 2020]

[3] Didactic techniques. Monterrey, México: *Sitios ITESM.* Retrieved from: http://sitios.itesm.mx/va/dide2/tecnicas_didacticas/aop/aop.htm, 2010.[retrieved: February, 2020]

[4] K. Ulrich and S. D. Eppinger, "Product Design and Development", 5th edn. McGraw-Hill, New York, 2012.

[5] "Microelectronics Integrated Systems", Datasheet: MLX90614 family, Melexis, 2006

[6] "Pulse oximeter". Retrieved from: https://www.howequipmentworks.com/pulse_oximeter/, [retrieved: March, 2020].

Creating Free, Interactive Resources to Support Student Success: Pilot Programs and Preliminary Findings

Tamara Powell
English Department
Kennesaw State University
Kennesaw, Georgia, USA
E-mail: tpowel25@kennesaw.edu

***Abstract*—The cost of higher education in the United States continues to climb. In addition to tuition prices, textbook prices have soared at alarming rates. In the US state of Georgia, the University System encourages and offers financial incentives to faculty to create their own course resources, including textbooks and ancillary materials. This program is called Affordable Learning Georgia, or ALG. Open Educational Resources, or OERs, have shown to support student success including retention, completion, satisfaction, and learning outcomes. At Kennesaw State University (KSU), faculty members have stepped up to create course materials, ancillary resources, and even student support materials. Early surveys have shown that students have been appreciative of the faculty efforts and have had positive responses to the various components faculty have created and provided. This innovation in the type of resources provided has boosted student satisfaction. In addition, the resource on academic integrity has reduced the amount of cheating through social media.**

Keywords-Affordable Learning Georgia; OERs; student success; textbooks; United States.

I. INTRODUCTION

The cost of higher education in the United States continues to climb. One area driving up costs is the constant reduction in each, individual state's contribution to higher education. "Overall state funding for public two- and four-year colleges in the school year ending in 2018 was more than $7 billion below its 2008 level, after adjusting for inflation" [1]. Students are asked to take on more and more of the cost burden, and they are encouraged to take out student loans to fund their educations. The average student loan debt, per person, in the United States is $31,172 [2]. An additional catalyst in the soaring prices is textbook publishers. These publishers saw that they had a captive market and took advantage, jacking up prices and churning out new editions every year or two just so they could force students to purchase new editions instead of saving money buying used copies. Textbook costs have soared, rocketing up past four times the rate of inflation between 2006 and 2016 [3]. Also, books are no longer always physical and made of paper. Publishers now "bundle" digital textbooks with unique access requirements that must be purchased new each time. This practice puts a stop to selling back textbooks and purchasing used, and more affordable, versions [4].

II. AFFORDABLE LEARNING GEORGIA

Compared to other US states, the state of Georgia contributes more than most to public higher education [5]. At the same time, political leaders still want to assure taxpayers that the state government is keeping prices down and taxes low. To that end, the state ended many endeavors that were funding the purchase of hardware and software for students. This effort returned the financial burden for expensive educational technology and student support software and programs back onto students' pocketbooks.

The state of Georgia's University System, also known as the University System of Georgia, or USG, also set aside small amounts of money to incentivize and compensate faculty and staff to create learning materials for students to replace commercial and publisher materials. This initiative is called Affordable Learning Georgia, or ALG. What this initiative means in reality is if a student needs a license for a software vital to his or her career success, he or she will have to pay for it out of pocket because the school no longer can provide a license. However, more classes are being taught with free textbooks, so textbook expenses are no longer hindering students.

While some faculty balked at this direction, remarking that it is not their job to do extra work to reign in publisher greed, many faculty noted that they had already created such materials and would be happy to get a little one time incentive from the state and recognition to share them. Also, quite a few faculty felt it was the right thing to use their skills to help defray costs for students. As of Spring 2020, 26 Georgia universities had earned ALG grants, benefiting 417,000 students and saving them a total of $69.19 million [6].

III. THE MAGIC OF OPEN EDUCATIONAL RESOURCES

A. Overview

The author is a faculty member in the state of Georgia who has enjoyed working with digital tools to create online learning experiences that replace commercial and publisher products. In this paper, we will describe the products created, the purpose of them, and the early student responses. This paper also includes links to the resources mentioned.

B. *Impact in the Classroom*

In 2015, the state of Georgia began pushing the use of Open Educational Resources or OERs. The USG established ALG to spread information about the benefits of OERs. Research shows students learn more, get better grades, save money, take more classes, graduate faster and are more satisfied with their experiences when their classes use OERs [7]. These results sound amazing, but they are a logical outcome. If a student starts the semester with the course materials, he or she will not get behind, and, therefore, will perform better. With the savings from not having to purchase the textbook or take on an extra job to pay for the textbook, students can take more classes and devote more time to those classes—thereby, graduating faster and with higher grades.

In fall 2015, we worked with a team of faculty and an instructional designer at KSU. The team received an ALG grant to create an open technical communication textbook, currently titled *Open Technical Communication* [8]. The textbook was piloted in a summer 2016 online course called WRIT 3140: Introduction to Technical Communication. WRIT is a prefix for a group of classes that emphasize writing. The number 3140 refers to the fact that the course is taught at a junior, or upper, level at the university. In this course, students are instructed in the basics of writing for the technical fields, including computer science and engineering. Students in the course were surveyed regarding their experiences with the open educational resource, which in this case was a free, open, online textbook called *Open Technical Communication.* Of the 21 students who responded to the survey regarding the textbook, 95% responded positively. To further evaluate the initial success of the endeavor, we compared the retention rate, average grade, and evaluation average with the same course taught the previous summer with a publisher textbook which cost around $140. Both courses were taught online. To put this data in clearer context, the retention rate with OER went down. However, the average grade went up. In this class, grades are calcluated as failing, or F (earning 0-58% of the points available in the course); D (earning 59-69% of the available points); C or average (earning 70-79% of the available points); B or good (earning 80-89% of the available points); A or excellent (earning 90-100% of the available points). The evaluation in this chart refers to the average score on the instructor's end of course evaluation. It is a measure of student satisfaction. In this case, one can see that the student satisfaction increased in the course with the open edutational resources. In the course using OERs, the retention rate was lower, and the grades and course evaluations were slightly higher. Also, "Sum" refers to the fact that the courses being compared were taught in the summer session of the university, which is 8 weeks instead of the usual 16 weeks in fall and spring. Table I shows the retention data.

TABLE I. RETENTION DATA FROM WRIT 3140 WITHOUT OERS AND PILOT SECTION WITH OERS

Table Showing Comparison of Online WRIT 3140 Course with OER vs. without OER		
	WRIT 3140 Sum 2015 (without OER)	WRIT 3140 Sum 2016 (with OER)
Retention Rate	40/42 (95%)	21/25 (84%)
Average Grade	74 C	78 C
Evaluation	3.56	3.75

IV. OPEN TECHNICAL COMMUNICATION: THE GATEWAY TEXT

The faculty team created *Open Technical Communication,* the free, online, technical communication textbook, by remixing a previously available, but not yet completed, free, online technical communication textbook created by Dr. David McMurrey. It is entitled *Online Technical Writing* [9]. Dr. McMurrey gave the KSU faculty team permission to use his work in the project. We completed or updated some of the existing chapters, authored original chapters, and added resources such as practice quizzes and supplementary videos. Thus, *Open Technical Communication,* a remix and derivative of *Online Technical Communication*, was born.

In addition to the webpages and examples created by Dr. McMurrey and the faculty team, the remix contains videos, interactive exercises, and assignment ideas to support the use of the text either by teachers and students or persons simply wishing to learn more about technical communication. This textbook continues to be in use at Kennesaw State University and has been adopted for use in a few institutions. It has had 7,946 downloads over the past four years, the majority of which are in the Eastern US. The textbook has been downloaded in 135 countries with the top three users being the United States (3813 downloads), India (644 downloads), and the Philippines (428 downloads). The most downloaded chapter is the one entitled "Ethics in Technical Communication" [10].

We also teach American literature and wanted to use freely available resources in our literature courses, as well. In 2015, the goal was a challenging one to achieve, as the state was encouraging faculty to create their own textbooks.

However, a professor cannot simply write 10 great American novels to use in American literature courses. But, by 2017, the needed resources were becoming available. It was possible to find a great deal of readings on the Internet. And in 2018, two OER literature textbooks were made available. These were *Becoming American: An Exploration of American Literature Precolonial and Post-Revolution [11]* and *Writing the Nation: A Concise Introduction to American Literature 1865 to Present [12]*. Both books are published and maintained by the University of North Georgia Press. With the publication of these works, it was possible for us to make one of our literature courses 100% OER, with the other requiring less than $5 in course material expenses.

A. *Moving from Publisher Resources to OERs*

There are many research-based, positive reasons to adopt OER. However, OERs are not a panacea. A critic of OERs might argue that OERs do not work for every course. Often, they require vetting, adaptation, and supplementation to work successfully in a course. As was described above regarding the open technical communication textbook, the free book available was not yet completed. The faculty at KSU who wished to use it had to take a semester, create a work schedule, and update and complete it themselves in order to provide the benefits to their students. Many of these reasons are given by faculty and publishers as reasons not to adopt OERs. To counter these arguments, one might consider that publisher textbooks, too, require vetting, adaptation, and often, supplementation. The difference is that once an OER is adopted and revised to suit an instructor, the instructor has control over the content.

B. *Filling in the Gaps*

While the American literature survey OER textbook provided these supplemental materials, such as author biographies, to a degree, we wanted additional support and more context for students. As a subject matter expert, we had the knowledge to share with students to support their learning. Using Articulate Storyline [13], we were able to create several support pieces for the OER American literature textbooks. Topics included Transcendentalism, the Enlightenment, and American Literature after World War II. These support pieces were entitled Read'n Quizzes because they presented very text-heavy slides to students, slide by slide. Periodically, there was a quiz question. Each student had to complete the Read'n Quiz in order to earn 10 points for the activity. The technology allowed the instructor to upload the Read'n Quiz into the Learning Management System (LMS), in this case Desire2Learn BrightSpace, or D2L [14], as a Shareable Content Object Reference Model, or SCORM module so that quiz grade is automatically transferred to the gradebook. SCORM modules are built to a standard that includes four traits: "First, sustainability. Teaching resources will not be invalid because of the update of technology. It can be used for a long time. Second, reusability. Teaching can basically be used without modification. It can be reused in different platforms, and can be combined with other teaching contents according to their needs. Third, interoperability. Because teaching materials follow a unified standard, it can be presented on any standard platform, or can be modified by editing tools that conform to the standard. Fourth, availability. With the platform, learners can read the learning and teaching resources through the Internet without any time and space constraints, so as to achieve the purpose of distance learning" [15]. Through creating Read'n Quizzes in SCORM format, we were able to create learning objects that can be shared freely and widely. Also, we were able to motivate students to take in the connecting information, something that is normally very boring and students are prone to skip, so that they could gain more context and learn more.

In a fall 2019 survey regarding the student opinions of the OER materials, students were asked their impression of the Read'n Quizzes. On the survey, presented to the course after the midterm exam, students were posed this question: To help support the OER materials, your professor created what she called Read'n Quizzes where you watched presentations that included questions and were counted for a grade. Would you recommend she continue using those materials? Of the nine out of 25 students who answered the question, 44% said they would recommend the instructor to continue using the Read'n Quizzes if they keep the cost of the materials down. Here is a breakdown of the survey results:

44%="Yes, if they keep the cost of materials down."
22%="Yes, I found them engaging."
22%-"No, I had a hard time accessing them."
11%="No, it wouldn't record my grade correctly."
0%="No, I found them boring."

Figure 1 shows the response breakdown to the question on the survey. As can be seen, 66% of students were willing to

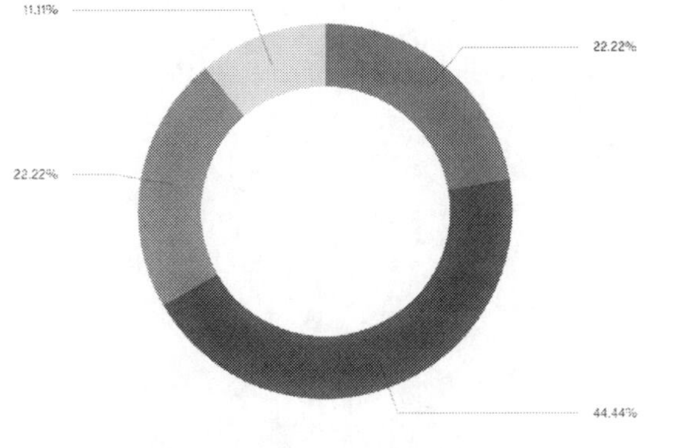

Figure 1. Graphic representation of student perceptions of Read'n Quiz activities.

tolerate the activities/actually liked them, while 33% had a hard time accessing the materials or could not get them to record their grades. The sample is small, but this pilot program shows that technical difficulties, not content, seem to be the deterrent to student approval. The materials are undergoing troubleshooting to improve the student experience.

V. Expanding the Student Support Resources

In the face of budget cuts mentioned in the introduction, software and student support programs had to be dropped. One of those was a commercial product that posed a series of questions to students and used analytics to help them to assess their readiness for online courses. It also had additional helpful features that were not available on the "Is Online Right for You?" helpsheets many institutions have on their websites. Those features included reading comprehension assessments, typing instruction, learning style assessments, and other information that was meant to benefit students and also provide instructors with an overview of what strengths and challenges students might be bringing to each class. Without that online readiness tool, many faculty members felt that students were not getting the preparation they needed to be successful in an online course. After all, KSU did not provide online students with any special orientation to ensure they understood what may be asked of them as online students. As this online orientation resource was created, it became clear that there were several additional resources that could help support student success: documentation and social media expectations.

A. Are You Ready for an Online Course?

To replace the commercial online orientation resource that was no longer affordable to the institution, a team in the College of Humanities and Social Sciences (CHSS) worked together. Using software such as Articulate Storyline, PowerPoint [16], Camtasia [17], and ShutterStock [18], the team created "Are You Ready for an Online Course?" [19]. Figure 2 shows the opening screen of the "Are You Ready for an Online Course" interactive presentation created by KSU faculty and staff to replace costly materials and support student success. This interactive presentation addresses tech-

Figure 2. Introductory image for the resource, "Are You Ready for an Online Course?"

-nology, communication, time management, goals and motivation, and other skills. It is KSU specific, but certainly any user might find helpful, research-based information there. Two versions are created. One is available on the open web for anyone to link to. A second, zip file is also available for anyone who might like to integrate it into an LMS using SCORM.

B. Documentation Resources

One of the goals for the student support resources was to find topics that were usable across a wide variety of courses in CHSS. A resource that had been requested for a while was a tutorial or other learning experience that helped students better understand documentation in research-based work, including how to avoid plagiarism.

CHSS courses mainly require Modern Language Association (MLA) and American Psychological Association (APA) documentation styles. Therefore, two documentation activities were created, one for MLA and one for APA. The activity starts with the Goblin Threat game created by Mary Broussard for Lycoming College [20]. Then it moves to the basics of MLA or APA, depending upon the presentation selected by the instructor. Like the online course readiness tool, it also includes a quiz question that can register in the LMS gradebook, should the instructor choose. The APA resource [21] and the MLA resource [22] are freely available.

Of course, this resource cannot replace the instructor's assignment guidelines or answer every documentation question, but it does help remind students that there are specific rules regarding plagiarism and documentation, and that they should heed those rules as they research and complete assignments.

C. Social Media Guidelines Regarding Academic Honesty

Finally, a new problem facing faculty and students at KSU has been misuse of social media, particularly GroupMe, a text-based chat platform that KSU students have adopted as their online community. For every course, a student automatically sets up a GroupMe and invites the entire class using the LMS classlist.

This GroupMe serves as a wonderful resource and support for students, particularly in online courses [23]. They go there to clarify assignments, ask about due dates, discuss issues in the class, and really engage in social learning and community building. However, it is also a place where students have the opportunity to engage in academic dishonesty. Many students didn't realize that the consequences for cheating on GroupMe were the same as cheating in the classroom. Students at the University of Texas at Austin, Ohio State University, and Louisiana State University have learned the hard way that social media can make cheating look too easy: "In 2017, Ohio State found 83 students in violation of 'unauthorized collaboration' via GroupMe" [24].

To help students to make good decisions regarding use of social media, we created an interactive presentation called "Academic Honesty and Social Media [25]. Figure 3 shows the opening screen of the "Academic Honesty and Social Media" interactive presentation designed to help students make informed decisions about social media use in courses.

Figure 3. Introductory image for the resource, "Academic Honesty and Social Media"

This presentation covers three scenarios that students may find themselves in on the GroupMe. The first describes a student posting unsolicited answers to assignments. The second details a student asking for answers on assignments. The third example features a good-hearted student posting "help" on the GroupMe that veers too close to academic dishonesty. As with "Are You Ready for an Online Course?" and the documentation resources, the "Academic Honesty and Social Media" resource also comes in a zipped file SCORM version that can be uploaded to an LMS where the quiz response can be registered in the grade book.

D. *Early Feedback*

The three resources discussed in this section were only implemented in fall 2019, and there has been no survey of either students or faculty to gauge whether or not they are helpful. However, early feedback from students in our midterm course surveys showed that the "Academic Honesty and Social Media" presentation has had mixed results. On the one hand, it has made students more aware of the penalties for academic dishonesty on social media, but on the other hand, it has stifled community building in the GroupMe because of anxiety surrounding innocent mistakes. That is an unintended and unfortunate consequence that hopefully future iterations of the resource can try to reverse.

VI. Conclusions and Future Work

In this work, we set out to examine the early impact of faculty innovations in the field of open educational resources. Specifically, what, if any impact, have these new efforts had on student success, particularly retention and satisfaction. With these forays into open educational resources and student success resources, it is too early to have more than individual student responses and pilot survey results. However, initial results show that students at Kennesaw State University are benefitting from adoption of OERs in the same way that students are showing benefits nationally. Also, while we will continue to update and improve the student success resources, we do feel that they are at least a helpful start. The faculty will continue to create open educational resources, including auxiliary materials and materials to support student success generally. We will continue to research the impact as the reach of these efforts becomes broader.

Acknowledgment

Special thanks to the College of Humanities and Social Sciences at Kennesaw State University, Georgia, USA for support, feedback, and resources to create these learning materials and conduct this initial research. The CHSS Resources are available [26].

References

[1] M. Mitchell, M. Leachman, K. Masterson, and S. Waxman, "Unkept promises: state cuts to higher education threaten access and equity." Center on Budget and Policy Priorities. October 4, 2018.[Online] Available from: https://www.cbpp.org/research/state-budget-and-tax/unkept-promises-state-cuts-to-higher-education-threaten-access-and Accessed February 3, 2020.

[2] N. Issa, "U.S. average student loan debt statistics in 2019." Credit.com. June 19, 2019. [Online] Available from: https://www.credit.com/personal-finance/average-student-loan-debt/ Accessed February 3, 2020.

[3] S. Etan and R. Donoghue, "Covering the cost: why we can no longer afford to ignore high textbook prices," Report, The Student PIRGs (Feb. 2016). [Online] Available from: www.studentpirgs.org/textbooks. Accessed February 3, 2020.

[4] G. Echevarria and J. Bowman, "Almost 80% of the textbook industry is dominated by 5 publishing companies that make books so expensive most students skip buying them." *Business Insider*. December 4, 2018. [Online] Available from: https://www.businessinsider.com/why-college-textbooks-expensive-textbook-publishing-2018-12.

[5] D. Tandberg and S. Laderman, "MHEC policy brief: evaluating state funding effort for higher education." June 2018. [Online] Available from: https://files.eric.ed.gov/fulltext/ED587428.pdf. Accessed March 16, 2020.

[6] "Textbook Transformation Grants: Spring 2020," Affordable Learning Georgia. University System of Georgia. [Online] Available from https://www.affordablelearninggeorgia.org/about/powerbi. Accessed March 17, 2020.

[7] N. B. Colvard, C. Edward Watson, and H. Park, "The Impact of open educational resources on various student success metrics," International Journal of Teaching and Learning in Higher Education, vol. 30, pp. 262–76, 2018.

[8] T. Reardon, T. Powell, J. Arnett, M. Logan, and C. Race, Open Technical Communication. [Online] Available from: http://open-tc.com/. Accessed February 2, 2020.

[9] D. McMurrey, Online Technical Writing. [Online] Available from: https://www.prismnet.com/~hcexres/textbook/. Accessed February 2, 2020.

[10] "Readership report," Author Dashboard. DigitalCommons@Kennesaw State University and Galileo Open Educational Materials. BePress. [Online] Available

from: https://readership.works.bepress.com/?authdash=1&userid=1727432&.authP=authdash%2Cuserid%2C.authTX&.authTX=1588379127&.authT=DN6zP7Z32IPB0Cike6pRA7v5WLfefw#/. Accessed November 22, 2019.

[11] W. Kurant, Becoming America: An Exploration of American Literature from Precolonial to Post-Revolution. University of North Georgia Press. [Online] Available from: https://ung.edu/university-press/books/becoming-america.php Accessed February 3, 2020.

[12] A. Berke, R. R. Bleil, J. Cofer, and D. Davis, Writing the Nation: A Concise Introduction to American Literature 1865 to Present. University of North Georgia Press. [Online] Available from: https://ung.edu/university-press/books/writing-the-nation-a-concise-introduction-to-american-literature-1865-to-present.php Accessed February 3, 2020.

[13] Articulate Storyline 360, [Online] Available from: https://articulate.com/360/storyline. Accessed March 17, 2020.

[14] D2L, Desire2Learn BrightSpace, [Online] Available from https://www.d2l.com/ Accessed March 17, 2020.

[15] Y. Shen, "Design of digital network shared learning platform based on SCORM standard." International Journal of Emerging Technologies in Learning, vol 13, pp. 214-227, 2018.

[16] PowerPoint, Microsoft Office. [Online] Available from https://products.office.com/en-us/powerpoint Accessed March 20, 2020.

[17] Camtasia, TechSmith. [Online] Available from https://www.techsmith.com/video-editor.html Accessed March 20, 2020.

[18] Shutterstock. [Online] Available from: https://www.shutterstock.com/ Accessed March 20, 2020.

[19] T. Powell, T. Reardon, J. Azriel, and S. Bartlett, "Are you ready for an online course?", Kennesaw State University College of Humanities and Social Sciences, July 2019. [Online] Available from: http://ode.hss.kennesaw.edu/Articulate/ReadyforOnline/story_html5.html Accessed February 3, 2020.

[20] M. Broussard and J. U. Oberlin, Goblin Threat. [Online] Available from: https://www.lycoming.edu/library/plagiarism-game/ Accessed February 3, 2020.

[21] T. Powell, "Plagiarism and documentation: APA." Kennesaw State University College of Humanities and Social Sciences. July 2019. [Online] Available from: http://ode.hss.kennesaw.edu/Articulate/PlagiarismDocumentationAPA/story_html5.html Accessed February 2, 2020.

[22] T. Powell, "Plagiarism and documentation: MLA." Kennesaw State University College of Humanities and Social Sciences. July 2019. [Online] Available from: http://ode.hss.kennesaw.edu/Articulate/PlagiarismDocumentationMLA/story_html5.html Accessed February 2, 2020.

[23] S. Gronseth and W. Hebert, "GroupMe: investigating use of mobile instant messaging in higher education courses." TechTrends: Linking Research and Practice to Improve Learning, vol 63, pp. 15-22, January 2019.

[24] W. Jenkins, "Has technology changed what qualifies as cheating?" The Chronicle of Higher Education, vol. 66, p. A28, October 4, 2019.

[25] T. Powell, "Academic honesty and social media." Kennesaw State University College of Humanities and Social Sciences. July 2019. [Online] Available from: http://ode.hss.kennesaw.edu/Articulate/AcademicHonesty_SocialMedia/story_html5.html Accessed February 3, 2020.

[26] Kennesaw State University College of Humanities and Social Sciences Office of Digital Education, Tutorials and resources. [Online] Available from: https://chss.kennesaw.edu/ode/tutorials.php Accessed February 2, 2020.

Solution for Real Problems through Research by Undergraduate Students

René Joaquín Díaz Martínez
Tecnológico de Monterrey
Torreón, México
email: renejdm@tec.mx

Rafaela Villalpando Hernández
Tecnológico de Monterrey
Torreón, México
email: rafaela.villalpando@tec.mx

Ramiro Saldaña Acosta
Tecnológico de Monterrey
Torreón, México
email: sramiro@tec.mx

Juan Francisco Medina Leal
Tecnológico de Monterrey
Torreón, México
email: A01234038@itesm.mx

Irene Reynoso Anguiano
Tecnológico de Monterrey
Torreón, México
email: A01232645@itesm.mx

Liliana Lizeth Luevano Rosales
Tecnológico de Monterrey
Torreón, México
email: A01231531@itesm.mx

***Abstract*— The present work gathers all the experience and knowledge from a group of students of last semester, taking the course entitled "Project of mechatronic engineering", which focused on actual problems of the local region. This class used an investigation method to approach these problems and teach students about self-learning. The objective of this project was to show students how the theory learned in school can be applied on the field.**

***Keywords*— inquiry-based learning; project; challenge; image processing.**

I. INTRODUCTION

In many situations, undergraduate students struggle to identify the relationship between the knowledge they have acquired throughout the course of their bachelor studies and their future jobs. Some manage to apply their studies through internships in their field, where they develop specific tasks for the companies they work for; others get involved in projects of interest to those entities and develop other abilities through research.

The current tendency to solve these problems is the linkage through university-industry projects that can occur through different pedagogical approaches, for example Research-Based Learning (RBL). This approach consists in applying teaching and learning strategies that aim to connect research with teaching. [1]. Berkeley, Warwick, MIT, Oxford, among others, are prestigious universities that promote this practice.

Pedaste et al. [2] identify and summarize the main characteristics of the RBL and set out the five phases and subphases, which are written in parenthesis, that distinguish it (see Figure 1): orientation, conceptualization (questioning and hypothesis generation), investigation (exploration, experimentation and data interpretation), conclusion, discussion (communication and reflection).

The authors did not find a framework which could gather and elaborate on the five phases and subphases exposed above, which allowed them to define the phases and subphases in what they called the Research Cycle, as shown in Figure 1.

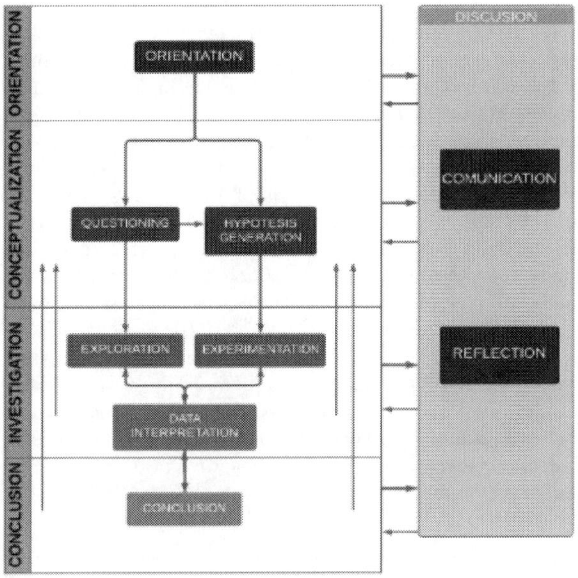

Figure 1. Research Cycle.

It is important to mention three elements of reference [2]:

1) The formulation of the technique is useful as guidance for those who desire to incorporate the pedagogical approach of RBL in their classes.

2) The presence of the discussion phase running parallel to the other phases provides a method in which designing is constantly happening, and it is not necessary to wait until the end to make adjustments because pondering and communication can be done at any moment.

3) Depending on the available information regarding the problem, three approaches can be proposed by students to develop the project: based on data, based on a hypothesis starting from a known theory, and based on questions that allow the formulation of a hypothesis. This last one is considered to come from the second.

Among the advantages that RBL offers, it can be mentioned that it allows better mentoring relationships between the professors and the students than traditional teaching, which results in improved learning and retention in undergraduate students. Also, enrollment in postgraduate education might be increased. In addition, students develop creativity, problem solving and intellectual independence; they also develop an understanding of research methodology. Finally, RBL promotes a culture oriented towards innovation. The other pillar that supports this work is Applied Research (AR). The term "Applied Research" was popularized during the twentieth century to refer to the type of scientific studies aimed at solving problems of daily life and controlling practical situations. It is currently a relevant topic, considering the close connection it has between education and industry. Its objective is to solve a specific approach focusing on the search and consolidation of knowledge for its application and, therefore, for the enrichment of cultural and scientific development [3].

Some important considerations about AR are highlighted below:

1) It can not be developed outside of theoretical and basic knowledge, which means that it is based on the results of Basic Research (BR), so that AR is the logical continuity of BR. However, the relationship between AR and BR is biunivocal, because the results of the AR help to rectify and expand the concepts emanating from the BR, thus contributing to the consolidations of a theory. As expressed in [4], many academics carry out the hybrid research, mixing both types of research, due to the need to obtain funds for their investigation, which can be provided by public or private institutions, letting them to test or apply what they have researched.

2) It allows to transform theoretical knowledge into concepts, prototypes, products, processes or services. This implies a close collaboration between the academy and higher education (teachers and students), industry and users. Therefore, there is a need for the participation of the end users and the industry responsible for verifying that it meets the needs.

This work gathers the experience carried out by mechatronic students, which allows them to identify the relationship between the knowledge acquired throughout their career, and an application in a real work environment. Part of the objective of devolving the current research work was to answer the question: "To what extent do the mechatronic engineering students recognize the link between the knowledge acquired in their career and the way they carry out an AR project associated with the solution of a real-world problem proposed by a company or an institution?"

First, the students were presented with a need from a company or institution, which must be solved by applying the knowledge gained throughout their career. After choosing a problem, the objectives were set. Table I shows the general objective and the specific objectives set.

The structure of the paper is as follows. In Section 2, we explain the approach taken to address the work and which projects arose from class. In Section 3, the results are explained and divided between each component of the project. We conclude in Section 4 with a summary of the work.

TABLE I. GENERAL AND SPECIFIC OBJETVIES OF THE WORK.

Main Goal	Determine the extent to which a mechatronic engineer student can manage to identify the relation between the knowledge of their profession and the surrounding environment, by carrying out an AR project associated with the solution of a real-world problem, proposed by a company or an institution.
Specific Objec-tives	1. Apply the RBL approach to develop AR projects 2. Identify the characteristics of an AR from this definition and its differences with an BR. 3. Design, build and test prototypes of mechatronic products that solve specific problems in their area of activity. 4. Promote the management of new knowledge not addressed in classes. 5. Encourage teamwork, so that this leads to the development of a functional mechatronic product, and to the elaboration of the descriptive memory that collects all the information corresponding to its design. 6. Expose the results achieved before a court of professors and experts.

II. METHODOLOGY

The RBL was developed through an AR in the class of "Project of mechatronic engineering", whose essence is precisely the solution of a real-world problem in a given context, seeking the implementation or the use of knowledge received or self-acquired. 13 students participated in this task, which were grouped into two teams at the beginning of the semester, and they had the full semester to complete the project.

TABLE II. PROBLEMS RAISED.

Problem	Research characterization
Tempera-ture measure-ment of stable cattle	Problem situation: problems with measuring the temperature of dairy cattle. Problem: there is no system capable of measuring in real time the temperature of a cow, which allows predicting diseases, stress or their mating season. Object of study: measurement of body temperature of living beings. Field of action: methods to measure the temperature of a dairy cow. Course objective: design, assemble and test a prototype system to measure the temperature of a dairy herd. Task: study of methods to measure body temperature; design prototypes based on image acquisition and processing acquired temperature measurements using thermal imaging cameras; make measurements with the prototype and process the data obtained. Hypothesis: with a system to measure in real time the body temperature of a cow, one can predict the caloric stress, symptoms of disease and the mating season of the animal.
Flow sensor for semi automated milking station	Problem Situation: Problems within the measurement of milk in a milking semi-automatic system. Problem: Lack of a device able to measure constantly the flow of the liquid, with a minimum error of 5%. Object of study: Study of the flow and measurement of fluids. Field of action: Methods to reduce the turbulence in flowing liquids. General objective: Design, mount and test a working prototype of a turbulent fluid flow sensor, with an error less than 5%. Tasks: Study the classical methods to reduce the turbulences on a fluid; design prototypes based on aerodynamic profiles and on the brachistochrone curve; characterize measurements using optoelectronics; measure with different prototypes and process the gained data. Hypothesis: Reducing the turbulence on the fluid will raise the precision and accuracy of the measurement, within a 5% error.

Of the three routes suggested in [9], the second one was chosen, where from a real known problem and an idea-solution based on a theory, a hypothesis is generated. The hypothesis triggers a research process based on experiments, tests and analysis of the results. Each team worked on a different problem, which is shown in Table II.

Both problems were worked on during the time given. The students had freedom to find their own solutions, in order to encourage the development of abilities and skills not seen in class, helping them to gain knowledge in other areas.

III. PARTIAL RESULTS OBTAINED

From the characterization discussed, the partial results obtained in the measurement of the temperature of the cattle are exemplified. Only these results will be explained in detail for conceptualization purposes.

After defining the method to use for the measurement of the temperature of the livestock, considering the economic resources, an approach was determined. The team decided to develop a prototype with cheap components, in a way in which it would show the main idea of the whole project.

A. Camera

Research was done in order to choose an accurate thermographic camera that fulfills the specifications of the project. After a thorough investigation, the Adafruit AMG8833 [5] was chosen, although the Flir E6 [6] is a better option technically, but it is too expensive for this project.

The AMG8833 camera complies with the needs of the project, although it has a poor accuracy of -+3°C, a maximum reach of 5 meters and a field of view of 60°. Table III was created to show how different the accuracy of the AMG8833 is, compared to other types of temperature sensors. For the camera the maximum measured temperature was considered. Also, a wet simulation was done in order account for the situation when an animal becomes wet when water it is sprayed on it.

TABLE III. TEMPERATURE MEASUREMENTS

Body Part	Digital Themom-eter	Distance	Laser		Camera	
			Dry	*Wet*	*Dry*	*Wet*
Hand	34.4°C	5 cm			34.5°C	32.75 °C
		30 cm	36.1°C	32.00°C	33.25°C	31.25 °C
Face	35.7°C	5 cm			35.25°C	
		30 cm	35.6°C	34.6°C	34°C	
Body	35.8°C	5 cm			35.75°C	33 °C
		30 cm	37.8°C	32.9°C	33°C	32.25 °C
		1 m	37.9°C	32.5°C	31.75°C	
		3 m	32.2°C	32.2°C	35.55°C	

The camera works with inter-integrated circuits (I2C) communication, which can be connected to a microcontroller. For this case an Arduino was chosen. As the Adafruit has open libraries for Arduino, it facilitates the use of this device. The sensor sends an 8x8 matrix of temperatures, which can be seen in Figure 2, where each number corresponds to a pixel of a picture.

```
-- Pixels Test --

[24.25, 23.50, 23.50, 23.50, 23.50, 23.50, 23.75, 23.00,
24.50, 24.25, 24.25, 24.50, 24.75, 24.50, 24.00, 24.50,
25.25, 25.25, 25.25, 25.00, 25.00, 24.75, 24.25, 24.25,
26.00, 26.75, 27.00, 26.75, 27.00, 25.50, 25.50, 24.00,
26.00, 28.25, 27.75, 28.00, 28.75, 28.50, 25.75, 24.50,
25.25, 27.50, 28.25, 29.25, 29.75, 28.25, 25.25, 24.25,
27.75, 27.75, 28.25, 29.25, 29.75, 28.75, 26.00, 24.50,
28.75, 26.75, 27.25, 28.75, 29.50, 26.50, 25.75, 24.75,
]
```

Figure 2. 8x8 Matrix example.

Although the sensor does not capture an image, only temperatures, the data was processed on MATLAB to create an image, which is shown in Figure 3. Due to the small number of pixels, the array had to be converted into a larger one. For this, a method called bicubic interpolation was used to create a 32x32 image and improve the quality.

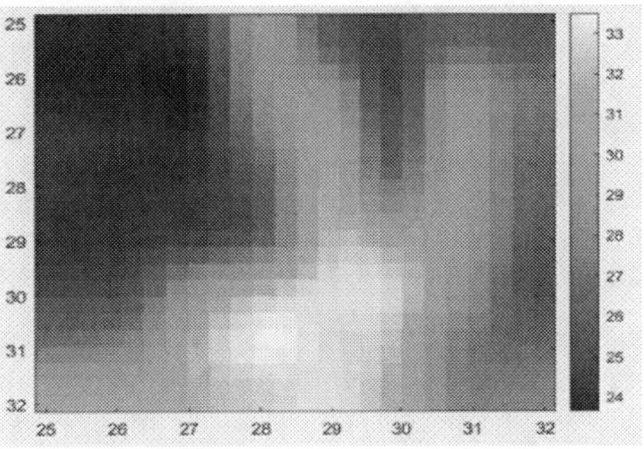

Figure 3. Thermographic image of a hand on MATLAB.

B. Identification System

The project is supposed to be operating in an establishment where there is a large amount of livestock. For this reason, an identification system had to be implemented, in order to identify the cow, in this case, as it gives helpful information to the carer. For identification, a radio frequency identification (RFID) RC522 module was used, but other methods can be used, such as image identification or magnetic sensor. The RFID module has a reach of approx. 5 cm [7]. Although is a short distance, these types of systems can be made so that they reach up to 10 meters, which is enough for projects implemented in the field. These systems identify pre-programmed identification cards that pass through the range of the RFID signal.

C. Mechanism

The location where the project would be placed is in a barn where livestock is kept. For this reason, the idea of mounting the camera with the identification system on a base, which would be held by a movement system involving a band that moves the system back and forth. It is supported by 2 rails. In addition to moving back and forth, the base of the camera can move on the spot 120° to increase the field of view. A 3D model was designed, as shown in Figure 4, before implementing it using specific materials. The materials used to create the prototype were: ABS plastic, wood, steel bars, toothed band, DC motor, servo motors, electric components (H bridge, resistors) and copper cable. The prototype range of motion was under 50 cm.

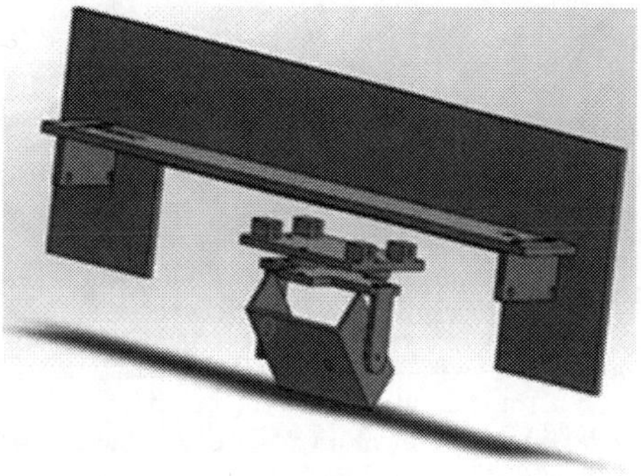

Figure 4. 3D model of the camera mount mechanism.

D. Data system

All the data is saved on a platform where a table of temperatures with their corresponding thermographic images is placed together with the date and time of the measurement. In this way, the end user can go back to past records or look into present ones. MATLAB was used to process the data and save such files into a specific folder in the computer.

E. Prototype

After consolidating all the parts of the system, the final prototype was created. An image of the result is shown in Figure 5.

Figure 5. Final protype of the temperature acquisition system.

As shown in Figure 5, the prototype was constructed at a smaller scale, so it can be tested in the classroom. In order to be tested in a barn, the prototype would need to measure at least 6 meters in length, to fit in the barn structure. For this reason, the team decided to first prove the mechanical and electronic functioning with a smaller size device, as a larger prototype would have the same principle.

IV. CONLUSION

The objective of this paper was to allow mechatronic students to relate the acquired knowledge throughout their career, with an AR project to implement a solution for a real-world problem. This was reached through the research done and with the reported results. The RBL approach was applied throughout an entire university semester as part of the course entitled "Project of mechatronic engineering".

Following this RBL approach, solutions were reached as well as some transversal key competences were developed, for example, teamwork, written, presentation skills, and abilities to solve complex problems. In addition to developing competences, the project's team gained knowledge regarding image processing and skills on the use of software for programming and data management, in this case were MATLAB and Arduino. The obtained results allowed the qualitatively evaluation of the students (final grades between 95 and 100), two rubrics were used to grade the written proof and the oral presentation.

The project allowed students to link applied investigation with the research-based learning method, achieving something that most desire, which is to solve problem based on an industry or company needs through an academic approach.

We suggest the following recommendations for the follow-up of the project:

1) Employ project management tools, for example: Wrike, Asana and Flow, in order to ensure a better control of the project phases.

2) Apply a survey to the students, where they state what have they learned, which challenges they have overcome and what area of opportunity they discovered. In the same way, apply other survey to the client, where he can express the level of satisfaction with the problem solution.

3) For the complexity of the problem, the prototype was constructed at a smaller scale, which is yet to be adapted, so it can be placed in a barn.

ACKNOWLEDGMENT

The authors would like to acknowledge the financial and the technical support of Writing Lab, TecLabs, Tecnológico de Monterrey, Torreón, México, in the production of this work.

REFERENCES

[1] "Edu Trends: Educational Innovation Radar," (2017), Monterrey: Instituto Tecnológico y de Estudios Superiores de Monterrey, https://observatorio.tec.mx/radar-de-innovacin-educativa-2017/, [retrieved: 02, 2020].

[2] M. Pedaste et al., "Phases of inquiry-based learning: Definitions and the inquiry cycle," Educational Research Review, vol 14, pp. 47–61, 2015.

[3] "Applied Research," (n.d.), Duoc UC, http://www.duoc.cl/biblioteca/crai/definicion-y-proposito-de-la-investigacion-aplicada, [retrieved: 02, 2020].

[4] P. J. Bentley, M. Gulbrandsen, and S. Kyvik, "The relationship between basic and applied research in universities," High Educ, published on line: 25 March 2015.

[5] "Adafruit AMG8833 8x8 Thermal Camera Sensor," (n.d.), Adafruit, https://learn.adafruit.com/adafruit-amg8833-8x8-thermal-camera-sensor, [retrieved: 02, 2020].

[6] "Flir E6 WIFI," (n.d.), Flir, https://www.flir.com.mx/products/e6-wifi/, [retrieved: 02, 2020]

[7] "RC522 RFID Module," (n.d.), Components101, https://components101.com/wireless/rc522-rfid-module, [retrieved: 02,2020]

Intelligent Tutoring Systems for Generation Z's Addiction

Ioana R. Goldbach
Center for Research and Studies in Management and Marketing
Valahia University of Targoviste
Targoviste, Dambovita, Romania
e-mail: ioana.goldbach@icstm.ro

Felix G. Hamza-Lup
Computer Science
College of Engineering and Computing
Georgia Southern University
Savannah, Georgia, USA
e-mail: fhamzalup@georgiasouthern.edu

***Abstract*— As generation Z's big data is flooding the Internet through social nets, neural network based data processing is turning an important cornerstone, showing significant potential for fast extraction of data patterns. Online course delivery and associated tutoring are transforming into customizable, on-demand services driven by the learner. Besides automated grading, strong potential exists for the development and deployment of next generation intelligent tutoring software agents. Self-adaptive, online tutoring agents exhibiting "intelligent-like" behavior, being capable "to learn" from the learner, will become the next educational "superstars". Over the past decade, computer-based tutoring agents were deployed in a variety of extended reality environments, from patient rehabilitation to psychological trauma healing. Most of these agents are driven by a set of conditional control statements and a large answers/questions pairs dataset. This article provides a brief introduction on Generation Z's addiction to digital information, highlights important efforts for the development of intelligent dialogue systems, and explains the main components and important design decisions for Intelligent Tutoring System.**

Keywords- intelligent tutoring systems; machine learning; adaptive systems; artificial intelligence.

I. INTRODUCTION

Driven by a large amount of data (i.e., training sets) available and the developments in neural-nets, a metamorphosis to *intelligent-like behavior* is catalyzed by the increase in the processing power of parallel systems. Generation Z (or Gen Z, commonly defined as people born between 1995 and mid-2010s) the "digital natives", are becoming more influential in dictating changes in education in the years to come. Like generation Y (i.e., Millennials [1]), Gen Z accelerates the changes in higher education by employing mobile, multimedia, and online technologies. It is the generation of online connection that collaborates and wants to learn fast, adapts and wants active participation in the learning environment. Gen Z students have already entered the university level and they adopt social learning environments that directly involves them. They are the generation of *demanders* as they request services that are available anytime, anywhere. Digital tools are an addiction to many, as they participate on a daily basis in social networking, specifically in scattered cities around the globe where the city architecture is not facilitating social face-to-face interaction.

Research from the Center for Generational Kinetics [2] shows that 95% of the Z generation has smartphones, 55% of them use phones around 5 hours a day, and 26% of them are addicted to digital content, as they spend more than 10 hours a day online. Addiction-like level involvement with digital content shows that 31% of them feel uncomfortable if they are disconnected from the phone for more than 30 minutes. A recent study on people aged between 14 to 40 in the US [3] was targeted towards the behavior, preferences, and attitudes of young people. The study revealed fundamental differences and similarities between the Y and Z generations. About 39% of Gen Z wants to learn with a teacher, while 47% of them spend more than 4 hours a day on video platforms. Compared to Gen Y, Gen Z tends to learn through self-guidance and prefers flexibility. Regardless of the differences between generations, 66% of Gen Z have a positive view of technology in education [3].

This paper is structured as follows: Section 2 provides an overview of an Intelligent Tutoring System (ITS) and the main actors involved in such systems. Section 3 highlights the main research efforts in the area, while the structure and the main components of an ITS are presented in Section 4. In the conclusion, future trends in ITSs evolution are highlighted and explained.

II. ARTIFICIAL INTELLIGENCE IN EDUCATION SYSTEMS

Artificial Intelligence (AI) mainly resorts to machine learning algorithms to transform data in decisions and provide meaningful user-computer interaction. At the core of the machine learning methodology is a set of statistical and prediction based algorithms or constructs that allow timely big data processing and extraction of meaningful patterns. Such patterns are used to predict (hopefully with high probability, e.g., 90%+) future events/values, hence allowing automated decisions (i.e., expert decision systems) to be taken by machines, providing the user with the impression that the computing device makes intelligent choices.

Particularly interesting is the recent application of AI in intelligent tutoring for education and, as a consequence, the proliferation of ITS. The basic principle of operation and the main actors involved in a possible AI-based ITS are depicted in Figure 1. Data about the learner may be collected from multiple venues (i.e., social networks, instructors, online course preferences, etc.) and recommendations are made based on the processing of collected information and other inputs (e.g., exam results, learner's past and current questions, instructor's feedback about the learner, peers feedback, etc.).

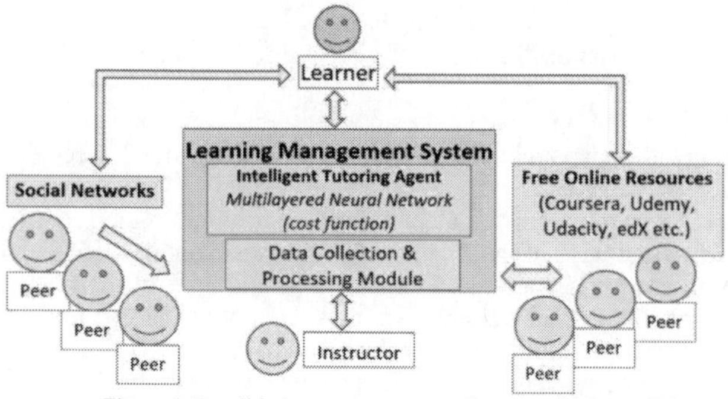

Figure 1. Possible interaction among the actors in future ITS

In the very near future, a data collection and processing module (illustrated in Figure 1) could potentially aggregate information from a variety of sources and could extract patterns specific to the learner, allowing the learner profile generation. Those patterns are further employed by the tutoring system to fine-tune the content of the conversation with the user in order to generate intelligent dialogue. A multilayered neural network, driven by a cost function, is constantly evaluating the learner's feedback and providing informed guidance to the learner.

III. Brief Review on Intelligent Tutoring

ITSs are not a new development, as early research efforts that focused on intelligent dialogue have been explored for several decades. Among the most notable efforts are the Hamburg Application-oriented Natural language System (HAM-ANS) project [4] at the University of Hamburg, the KLAUS project at the Scientific Research Institute (SRI) International [5] and the XCALIBUR project [6] at Carnegie-Mellon University. Central to these systems was always the requirement for interaction through sequential dialogue with a human operator and the capacity of the system to generate meaningful dialogue based on the collected data.

The rapid proliferation of automated and online learning systems has spawned in the last decade a large number of ITSs with the main goal of enabling the student to successfully solve problems. Among them, AutoTutor [7] is an intelligent guidance system that stimulates dialogue and has the pedagogical strategies of a human tutor. It was designed to help students learn the basics of hardware, operating systems, and the Internet, and enhances the learning technology in the following areas: computer literacy, critical thinking, and physics. AutoTutor focuses on meditation and pedagogical strategies and was designed using human tutor strategies to identify motivational factors for students. AutoTutor was the basis for the development of other intelligent systems such as: AutoManager, AutoTutor-Sensitive, AutoTutor-3D [8] with interactive 3D embedded simulation, DeepTutor, AutoTutor-Lite, GnuTutor, MetaTutor - metacognition self-learning, Human Use Regulatory Affairs Advisor (HURAA) Web Counselor on ethical treatment of experimental subjects, iDRIVE - Learning to Ask Deep Questions about Science, Center for the Study of Adult Literacy (CSAL) and Operation Acquiring Research, Investigative, and Evaluative Skills (ARIES) [9].

Another prominent example is SmartTutor [10] an intelligent system that addresses two basic elements in continuous education: personalization and intelligent guidance. It contains a database of over 3000 reading and math lessons. The effectiveness of the system has been evaluated and the results have been exceptional at the K8 level. The system is based on the fact that learners' answers can provide a lot of information about the current state of their conceptual understanding. The syntactic dimension is explored in Why2-Atlas [11], an intelligent system that analyzes students' explanations of physics principles through various mechanisms. Students introduce their essays into the system as a paragraph, and the tutor uses syntactic analysis to proofread the essays and find misconceptions, as well as incomplete explanations. If the tutor identifies certain mistakes in the essay, it generates a dialogue regarding the wrong or non-existent requirements and then asks the student to correct the essay. Several iterations and dialogues can take place before the process is completed.

Along the same lines, ElectronixTutor [12] is a fully integrated system based on many intelligent learning systems (e.g., AutoTutor, Dragoon, LearnForm, ASSISTments, BEETLE-II). The system includes a student model that has knowledge of electronic circuits and guides other learners in the electronics field providing feedback. Like ElectronixTutor, e-Teacher [13] automatically builds student profiles while studying online courses and detecting the student's performance. The system suggests a customized course of action designed to support each learner.

Introductory knowledge helps learners navigate basic concepts in different disciplines. ZOSMAT [14] has been developed as an intelligent introductory system in response to the student's needs of individual learning. The role of the system is the tracking and the guidance of the learning process. It identifies and records student progress and changes the study program according to the learners' effort. It can be used for individual learning purposes, but it also provides a feature that makes it different from other intelligent guidance systems: it can be used in class under the guidance of a human tutor.

While some of these research efforts are still in the preliminary phases, there are several successful commercial applications, particularly targeted at teaching basic concepts and addressing large groups of learners, specifically at the K-12 level.

IV. INTELLIGENT TUTORING SYSTEMS STRUCTURE

Intelligent tutoring systems consist of four important components [15]: (1) an Expert Model (EM), (2) a Student Model (SM), (3) a Tutoring Model (TM) and (4) the User Interface Model (UIM), as illustrated in Figure 2. The data flowing among these components is constantly fine-tuned based on the system and the target users group.

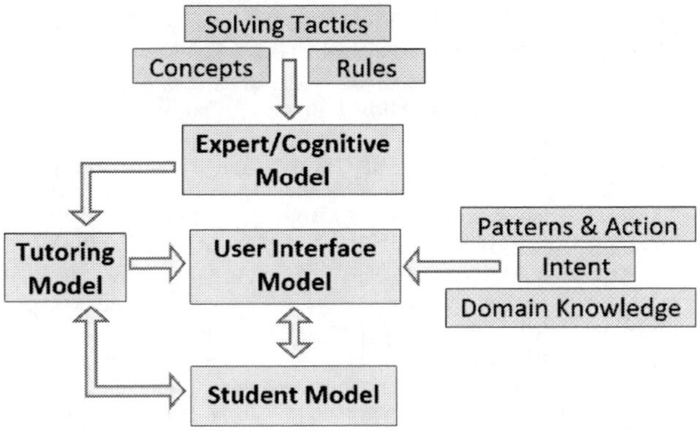

Figure 2. ITS – Generic Structure and Data Flow

The expert model (cognitive/domain model or expert knowledge model) is built on learning theories that consider all the steps required to solve a problem and contains the concepts, rules, and problem-solving tactics of the domain to be learned. The EM also contains the mal-rules and misconceptions that students occasionally exhibit. EM can fulfill several roles: a source of expert knowledge, a standard for evaluating the student's performance or for detecting errors and fallacies. Another approach for developing the EM is the constraint-based modeling approach [16], presented as a set of constraints on correct solutions [17].

The student model can be thought of as a cover on the EM. It is considered as the central component of an ITS, focusing on the student's cognitive and affective states and their evolution as the learning progresses. As the learner works step-by-step through their problem-solving process, the ITS employs a model tracing approach. If the SM deviates from the EM, the system triggers a warning and particular actions. In contrast, in constraint-based tutors, the SM is represented as an overlay on the constraint set [18] and they evaluate the student's solution against the constraint set, to identify satisfied or violated constraints. Violated constraints trigger the ITS feedback on those constraints [19], providing the learner with immediate feedback. The SM builds a profile of strengths and weaknesses for each learner relative to the EM.

Next, the tutor model (or pedagogical model or instructional model) accepts information from the EM and the SM and makes choices about tutoring strategies and actions. The TM contains several hundred production rules that exist in one of two states: learned or unlearned. Every time a student successfully applies a rule to a problem, the system updates a probability estimate that the student has learned the rule. The system continues to drill students on exercises that require the effective application of a rule until the probability that the rule has been learned reaches the 95% threshold [20].

Last but not least, the UIM interprets the learner's contributions through various input media (speech, typing, clicking) and generates output in different media (text, diagrams, animations, agents). It integrates the following information: knowledge about patterns of interpretation (to comprehend the speaker) and action (to generate meaningful expressions) within dialogues, domain knowledge needed for content communication, and knowledge for communicative intent [21]. The communicative intent is the use of gestures, facial expressions, articulations, and/or written expressions to deliver a message and, sometimes, the ITS presents an avatar embodiment to facilitate the user interaction.

ITS are expensive systems to develop both from the complexity and development time perspectives. Attempts to develop authoring tools [22] have looked into various ways to develop agent-based tutors and dialogue-based tutors. Significant research has ensued an array of theoretical frameworks that remain enthusiastically investigated to this day. Reviews of the expert model design in [23]-[25] point to the need to extract domain based features. A review of student modeling [26] reveals the importance of specific learner's characteristics and also points out the requirement for a reward system. A detailed review of tutoring strategies is presented in [27].

Among the most important categorization dimensions for an ITS is the fundamental learning component. Three directions are possible:

- *Simulation-based* learning environments. Here, the general paradigm of a simulated world is captured in the term *reactive environment* [28] to describe an ITS in which the system responds to learners' actions in a variety of ways catalyzing learners' concepts understanding.
- *Discourse-based* learning environments. Natural language interactions have enabled more conversational forms in such environments. Discourse as a tutorial approach, is intended to operate in an ITS much like it does when practiced by a skilled human tutor.
- *Situation-based* learning. Instructional systems may be more effective when coupled with situations in which the users naturally encounter, learn, and apply the skills and knowledge being taught.

A prominent research effort, the Generalized Intelligent Framework for Tutoring (GIFT) [29] is oriented around providing three services: authoring of components, management of instructional processes, and an assessment methodology [30].

V. CONCLUSION

The paper presents several statistical facts about Generation Z as it pertains to the use of technology for learning tasks, culminating with the need for customized intelligent tutoring systems. A brief review of the existing ITSs, as well as the fundamental structure of the ITS, is presented with a brief description of each structural component.

The relatively high cost of building an ITS makes it a viable option only for situations such as simultaneous tutoring of large groups, or in cases when tutoring redundancy is necessary and can generate significant savings (i.e., reducing the need for human instructors or freeing human instructors time and resources). With advances in processing speed and machine learning algorithms, we foresee an increase in the online deployment of ITSs and, possibly, a wider adoption of such systems among generation Z's learners.

REFERENCES

[1] https://www.inc.com/ryan-jenkins/generation-z-vs-millennials-the-8-differences-you-.html/ [retrieved: 2020-01-23].

[2] https://genhq.com/top-10-ways-gen-z-is-shaping-the-future/ [retrieved:2020-01-22].

[3] https://www.pearsoned.com/generation-z-millennials-expect-technology-education/ [retrieved: 2020-01-31].

[4] J. A. Mason and J. L. Edwards, "Surveying projects on intelligent dialogue," International Journal of Man-Machine Studies, vol. 28 (2-3), Feb-Mar, 1988, pp. 259-307, https://doi.org/10.1016/S0020-7373(88)80038-5/ [retrieved: 2020-01-25].

[5] D. Appelt et al., "Research on Natural-Language at SRI," TechNote 257, 1981, pp. 5-7.

[6] J. G. Carbonell, W. M. Boggs, M. L. Mauldin and P. G. Anick, "The XCALIBUR project: a natural language interface to expert systems," Proceeding IJCAI'83 Proceedings of the Eighth International Joint Conference on Artificial Intelligence, vol. 2, 1983, pp. 653-656.

[7] A. C. Graesser, "Conversations with AutoTutor Help Students Learn," International Journal of Artificial Intelligence in Education," vol. 26, 2016, pp. 124-132.

[8] A. C. Graesser, "Learning, thinking, and emoting with discourse technologie," American Psychologist, 66, 2011, pp. 743-757.

[9] B. D. Nye, A. C. Graesser and X. Hu, "AutoTutor and Family: A Review of 17 Years of Natural Language Tutoring," International Artificial Intelligence in Education Society, 24, 2014, pp. 427-469.

[10] B. Cheung, L. Hui, J. Zhang and J. S. M. Yiu, "SmartTutor: An intelligent tutoring system in web-based adult education," Journal of Systems and Software, vol. 68, 2003, pp. 11-25. URL: https://doi.org/10.1016/S0164-1212(02)00133-4, [retvd: 2020-01-30].

[11] K. VanLehn et al., "The Architecture of Why2-Atlas: A Coach for Qualitative Physics Essay Writing," In: Cerri S.A., Gouardères G., Paraguaçu F. (eds) Intelligent Tutoring Systems. ITS 2002, Lecture Notes in Computer Science, vol. 2363, 2002, Springer, Berlin, Heidelberg, URL: https://doi.org/10.1007/3-540-47987-2_20, [retrieved: 2020-01-30].

[12] A. C. Graesser et al., "ElectronixTutor: an intelligent tutoring system with multiple learning resources for electronics," International Journal of STEM Education, 2018, vol. 5, URL: https://doi.org/10.1186/s40594-018-0110-y/ [retrieved: 2020-01-25].

[13] S. Schiaffino, P. Garcia and A. Amandi, "eTeacher: Providing personalized assistance to e-learning students," 2008, Computers & Education, vol. 51, pp. 1744-1754.

[14] A. Keleşa, R. Ocakb, A. Keleşc and A. Gülcü, "ZOSMAT: Web-based intelligent tutoring system for teaching-learning process," Expert Systems with Applications, vol. 36, Issue 2, Part 1, vol. 1229-1239, URL: https://doi.org/10.1016/j.eswa.2007.11.064/ [retrieved: 2019-09-27].

[15] R. Nkambou, R. Mizoguchi and J. Bourdeau, "Advances in intelligent tutoring systems," 2010, Heidelberg: Springer, ISBN 9783642143632, https://link.springer.com/book/10.1007%2F978-3-642-14363-2/ [retrieved: 2020-01-30].

[16] S. Ohlsson, "Constraint-based Student Modeling. Artificial Intelligence in Education," 1992, vol. 3(4), pp. 429-447.

[17] A. Mitrovic and S. Ohlsson, "Constraint-Based Knowledge Representation for Individualized Instruction," Computer Science and Information Systems, vol. 3(1), 2006, pp. 1-22.

[18] A. Mitrovic, "Fifteen years of Constraint-Based Tutors: What we have achieved and where we are going," User Modeling and User-Adapted Interaction, 2012, vol. 22(1-2), pp. 39-72, https://doi.org/10.1007/s11257-011-9105-9/ [retrieved: 2020-01-28].

[19] A. Mitrovic, B. Martin, P. Suraweera, "Intelligent tutors for all: Constraint-based modeling methodology, systems and authoring," IEEE Intelligent Systems, 2007, vol. 22(4), pp. 38-45.

[20] A. T. Corbett and J. R. Anderson, "Student modeling and mastery learning in a computer-based programming tutor," Proceedings of the Second International Conference on Intelligent Tutoring Systems, 1992.

[21] I. Padayachee, "Intelligent Tutoring Systems: Architecture and Characteristics," In: SACLA 2002 Proceedings of 32nd Annual Conference of the Southern African Computer Lecturers' Association, 2002.

[22] R. A. Sottilare, A. C. Graesser, X. Hu, K. Brawner. "Design Recommendations for Intelligent Tutoring Systems," vol. 3 Authoring Tools and Expert Modeling Techniques, Publisher: US Army Research Laboratory, Editor: Sottilare, Graesser, Hu, and Brawner, 2015, ISBN: 978-0-9893923-7-2.

[23] N. J. Ahuja and R. Sille, "A Critical Review of Development of Intelligent Tutoring Systems: Retrospect, Present and Prospect," International Journal of Computer Science Issues, vol. 10, no 2, July 2013, pp. 39-48.

[24] G. Paviotti, P. G. Rossi and D. Zarka, "Intelligent Tutoring Systems: An Overview," Lecce: Pensa Multimedia, Italy, Google Scholar, 2012.

[25] S. Sani and T. N. M. Aris, "Computational Intelligence Approaches for Student/Tutor Modelling: A Revie," In Proceedings of the 2014 Fifth International Conference on Intelligent Systems, Modelling and Simulation, Langkawi, Malaysia: IEE, 2014.

[26] P. I. Pavlik Jr., K. W. Brawner, A. Olney and A. Mitrovic, "A Review of Learner Models Used in Intelligent Tutoring Systems," In R. A. Sottilare, A. Graesser, X. Hu, & H. K. Holden (Eds.), Design Recommendations for Adaptive Intelligent Tutoring Systems Learner Modeling, Army Research Labs/ U. of Memphis, 2013, pp. 39-68.

[27] R. A. Sottilare, J. A. DeFalco and J. Connor, "A Guide to Instructional Techniques, Strategies and Tactics to Manage Learner Affect, Engagement and Grit," In R. Sottilare, A. Graesser ,X. Hu and B. Goldberg (Eds.), Design Recommendations for Intelligent Tutoring Systems: Instructional Management, US Army Research Laboratory, vol. 2, 2014.

[28] V. J. Shute and J. Psotka, "Intelligent tutoring systems: Past, present, and future," In D. Jonassen (Ed.), Handbook of research for educational communications and technology, New York, NY: Macmillan, 1996, pp. 570-600.

[29] https://gifttutoring.org/projects/gift/wiki/Overview. [retrieved: 2020-01-25].

[30] R. A. Sottilare, B. S. Goldberg, K. W. Brawner and H. K. Holden, "A modular framework to support the authoring and assessment of adaptive computer-based tutoring systems (CBTS)." Interservice /Industry Training, Simulation, and Edu. Conf., 2012, pp. 1-13.

Evaluating Virtual Reality as a Learning Resource: An Insight into User Experience, Usability and Learning Experience

Katherina Gallardo
Tecnologico de Monterrey
School of Humanities and Education
Monterrey, Mexico
Email: katherina.gallardo@tec.mx

Nohemi Rivera
Tecnologico de Monterrey
School of Humanities and Education
Chihuahua, Mexico
Email: nohemi_rivera@tec.mx

Abstract—**Information and Communication Technologies (ICT) are powerful tools that support teaching and the case of Virtual Reality (VR) is especially promising because of its unique characteristics. In this paper, we report on a project that aims to describe how variables such as usability, user experience and learner interface experience might affect learning results while using VR resources. We present the preliminary results of a mixed-methods study, including the students' perceptions collected in two focus groups. These undergraduate students were exposed to the use of VR resources for learning purposes. These preliminary results invite us to think about the inclusion of different indicators to strengthen the VR resources evaluation process in higher education.**

Keywords-Learning assessment; Learning interface experience; Usability; User experience; Virtual reality; Higher education; Educational innovation.

I. INTRODUCTION

Information and Communication Technologies (ICT) are powerful tools to support learning because they allow students to be reached at any place and time, reducing the costs of traditional learning methods. Digital technologies provide materials for active learning that more fully engage learners [1]. The case of Virtual Reality (VR) is especially promising because of its unique characteristics. VR is a term used to describe an absorbing, interactive, computer-generated 3D virtual experience in which a person interacts in real time with simulated objects that seem real [2], and it can be used as a learning environment for different levels and disciplines [3]. Most VR environments are primarily visual experiences, but they may also include auditory simulation, which is very useful because vision provides the most information, followed by hearing; probably 90% of our world perception is visual or auditory [2]. Furthermore, the VR content can be delivered in a variety of ways, including specially made VR headsets, smartphones and computers [1]. We can group the VR systems depending on the level of immersion they offer to the user. There are different kinds of immersions that can be achieved in a virtual environment [2]:

- Tactical immersion: Experienced when performing tactile operations.
- Strategic immersion: Related to mental challenge.
- Narrative immersion: When players become invested in a story (like reading a book).
- Spatial immersion: When the simulated world is perceptually convincing (feeling of being there).
- Psychological immersion: When a player confuses the game with real life.
- Sensory immersion: Experiencing a unity of time and space (fusing with the image medium).

VR headsets (immersive system) provide the greatest sense of immersion by completely replacing the real world with the virtual one, but they are also the most expensive way to deliver it [1]. This type of system provides a stereoscopic view of the scene according to the user's position and orientation [2]. Computers (non-immersive system), on the other hand, are the simplest and most readily available method for VR playback, but they greatly reduce the sense of immersion [1]. In this case, the user views a virtual environment through one or more computer screens and is able to interact with the environment without being immersed in it [2].

The rest of the paper is structured as follows. In Section II, we present the related work. Section III presents the structure of the project, as well as the research methods and instruments used in the gathering and analysis of the preliminary data. Section IV presents the most relevant results of the two focus groups, and Section V critically analyzes the main findings and the future work to be done.

II. RELATED WORK

The immersion, presence and interactivity are some of the features that make VR different from other traditional media. Furthermore, the autonomy, the free navigation in a 3D space, the intuitive and realistic interaction with virtual objects and the first-person point of view are some of the VR features that contribute to a sense of presence inside the virtual environment and make the users feel as being in a real laboratory [2][3]. Mikropoulos and Bellou [3] found that all these VR features play an important role for knowledge construction, and presence is the principal feature that contributes to positive learning outcomes. Thus, these features should be taken into consideration when designing virtual environments, in combination with the discipline and specific content under study. VR implementation is mainly found in high school, college and university; with healthcare and engineering being the most investigated subject areas, followed by computer sciences, culture, history and automotive. In addition, professional education domains are now incorporating VR technologies to train their employees [4].

The implementation of VR in education is based on constructivism, which emphasizes the dynamic aspect of learning. Experiential learning is constructivist, and it emphasizes the central role that experience plays in the learning process [5]. Unlike passive information transference methods (such as lectures), VR experiences allow the learner to control the pace of the process and make decisions that influence the outcome, making a virtual world feel real and increasing memory retention [1]. When the learning process involves learners' emotions and social life, they can better master the knowledge. Using VR allows learners to gain information from an experience that is not easily accessible or does not exist in real life, and encourages them to use their imagination when manipulating the environment, which eases the active construction of models and the skills development [2][6]. Also, creative learning and the ability to innovate can be stimulated and improved. Another advantage is that there is no risk in virtual training, learners can practice repeatedly until they master a skill [6]. For example, Tsai [7] found that using VR during training could reduce the anxiety caused by emergencies. In short, immersion in a virtual world allows us to construct knowledge from direct experience, not from descriptions of experience [8].

Durrani and Pita [4] found that VR has a very positive effect on learning. 92% of the studies they analyzed showed a positive impact of integrating VR, and the other 8% of the studies showed a neutral effect. In line with this, Marks [9] found that the exploration of a 3D model really helped students to understand the spatial structure. In addition, the VR application promoted discussions among the students and, when compared with the group using traditional materials, they showed a higher cooperation. Moreover, the VR group showed the most significant difference in the question about stimulating interest in the topic. This is where VR seems to show more promise [9]. Hence, VR can enhance the learning process, but it is not appropriate for every instructional objective or learning content. Therefore, to decide if using VR is the best option, it is necessary to evaluate the type of contents that will be taught and identify the experiences that would be difficult, dangerous or impossible to provide in formal education. Strategic and descriptive knowledge can often achieve good results without using a virtual experience. Furthermore, it is crucial to consider if creating a simulated environment is relevant to the learning objective [6][10]. Creating a pedagogical foundation when designing VR modules is an important step in their development. This process requires script writing and expert content evaluation before the modules can be recorded. Students may benefit greatly if provided with safe and effective experiential learning opportunities through VR [1].

Besides the pedagogical foundation, the application of VR technology to education requires students to be autonomous learners and to have learning initiative. This learning way is student-centered, emphasizing that students need to demonstrate their enthusiasm and initiative in the learning process [6]. However, it is important to consider that a purely exploratory tool, such as a VR application, is not sufficient to guide the students through the whole learning process. Marks [9] discovered that even though the 3D model they used in the VR tool presented all the necessary information, not all of it was discovered or remembered correctly by the students. Therefore, teachers should not think that using VR can be enough for students to finish learning. On the contrary, the use of VR in education has high requirements for teachers, who play a guiding role in the entire process and must constantly improve themselves and adapt to the needs of future teaching [6]. It is also helpful to have some guidance in the VR application besides previous oral indications delivered by teachers, such as a list of items to work through or an audio or textual narrative. Regarding this, the majority of the participants in Marks' [9] study requested a guidance mechanism for the exploration process and short comprehension tests of the content before unlocking the next part of the tour. In conclusion, VR is a promising tool for educators, presenting important advantages like the ease of use, the increased motivation and the non-symbolic, first-person experience. However, to maximize the benefits, it is important to consider the whole context of the education process in the design of any VR application [8][9] as well as the instructional decisions teachers take to insert this kind of material for learning purposes.

As mentioned previously, many authors have evaluated the usability of VR technology [9] and the students' experience when using it as a learning tool [11], but there is very little research on its instructional usability, which is the degree in which the tool is really motivating and helping students to achieve the learning objective. In this sense, the objective of this paper is constructing an evaluation process for VR resources that considers all the aspects of the learning process.

III. Methodology

A. Design

This is a mixed-methods study [11]. The objective is to describe how variables such as usability, user experience and learner interface experience might affect learning results while using VR resources.

B. Context and participants

This study took place in a private university located in northeastern Mexico. Undergraduate students from different programs such as engineering, medicine and business were exposed to the use of VR resources for learning purposes. The results presented in this paper focus on a VR resource that was designed to collect, calculate and estimate data from a daily activity: going to buy groceries at a supermarket. This VR tool attempted to achieve spatial immersion (a simulated world that is perceptually convincing).

In sum, 268 students from engineering and business that were taking the course "Mathematics and Data Science" used the VR tool in Monterrey; 76 students were studying at the campus in a presence-based modality and the rest were online students. The students used the VR tool for about an hour and, during this time, they had to choose 5 foods, trying to get the smallest number of calories possible. The objective of the VR tool was to help students to calculate their caloric intake and stimulate their interest in the nutritional value of the food they choose.

C. *Instruments*

Two instruments were adapted for responding to research questions: The first instrument was a questionnaire with 21 items using Likert scale (1= completely disagree, 2= disagree, 3=somewhat disagree , 4=somewhat agree, 5= agree, and 6= completely agree) divided into two sections: usability and user experience statements [9][12]–[15]. The quantitative results obtained from this questionnaire will be presented in future work. The second instrument was a mixed questionnaire [9], [12]–[16]. In this case, this instrument was applied in a focus group technique. The instrument was divided into four sections.

- Section 1: contains 6 items about usability and 5 items about user experience. All of them are open-ended questions.
- Section 2: contains 12 items related to instructional issues and learning experience. These items use a six-point Likert scale (1= little 6= a lot), open-ended questions and statements that need to be qualified according to a scale in consensus.
- Section 3: Contains one open-ended question to make a global appreciation of students' perception of the learning experience using VR and how to improve it.
- Section 4: Contains a single-word multiple choice question that asks to select the word that best represents how they felt about the learning experience with VR. There are eight possible options that go from positive to negative emotions or feelings. A mode value is obtained after voting.

Five educational experts in tertiary education and educational technology usage made a first validation procedure for both instruments before application.

D. *Procedures*

At the time this contribution has been written, we had some partial results, as this research project is still in progress. Thus, two focus groups were formed. 13 students were randomly chosen to participate in the two focus groups. The application of the questionnaire using Likert scale is still open for collecting data and two other focus groups are pending.

The steps corresponding to the methodology procedures of this study are the following:

- Design of the instruments.
- Validation of each instrument by experts.
- Adjustment of the instruments according to expert's opinion and suggestions.
- Application of the questionnaire using an electronic format for collecting data.
- Application of focus group, with the participation of at least 7 students in each one.
- Transcription of focus group dialogues using the Amberscript online service.
- Ensure transcription in verbatim format corresponding to the content of each audio files.
- Analysis of data using IBM SPSS and ATLAS.ti software respectively.

IV. Results

The preliminary qualitative results of the study are presented in this section. The expected and emergent categories are presented, along with the most representative students' comments, which invite us to think about the inclusion of different indicators to strengthen the evaluation process of these resources, considering three dimensions: usability, user experience and learning experience.

Usability: The majority of the students said that adapting to the VR was a trial and error process because people guiding them could not know for sure what they were going to do; but they felt this adaptation process was pretty fast; they agreed that the interface was very simple and easy to use. Even though the interface was perceived as very simple, students agreed they needed someone to tell them how to use it, and some of them faced some issues at the beginning and at the end of the activity and needed further instructions. They mentioned the end of the activity was confusing because it was not well defined. Students who saw their classmates do the activity first or had previous experience using VR technology were more comfortable with the environment from the beginning, but all of them would have preferred to have more instructions included directly in the VR.

With respect to the complexity of the environment, the students mentioned it was comfortable and practical. Some students perceived this simple interface as an advantage. They said supermarkets are a lot bigger compared to the one in the VR, so, this simplified things for people that do not know how to use it because they could easily reach and count everything. However, other students perceived this simplicity as a disadvantage because they felt it limited their options or made it less realistic.

User experience: Students agreed that it was an attractive experience that excited them. They were glad to have the opportunity to do something new and go out of the regular classroom activities. Some of them said the VR exceeded their expectations and they never imagined being able to have something like this in a class. They felt having VR tools is an advantage and the school should invest more in this technology. A few students said they even took some extra time after finishing the activity to explore the environment.

Regarding immersion, students said they were not conscious of what was happening around them, just the VR, so they felt they were the character they were controlling. They liked the 360 degrees view because they could turn their head anywhere, which made them feel immersed in the environment. The students also mentioned it was important not being told what to do, in order to feel free to experiment in the environment; they liked to have a feeling of control.

One of the issues that affected their sense of presence was that they could not find everything they were looking for, which made the experience less real. Also, they mentioned they would have felt more immersed if they had been able to walk and listen to the kind of music you find in a supermarket. Not being able to walk also made some students feel dizzy after the experience. Furthermore, they mentioned that the quality of the graphics is a key element to experience inside the game; as well as being able to do all the normal activities one can do in the real environment and interacting with the objects in a natural way, like placing the products in a shopping cart and paying for them at the cashier, in this case.

Learning experience: In general, students thought that using VR is a good way to learn because it takes them out of their routine. They also thought the learning objective was clear, the activity was related to their class and the VR complexity was adequate for the purpose of the activity. About the effort they had to do to learn, they said they did not have to focus a lot because the objective was clear, they were familiar with the context and they were comfortable with the use of technology. They added that the mental effort would have been a lot greater if they had not had any instructions. In relation to the physical effort, they said no effort is needed and anyone can do it, even a person with a physical impairment can enjoy it.

Although students thought the VR experience was related to their class, the majority expected a more analytic experience, in which they could see graphics and interpret information. Considering this, the majority of the students agreed this experience is more relevant as an introductory activity, to learn a new concept, rather than a practice. In addition, they thought having more products in the supermarket would have also enhanced their learning experience because they would have been able to analyze more data. They also emphasized having the right calorie values is important in order to use those values in their analysis.

With respect to the time they had for the learning experience, students in the two groups had different opinions. In one of the groups there were more students, so they felt they did not have enough time to interact with the VR tool. The other group had very few students and they felt they had a lot of time for the activity, they even mentioned the activity should have a limited amount of time in order to be more like a game and compete with their classmates. In addition to the competition, students also mentioned they would like this tool to allow a more social learning. They said they would like to have more people connected in the same virtual environment, including the teacher.

Students concluded this tool should be used in more subjects at the university, and they should be able to use it more frequently. They even mentioned they would be able to learn more and benefit more from the tool if they could access it at any time, using it as a reference material. Students say they can not really learn anything if they only use the tool once.

Table 1 summarizes the most relevant students' comments for each dimension.

TABLE I. STUDENTS' PERCEPTIONS

Dimensions	**Students' comments**	
	Features appreciated in the VR	***Missing features in the VR***
Usability	"I adapted very fast, it was really easy to use and simple" "I had seen others do it, so it was easier" "I feel that if more things are added, people who don't know how to use the VR will start to get confused"	"If there had not been a professor explaining everything, I wouldn't have known what to do" "I finished and I did not know what to do next" "The game does not have a lot of food options, so it is easy to repeat other's actions"
User experience	"I really liked the experience, and when I finished, I wandered around to see the products" "It is a new experience for many of us and you go out of the classroom, because it is very tedious to be in the classroom all the time" "What made me feel immersed is the fact I could turn my head anywhere freely, see everything, and move anywhere I wanted to"	"I could not find meat, chicken or something more similar to what I really eat" "I would have preferred to walk instead of teleporting" "The music of a normal supermarket, or hearing people talking would have made me feel inside a supermarket" "To be like a supermarket, we should have been able to pay for the products, having a shopping cart and going to the cash register"
Learning experience	"The program was simple, but we did not need a lot more detail for the learning objective we had" "It meets the objective and it's very simple" "The way to use it was so simple and clear that it did not require a lot of mental effort to understand what you were doing, maybe you need a little bit more effort to apply it in class"	"We understood the data collection, but not its analysis, which is the focus of the course" "I would prefer to have this activity starting the semester and build on this experience to do further activities" "I did not like to feel pressured by the time" "I would like it to be more competitive" "I imagine having a digital class with everyone connected; like an interactive classroom" "We should be able to access the resource freely"

This preliminary qualitative analysis allows us to rethink about the indicators that should be considered to evaluate a VR didactic resource for learning processes in higher education.

V. CONCLUSION AND FUTURE WORK

These preliminary results seem to confirm that the features proposed by Mikropoulos and Bellou [3] strongly contribute to a sense of presence when using a VR tool. Students agreed that the free navigation, the autonomy, the 360 degrees view and the interaction with the objects made their experience more realistic. They also mentioned they would have appreciated involving more senses in the experience, for example listening to the type of music they would hear if they were really in the place.

However, VR tools should be used carefully because they are not appropriate for every instructional objective. The students in this study said that they would have preferred to have this experience at the beginning of the semester and build on it for further activities. In addition, they felt that the resource objective was limited; they would have appreciated analyzing the data they collected during the experience. This supports Pantelidis [10] suggestions about creating a pedagogical foundation when designing VR modules; the interaction with 3D objects by itself will not be enough to achieve better learning outcomes.

Furthermore, this study corroborated that teachers play an essential role when using this technology [6]. Teachers should clarify the learning objective of the resource before using it, and they should also define the steps students should follow and what is expected from them. After the experience, it is also important for teachers to engage students into a discussion about what they learned and how they can apply it to further class activities and to their daily life.

This study presents qualitative preliminary results, but the three dimensions will be evaluated using quantitative data, and interviews with teachers will be done. VR resources have demonstrated to have a great potential to enhance the learning process, but we must carefully define the learning objective and guide the students' experience. It is important to continue evaluating the characteristics that must be considered when using VR tools in higher education.

In this respect, future work must consider students' characteristics, analyzing any differences in the VR experience related to their gender, the program they are studying, their previous experience using VR, and their learning styles. In order to generalize results, it is important to include larger samples of students in different disciplines and with different characteristics. This could also allow measuring other variables such as acceptability of VR tools and user satisfaction.

ACKNOWLEDGMENT

The authors would like to acknowledge the financial and the technical support of Writing Lab TecLabs, Tecnologico de Monterrey, Mexico in the production of this work.

REFERENCES

[1] L. Hickman and M. Akdere, "Developing intercultural competencies through virtual reality: Internet of Things applications in education and learning," 2018 15th Learn. Technol. Conf. L T 2018, pp. 24–28, 2018.

[2] S. Mandal, "Brief Introduction of Virtual Reality & its Challenges," Int. J. Sci. Eng. Res., vol. 4, no. 4, pp. 304–309, 2013.

[3] T. A. Mikropoulos and J. Bellou, "The unique features of educational virtual environments," Teach. Learn. with Technol. Beyond Constr., no. January 2006, pp. 249–258, 2010.

[4] U. Durrani and Z. Pita, "Integration of Virtual Reality and Augmented Reality: Are They Worth the Effort in Education?," in Proceedings of 2018 IEEE International Conference on Teaching, Assessment, and Learning for Engineering, TALE 2018, 2019, no. December, pp. 322–327.

[5] D. A. Kolb, R. E. Boyatzis, and C. Mainemelis, "Experiential Learning Theory: Previous Research and New Directions," Perspect. Thinking, Learn. Cogn. Styles, no. January, pp. 227–248, 2018.

[6] J. Jiang, L. Zhi, and Z. Xiong, "Application of Virtual Reality Technology in Education and Teaching," Proc. - Int. Jt. Conf. Information, Media Eng. ICIME 2018, pp. 300–302, 2019.

[7] H.-H. Tsai *et al.*, "An Interactive Virtual Reality Application in Education for Soil and Water Conservation," 2019 Int. Symp. Educ. Technol., pp. 60–64, 2019.

[8] W. Winn, "A Conceptual Basis for Educational Applications of Virtual Reality," Washingt. Technol. Cent. Univ., no. R-93-9, p. 0, 1993.

[9] S. Marks, D. White, and M. Mazdics, "Evaluation of a Virtual Reality Nasal Cavity Education Tool," Proc. 2018 IEEE Int. Conf. Teaching, Assessment, Learn. Eng. TALE 2018, no. December, pp. 193–198, 2019.

[10] V. S. Pantelidis, "Reasons to Use Virtual Reality in Education and Training Courses and a Model to Determine When to Use Virtual Reality," Themes Sci. Technol. Educ., vol. 2, no. 1–2, pp. 59–70, 2010.

[11] F. Serenelli, E. Ruggeri, A. Mangiatordi, and P. Ferri, "Applying the multimedia learning theory in the primary school: An experimental study about learning settings using digital science contents," Proc. Eur. Conf. Games-based Learn., vol. 2, pp. 943–952, 2011.

[12] R. B. Johnson and A. J. Onwuegbuzie, "Mixed Methods Research: A Research Paradigm Whose Time Has Come," Educ. Res., vol. 33, no. 7, pp. 14–26, 2004.

[13] B. G. Witmer and M. J. Singer, "Measuring presence in virtual environments: A Presence Questionnaire," Presence, vol. 7, no. 3, pp. 225–240, 1998.

[14] M. Usoh, E. Catena, S. Arman, and M. Slater, "Using presence questionnaires in reality," Presence Teleoperator Virtual Environ., vol. 9, no. 5, pp. 497–503, 2000.

[15] B. Sun, U. Chikwem, and D. Nyingifa, "VRLearner: A Virtual Reality Based Assessment Tool in Higher Education," pp. 1640–1645, 2019.

[16] P. Truchly, M. Medvecký, P. Podhradský, and M. Vančo, "Virtual Reality Applications in STEM Education," ICETA 2018 - 16th IEEE Int. Conf. Emerg. eLearning Technol. Appl. Proc., pp. 597–602, 2018.

[17] S. G. Hart, "NASA-task load index (NASA-TLX); 20 years later," Proc. Hum. Factors Ergon. Soc., pp. 904–908, 2006.

DEKXTROSE: An Education 4.0 Mobile Learning Approach and Object-Aware App Based on a Knowledge Nexus

Roy Oberhauser[0000-0002-7606-8226]
Computer Science Dept.
Aalen University
Aalen, Germany
e-mail: roy.oberhauser@hs-aalen.de

Abstract—**The exponential growth in knowledge coupled with the decreasing knowledge half-life creates a challenging situation for educational programs - particularly those preparing software engineers for their very dynamic high-technology field. Teachers in high technology education areas are challenged in selecting and making relevant knowledge intuitively accessible to students, especially with regard the highly dynamic digital and software technologies. This paper contributes a knowledge nexus-based multimedia approach aligned with Higher Education 4.0 for creating learning apps on mobile devices that support multiple didactic models, leverage intrinsic curiosity and motivation, support gamification, and enable digital collaboration. Object recognition is used to trigger learning paths, and various didactic methods are supported via workflow-like learning flows to support group or team-based learning. A prototype app was realized to demonstrate its feasibility and an empirical evaluation in software engineering shows the didactic potential and advantages of the approach, which can be readily generalized and applied to the arts, sciences, etc.**

Keywords - Higher Education 4.0; e-Learning; mobile learning; m-Learning; computer science education; software engineering education; mobile app.

I. INTRODUCTION

We are experiencing an exponential growth in knowledge, articulated by Buckminster Fuller [1] and known as the knowledge-doubling curve. IBM extrapolated that by 2020 knowledge would be doubling in a matter of hours [2]. Among the factors fueling this trend are the digital and interconnected global access to knowledge, the transition from industrial to knowledge- and service-based societies, the advancement of science and invention, collaborating teams, computer-based data analysis of big data and that generated by sensors and devices, etc. However, not all knowledge remains stable, valuable, useful, and accurate for long, but goes through a process of knowledge decay or obsolescence, implying that some subset of our knowledge has a "half-life" as articulated by Fritz Machlup, and this half-life is correspondingly decreasing [3]. One can view this trend to be exacerbated for high-technology fields and related education and training.

As to the background context for this paper, Software Engineering (SE) can be viewed as a subset of Computer Science (CS) and Systems Engineering (SysE) as a related field. Because SE is a high technology field and software exists in an artificial man-created environment, it is perhaps even more susceptible to accelerated knowledge dynamics versus other fields. This creates a challenge for educating and training software engineers to acquire relevant knowledge and skills that are not obsolete when conveyed or soon thereafter, and perhaps not yet obsolete by the time they enter the marketplace.

A correlating concept to Industry 4.0 is the concept of Education 4.0 [3], or more specifically Higher Education 4.0 [4], which aims to better align humans and technology in the area of tertiary education. It involves various aspects that are values of a digital native culture, including: student-centric approaches instead of traditional lectures, individualistic (customized) learning, internet and multimedia usage, collaborative peer emphasis, mobile device usage, and leveraging learning analytics to customize experiences.

To deal with these situations, it is imperative that CS, SysE, and SE education (SEE) embrace more technologically sophisticated approaches for conveying and transferring knowledge, especially for the fast-changing area of digital technologies. Despite the budding digitalization, knowledge, particularly related to some high-technology object in our nearby environment, often remains abstract and scattered and hidden within literature or scattered on the web. Learning or direct connections of knowledge and questions regarding visible objects in our environment is not triggered automatically by visible objects in our environment, e.g., Wikipedia expects a search term and Amazon Alexa expects a question or command. In addition, it is becoming increasingly difficult to keep track of the flood of information and to perceive open questions and problems with other questions, including time-delayed ones, and to develop solutions and incorporate new knowledge in a co-operating manner. Emails, social networks (Slack, WhatsApp), and Learning Management Systems (LMS) are not really conducive to linking knowledge to certain objects of interest in a time-delayed manner. The attention and concentration on a topic and the motivation and interest can also be awakened and held by visible objects (such as Internet-of-Things devices), and thus offers an additional tactile incentive to acquire the knowledge behind it.

In previous work [5], our edutainment approach called Software Engineering for Secondary Education (SWE4SE) combined short informational videos and various simple digital games. This paper contributes a knowledge nexus-based multimedia approach for creating mobile learning (mLearning) apps that support augmented reality object identification, multiple didactic models, leverage intrinsic curiosity and motivation, support gamification, and enable digital collaboration. Object recognition is used to trigger learning paths, and various didactic methods support group or team-based learning via learning workflows. A prototype app was realized to demonstrate its feasibility and an empirical evaluation shows its potential and the advantages of the approach for supporting SEE. We call it DEKXTROSE (Didactic-Enhancing Knowledge-neXus TRail-enabled Object-aware Software for Education), which can be viewed as a sweetener for education and training.

The paper is organized as follows: the next section describes related work; Section 3 describes our mLearning solution approach; Section 4 provides details about ou5 realization, which is followed by our evaluation in Section 4; finally, a conclusion is provided.

II. Related Work

Various systematic reviews of mLearning have been performed. Zydney & Warner [7] studied 37 articles, of which three focused on tertiary students. Technology-based scaffolding was used in 23 apps to guide students with mLearning, and 19 apps gave users the ability to digitally construct knowledge. 12 apps supported digital knowledge sharing. Krull & Duart [8] provide a systematic review of the use of mobile devices in higher education. Among their findings was that more research and practice is required in themes related to innovative approaches (such as context-awareness, augmented reality, and gamification). The most common research theme was enabling mLearning applications and systems. Chang & Hwang [9] performed a systematic review of journal publications regarding digital game-based learning in the mobile era. Most of the 113 papers involved role-playing games (41), followed by simulation games (23), and then gamification (20). In their systematic review, Anohah et al. [10] analyzed 86 articles regarding mLearning in computing education, and found the following learning effects reported: knowledge, experience, engagement, interest/attitude, motivation, confidence, interactivity, enthusiasm/excitement, critical thinking, problem solving skills, team work, and analytical skills.

Khaddage et al. [11] proposed an approach for seamlessly blending formal and informal learning in mLearning based on science, technology, engineering, art and mathematic subjects to achieve some required learning outcome in informal settings. Schefer-Wenzl & Miladinovic [12] provide an approach for teaching software development topics that combines mLearning with just-in-time teaching, industry-like student projects and peer assessment. No specialized app was presented to realize their approach.

We found no mLearning work that is specifically focused on the CS/SE/SysE domain with a single app that holistically supports a potpourri of didactic methods via learning workflows, utilizes a collaboratively taggable knowledge nexus with multimedia content, supports social networking via chat and object-aligned commenting, utilizes object recognition for triggering learning paths, integrates quizzes for immediate learning feedback, and supports gamification as a motivational factor for informal learning.

III. mLearning Approach

Our solution concept and investigation were motivated by several questions and factors. We wanted to determine to what extent is object recognition currently practical for didactic applications, and if the recognition rate good enough for real usage. Furthermore, can digital learning and knowledge content be connected to physical objects and triggered by users in context? How can knowledge and practice (from research and professional practice) be efficiently and effectively modularized into digital units, reused, and linked in a nexus-like way? How can digital long-lived sequential learning trails (routes through knowledge) be technically realized? How can complex learning flow templates (to actively support methods such as research learning, problem-based learning, project learning, experiential learning with assistance and navigation suggestions ("guidance") be technically implemented? To what extent can technically supported learning flows support creative thought processes? Additionally, is gamification motivating for all users, or are some primarily intrinsically motivated? And finally, can we easily reuse digitally available information material in a way that: leverages intrinsic curiosity and motivation, visually shows how one knowledge granule relates to another - and helps users find the next interesting knowledge granule; enables users to add and share their own knowledge or opinions onto a knowledge node; and facilitates individual customized learning and flipped classroom approaches that put the student in the driver's seat.

Underlying presuppositions for our solution include:

1) Individualized (no single one-size-fits-all): For certain courses or training - especially higher-semester courses, a one-size-fits-all didactic model is not effective nor efficient with regard to the post-course relevance of transferred knowledge. Each individual has personal preferences, pre-existing knowledge, competencies, learning styles, etc.
2) Disparate, unpackaged knowledge: Much of the knowledge that "should" be distributed to an individual is not exclusively available from the mind of the expert, but also digital sources, especially in the SE domain. However, the knowledge has typically not been fashioned in a way that lends itself to efficient learning. Web search engines, while designed to quickly find relevant web pages, are not designed to support efficient learning.
3) Networked-knowledge: knowledge is not isolated and (mostly) not immutable, but rather relevant or connected to other knowledge to some degree. Certain knowledge objects have multiple possible representations and ways they can be consumed (e.g., media formats). Digitally accessible resources should be reused if possible.

Figure 1 depicts DEKXTROSE, which incorporates the following capabilities and concepts:

- Scanned object recognition (object-awareness)
- LearningPaths (trails) with the integration of web/video/photo content as tags

- LearningFlows (process stencils) that comply with specific didactic methods
- Gamification via quizzes and badges is supported.
- Data/learning analytics available

Figure 1. DEKXTROSE mLearning approach.

LearningPaths are trails that explain knowledge in a predetermined sequential order using multimedia offers (e.g., about certain technologies that users do not yet know) and contains a quiz at the end. It can be started by object recognition in order to acquire knowledge by curiosity about possibly unknown objects, or by choosing a LearningPath directly from the menu. Users can acquire requisite knowledge and skills using LearningPaths.

LearningFlows are learning workflows that enable different didactic methods (research learning, problem-based learning, project learning, experience-based learning) to be quickly understood and self-directed, alone and as a team, methods previously unknown to users. Thus, by providing students a goal and LearningFlow (process), a team of students is provided with a framework with which they can achieve some goal.

DEKXTROSE links digital knowledge and questions with real objects in the immediate environment using the device's camera together with an object recognition service. Thus, objects can be recognized, parts of such a knowledge nexus can be triggered and visualized, and curiosity can be aroused. Passive LearningPaths provide sequential learning of expertise in these objects using self-motivation; by means of more complex LearningFlows, different didactic methods can be applied in a self-directed fashion to knowledge processes.

Didactically, our solution approach involves cognitive aspects that relate to basic knowledge concepts conveyed via networked knowledge nodes (knowledge granules). It is also instrumental in that it utilizes LearningPaths, quizzes, and badges to motivate. It is formative-educative in supporting the development of skills and abilities and the achievement of educational objectives. Both the LearningPath and LearningFlow facilitate the flipped classroom learning approach, allowing the students to be in the driver's seat and a teacher to take on the role of a facilitator.

As to the applicability to SE, the concepts inherent in SE are exemplified in the SWEBOK [13] and for SysE in the SEBoK [14]. The objectives of the SWEBOK include promoting a consistent view of SE, clarifying the bounds of and characterizing the contents of SE with respect to other disciplines, and providing a topical access to the SE Body of Knowledge (BOK). Knowledge areas (KAs) have a common structure, including a subclassification of topics and topic descriptions with references. Available technologies play a key role in creating viable systems and software that address stakeholder needs, and software and systems engineers need to be aware of current available technologies, understand what they are – including in relation to one another, and to a certain degree how they work. The SWEBOK references technologies and aspects at various points, which are suitable for knowledge our approach can convey. These including Construction Technologies (3-8) as well as various Computing Foundations (13), including Computer Organization (13-13), Network Communication Basics (13-19), the Internet and Internet-of-Things (13-20), Operating Systems Basics (13-16), Basic Concept of a System (13-11), Parallel and Distributed Computing (13-21), Basic User Human Factors (13-22), etc. While the SWEBOK is currently published in a static format, a more dynamic wiki-like format could support more SE community involvement and knowledge updates.

Geddes, Cannon, and Cannon [15] articulate the concept of individual absorptive capacity (IAC), and we argue that education should further students' ability to acquire new knowledge and skills rapidly - even beyond the confines of their current course or curriculum. In our view, our solution approach can be used to further the IAC for students.

IV. Realization

To realize DEKXTROSE, we developed a cross-platform tablet app for iOS and Android using Flutter, the Google Firebase ML Kit service for machine-learning-based object recognition, the mlkit-custom-image-classifier for custom image/object training on a set of images taken of an object, and the Google Firebase Cloud Firestore service for backend data storage.

A graph of knowledge nodes is manually realized (see Figure 2), implemented as a set of JSON documents that contain links to other related knowledge nodes, as well as detailed information and media pertaining to that node (see Figure 3 left). In order to easily add information (e.g., comments, links to external site or photos, etc.), the concept of tags are used. From a technical perspective, our use of cloud storage as a backend for the app permits us to easily add to or adapt the knowledge nexus at any time without requiring the app software to be updated. This supports longer-term sustainability of the knowledge network. Furthermore, moderators, analogous to Wikipedia, can be utilized for certain areas of expertise to validate entries, add new knowledge, and maintain the network.

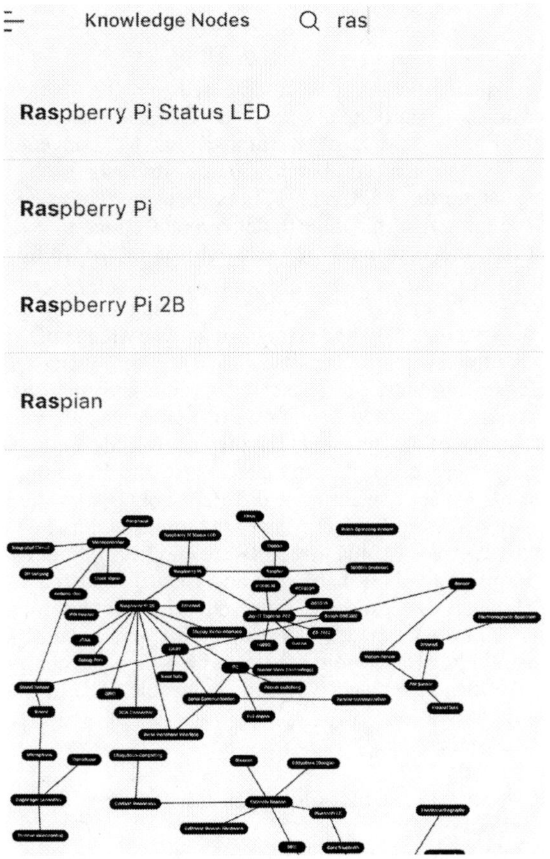

Figure 2. Knowledge nodes can be browsed, searched, and viewed as a list (top) or nexus (bottom, network overview).

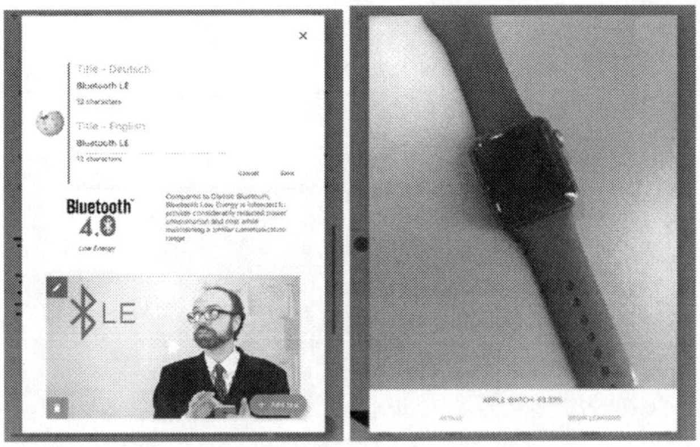

Figure 3. Descriptive information and multimedia can be added via tagging (left); screenshot of object recognition via camera (right).

LearningPaths, a sequence/path of knowledge nodes, can be specified by an administrator (Figure 4 top). Object recognition can be used to trigger a LearningPath, (Figure 3 right), which is implemented using machine learning on a set of images with the ML Kit.

Private and public tags can be added (Figure 5) - must be approved by a moderator before visible to other users, and these can include text, images, and video or other web links.

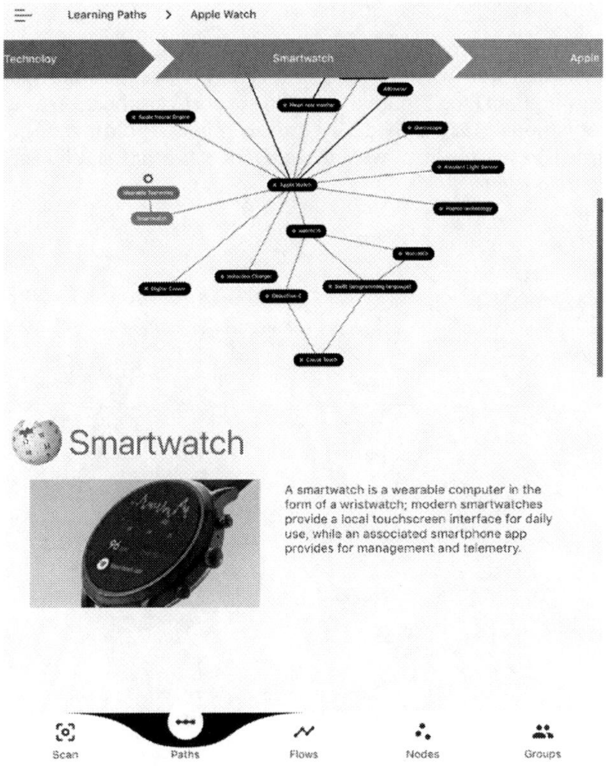

Figure 4. LearningPath is shown on top with the Knowledge Nexus for context (current node in blue) and Knowledge Object details (bottom).

Figure 5. Tagging options with various tag types.

Quizzes provide quick feedback and provide an orientation for users on the relevant knowledge for that LearningPath (see Figure 6 left). To support gamification as a motivational factor, badges (bronze, silver, gold) can be earned based on how well the quizzes were answered (see Figure 6 right).

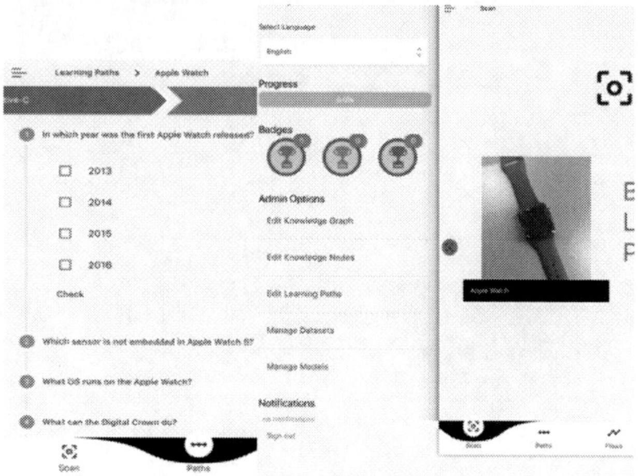

Figure 6. A quiz (left) includes questions such as: What sensor is not embedded in the Apple Watch? Which OS runs on Apple Watch? Depicted on the right are a progress bar and the badges.

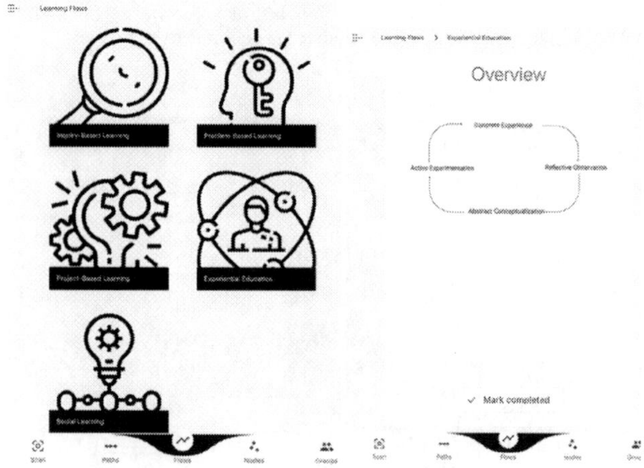

Figure 7. LearningFlow choices (left) and LearningFlow step, completed button, and textual explanation (right).

Once LearningFlows is selected, the set of possible LearningFlows is shown (see Figure 7 left). Once a specific LearningFlow is selected, an initial overview (see Figure 7 right) provides users with quick insights into the intent that particular learning technique. Via swiping the next is shown. Any step can be marked as completed. Details on any step in LearningFlow are provided: the left displays the overall process, while on the right further details and resources can be seen.

To facilitate collaboration, chat functionality is supported directly in the app.

V. EVALUATION

Our qualitative evaluation focused on the subjective impressions of participants in three areas: LearningPaths, LearningFlows, and general impressions. A convenience sample of thirteen computer science students took part (average semester = 5.8, min=3, max=8) using iPads or Sony tablets running Android. Due to data privacy concerns, we did not utilize the data analytics capabilities in the following evaluation.

For the LearningPaths feature, participants only chose paths about topics they had no significant knowledge of. First, they attempted a learning path without our app using URLs only for 15 minutes. They selected a topic and then visited URLs related to that topic (one's we had prescreened) without the assistance of our app, and then they answered a quiz. After that, they were given 15 minutes to use the LearningPath feature of our app, selecting a different unknown topic and then answer the built-in quiz. As to the topics and content we chose to offer, we assume that software engineers should have some knowledge about hardware and electronics (to a slight degree) when for example involved with the Internet-of-Things (IOT) or embedded systems. This also ensured that there would be at least some topics with which the computer science students were not yet knowledgeable. The available LearningPaths were:

- Beacon technology
- Raspberry Pi
- Raspberry Pi Internet-of-Things extension board
- Android
- Apple Watch
- Various hardware sensors (light, temperature, motion, sound, moisture)

TABLE I. DEKXTROSE QUESTIONNAIRE RESULTS

Area	Question	Average[a]
LearningPath	How helpful was the LP in learning?	4.00
	How much fun was using a LP?	4.08
	Were the quizzes motivating?	3.69
	Did quizzes provide helpful feedback when learning?	4.23
	Was earning badges motivating?	2.69
	How better/worse was the learning experience with app vs. without an app? (worse=-1, 0, better=+1)	0.85
Learning Flow	How helpful was the LF in learning?	3.15
	How much fun was it to use the LF?	3.69
General	Did you learn things you wouldn't have learned otherwise?	92% Yes
	Intuitiveness?	3.54
	How efficient was learning something new w/ app?	2.23
	Curiosity aroused about new technical knowledge?	3.15
	What was more fun?	100% app
	What would be your preference?	100% app
	What was the overall learning experience like?	4.00

a. Unless indicated, scale 1-5 where 1=Little, 5=Very

Subsequently, the learning experience (with and without app) was evaluated by means of a paper-based questionnaire. The results are shown in the "LearningPath" (LP) area in Table 1. To evaluate LearningFlows, the participants self-formed groups of 2-3 people and were directed to apply the learning flow "Experiential learning" with our app, going through all the steps at least once, in order to optimize a simple paper-based product within 15 minutes. Only one of the participants had prior knowledge of experiential learning. Then they answered questions about the learning experience, the results of which are shown in the "LearningFlow" (LF) area of Table 1. Finally, general questions on the entire learning experience were answered as shown in the "General" area of Table 1.

A selection of participants comments included:

- Can easily & quickly dive into new topics; greater depth of information is available when needed
- App summarizes knowledge compactly & very well; mostly intuitive to use.
- Topic overview via nodes was good and encouraged dig further into the topics of interest
- Learning path is very useful/helpful for unknown topics
- Prepared content is very good
- Graph view of knowledge nodes useful

The evaluation shows DEKXTROSE to be a viable approach. It that be used to support aspects of Education 4.0, including self-directed learning such as the flipped classroom approach, internet-connected multimedia, internet-based collaboration, and student data analytics that can be used to further customize the user learning experience.

VI. Conclusion and Future Work

Our DEKXTROSE Education 4.0 mLearning approach shows how relevant knowledge regarding technologies can be conveyed with a mobile app on a tablet while reusing digitally available knowledge organized in a knowledge nexus. The knowledge nexus can be explored for inquisitive learners. LearningPaths provide guided journeys through knowledge and are followed with a quiz to provide instant feedback and badges to support gamification. Objects in the environment can be used to trigger a LearningPath. LearningFlows support the use of didactic methods by individuals or teams, explaining the steps and tracking the state. Thus, it supports self-directed learning and flipped classroom approaches. Aspects of Education 4.0 are supported, providing digital natives a multimedia self-directed learning experience. The evaluation showed a strong approval and interest by students and shows its potential to help produce career-ready technology professionals who are aware of and knowledgeable about current technologies to "hit-the-ground-running." We believe the approach is generalizable to various other domains, including art, science, etc., and would be beneficial for education and training.

Future work includes: weighting the degree of connectedness between knowledge nodes based on a variable function of user-configurable parameters; utilizing the data and learning analytics to customize the learning experience, including adjusting paths based on a student's profile and career, role, and other interests; applying the approach in other domains; and a comprehensive empirical evaluation.

Acknowledgment

The author thanks Julian Eger-Benninger for his assistance with the design and prototype implementation. This project was partially funded by "Programmlinie „Lehr- und Lernlabore“ – Projekt „HUMUSPlus – Hochschuldidaktisch und -methodisch unterstützte Selbstinitiierung von Lernprozessen an Hochschulen für Angewandte Wissenschaften in Baden-Wuerttemberg."

References

[1] B. Fuller, Critical Path. St. Martin's Griffin, 1981.

[2] D. R. Schilling. *Knowledge Doubling Every 12 Months, Soon to be Every 12 Hours.* [Online]. Available from: http://www.industrytap.com/knowledge- doubling-every-12-months-soon-to-be-every-12- hours/3950 2020.10.20

[3] M. Ciolacu, P. M. Svasta, W. Berg, and H. Popp, "Education 4.0 for tall thin engineer in a data driven society," 2017 IEEE 23rd International Symposium for Design and Technology in Electronic Packaging (SIITME), 2017, pp. 432-437.

[4] S. Jeschke and U. Heinze, Higher Education 4.0 – Trends and Future Perspectives for Teaching and Learning, 2014. doi:10.13140/RG.2.1.1509.0002.

[5] R. N. Charette, *An engineering career: Only a young person's game? Half-life of knowledge pressures employers to seek out young engineers.* IEEE Spectrum 4, 2013. [Online]. Available from: https://spectrum.ieee.org/riskfactor/computing/it/an-engineering-career-only-a-young-persons-game 2020.10.20

[6] R. Oberhauser, "Gamifying and Conveying Software Engineering Concepts for Secondary Education: An Edutainment Approach,"10th Int'l Conf. on SW Eng. Adv. (ICSEA), IARIA, 2015, pp. 432-437, ISBN: 978161208367-4.

[7] J. M. Zydney and Z. Warner, "Mobile apps for science learning: Review of research," Computers & Education, vol. 94, pp. 1-17, 2016.

[8] G. Krull and J. Duart, "Research Trends in Mobile Learning in Higher Education: A Systematic Review of Articles (2011 – 2015)," Int'l Review of Research in Open and Distributed Learning, 18(7), 2017. doi:10.19173/irrodl.v18i7.2893

[9] C. Y. Chang and G. J. Hwang, "Trends in digital game-based learning in the mobile era: a systematic review of journal publications from 2007 to 2016," International Journal of Mobile Learning and Organisation, 13(1), pp. 68-90, 2019.

[10] E. Anohah, S. S. Oyelere, and J. Suhonen, "Trends of mobile learning in Computing Education from 2006 to 2014: A systematic review of research publications," Int'l J of Mobile and Blended Learning (IJMBL), 9(1), pp. 16-33, 2017.

[11] F. Khaddage, W. Müller, and K. Flintoff, "Advancing Mobile Learning in Formal And Informal Settings via Mobile App Technology: Where to From Here, and How?" Educational Technology & Society, 19(3), pp. 16–26, 2016.

[12] S. Schefer-Wenzl and I. Miladinovic, "Game changing mobile learning based method mix for teaching software development," Proc. of the 16th World Conference on Mobile and Contextual Learning, pp. 1-7, 2017.

[13] P. Bourque and R. Fairley (editors), "Guide to the Software Engineering Body of Knowledge (SWEBOK): Version 3.0," IEEE Computer Society Press, 2014.

[14] SEBoK Editorial Board. *The Guide to the Systems Engineering Body of Knowledge (SEBoK), v. 2.2.* [Online]. Available from: www.sebokwiki.org 2020.10.20

[15] B. C. Geddes, H. M. Cannon, and J. N. Cannon, "Addressing the Crisis in Higher Education: An Experiential Analysis," Developments in Business Simulation and Experiential Learning: Proc. of the Annual ABSEL Conf., vol. 45, pp. 265-279, 2018.

Conversational Robot for Practice Interviews in Creative Industries

Maria Leticia Flores-Palacios
Media and Digital Culture
Tecnologico de Monterrey
Monterrey, México
e-mail: lflores@tec.mx

Claudia Alicia Lerma-Noriega
Media and Digital Culture
Tecnologico de Monterrey
Monterrey, México
e-mail: clerma@tec.mx

Genaro Rebolledo-Mendez
Writing Lab, TecLabs
Tecnologico de Monterrey
Monterrey, México
e-mail: g.rebolledo@tec.mx

Abstract—**Technology must help information professionals collect data and analyze it. For this reason, a robot called Chatcontext, programmed with Artificial Intelligence (AI), was developed in order to promote interview mastery among students in the creative industries. This technology responds to the need to develop the ability to prepare clear and relevant questions that address various types of sources. The information compiled must serve to generate journalistic texts and research reports of a qualitative nature. Students of journalism and qualitative research courses at Tecnologico de Monterrey, Mexico, worked during the February-June 2020 semester with Chatcontext. The results indicated an improvement in the ease of learning and the usability of the chatbot tool. In this sense, it was observed that the use of technology keeps university education up to date and facilitates the evaluation of qualitative factors.**

Keywords- Chatbot; Interview; Journalism; Research Methodology; Education Technology; Higher Education; Educational Innovation.

I. INTRODUCTION

It is common for students to be tasked with seeking information directly from a primary source in communication and journalism courses. They must conduct interviews with their informants to collect data that will allow them to write various articles and develop qualitative research. In this data collection process, they face different challenges because the interviewees do not always have the interest or willingness to provide the information.

Based on this need, a chatbot called *Chatcontext* was developed to help students practice their interview techniques for research and journalism courses. This robot aims to improve students' performance, reformulate their questions using Artificial Intelligence (AI), and provide a platform for several practices. As an educational tool, its principal objective is to help students improve their interviews using robots to practice beforehand.

The use of technological resources in communication and journalism courses allows students to work outside of the classroom and without their teacher's presence. Practicing with the robot can generate more commitment to mastering the technique than simply receiving instructions and recommendations from their teachers. This is especially relevant during the COVID-19 pandemic because autonomous practice is possible at any place and time.

The use of technology goes hand-in-hand with the development of digital culture and communication skills that allow a person to recognize the particular characteristics of real informants; this is imperative in the journalism field. Also, technological tools must be intuitive and easy to learn.

This paper presents the results of our study as follows. Section II provides a theoretical background. Section III gives a description of the methodology employed. Section IV presents the research results and Section V presents the conclusion of this work.

II. THEORETICAL BACKGROUND

The technological competencies that students already have equip them to work using their cell phones and other tools, which, if combined with a chatbot developed for academic use, would allow them to improve communication and acquire ethical skills that are necessary post-graduation. These competencies, aligned with the institution's educative model, are necessary for the multimedia and multi-informed international society that awaits them.

Reen and Ramnarayan [1] conducted research at Manipal University, India, with medical students who were allowed to generate their learning products and add them to the work on social media. The authors concluded that this stance, coupled with technology, allowed the students greater autonomy, promoted critical thinking, and was conducive to immediate feedback from teachers and classmates.

Sutcliffe and Albeanu [2] mention that the journalist must also be able to create multimedia stories using mobile devices having relevant applications. These are useful to researchers, considering that much contact with informants is through face-to-face or virtual interviews, where creating empathy is vital to building trust and obtaining information.

The task involves practicing the technique, but it also requires considering ethics because respect for the person who becomes the source of information is indispensable.

III. METHODOLOGY

A. Overview of the research difficulties

This study sought to measure the ease of learning and the usability of the chatbot using the Systems Usability Scale (EUS from its name in Spanish), created by Brooke in

1996 to measure this type of tool, and which was adapted in Mexico by Hedlefs Aguilar & Garza Villegas [3]. This scale measures ten aspects of using a robot developed with Artificial Intelligence on a Likert Scale. The robot was developed using the IBM-Watson system, and a hybrid application for mobile devices was generated using the system's resources. This application was available in ANDROID and iOS portals. The use of AI modules allowed structuring a conversation between the student and the bot as if it were a real conversation, mediated by technology, between two people, the interviewer and the interviewee.

B. Procedure

The EUS was applied at two different times using Qualtrics software [11] to 112 students from the *Journalism* and *Qualitative Research Methodologies* courses at Tecnologico de Monterrey on the Monterrey Campus (see Table I).

The students were previously informed about the privacy of their answers and the objectives of the research project.

Two measurements were carried out in April and May 2020. Both measurements permitted observing the usability of the chatbot and determining if it favored learning.

TABLE I. NUMBER OF STUDENTS WHO USED THE BOT

Class	Table I	
	1st measurement	*2nd measurement*
Journalism course	n=20	n=18
Research course	n=35	n=39

For the first measurement (see Table II), the bot was fed a series of basic questions. The students could interview four robots, two men and two women, about their opinions on the importance and implications of two different topics.

TABLE II. MEASUREMENT RESULTS OF USING THE CHATBOTS ON THE EUS SCALE

Topics	Table II			
	Bot 1	*Bot 2*	*Bot 3*	*Bot 4*
1st measurement				
Diversity at the Oscars	Film critic	Female film director		
Music streaming services			Audio graduate	Stay-at-home woman
2nd measurement				
Immigration	Priest	Female senator		
The wage gap between male soccer players and female soccer players			Soccer coach	Female soccer player

In the second measurement, another four robots were also programmed to answer what they thought would happen in the near future regarding the topic.

The selection of the topics was made based on currently relevant issues in Mexico. The choice of the robots' sex and professions in the exercises followed what was customarily associated with these topics. Doing this allowed verifying whether the students chose bots according to gender or by popular topics.

In both exercises, the students extracted information that they later used to carry out class activities. These were graded and weighted according to the academic objectives of each activity.

C. Tools

The *ChatContext* access screen to illustrate how students access the app is presented in Figure 1.

Figure 1. Android Play Store screen, where the students can access the bot.

IV. RESULTS

After applying the EUS, the students' means improved in the second interaction with the bot for both factors considered in this study (see Table III). This is observed for usability (means of items 1, 2, 3, 5, 6, 7, 8, and 9), denominated as Factor 1. Those that represent the ease of learning (items 4 and 10) are grouped under Factor 2. When analyzing the means with a T-test, it was determined that there was a significant difference ($t = -2.7$, $p = .007$) for the means of Factor 1 as well as a significant difference for Factor 2 ($t = -3.47$, $p = .001$). It is important to note that in the interview exercise that led to the first EUS measurement, each student was assigned a particular gender of bot for gender balance. However, in the second exercise carried out a week later, the selection of both the topic and bot gender was free-choice on the students' part.

TABLE III. MEASUREMENT RESULTS OF THE USE OF CHATBOT ON THE EUS SCALE

Factor	Table III		
	Moment of measurement	***n***	***Mean***
1 (Usability)	1	55	3.1818
	2	57	3.6776
2 (Ease of learning)	1	55	3.2818
	2	57	3.8596

A. Discussion

The results showed that using a chatbot allows immediate feedback about oral communication skills in the interview because the bot contains prepared responses for reacting appropriately in different scenarios. Qualitatively, it can be seen that as the tool is used more frequently, the students' knowledge of the platform increases, and the results demonstrate this. The application of Artificial Intelligence aims to achieve independent learning and self-reflection, in line with the needs of professional life in the 21st century.

The practice of journalistic work inside the academic field allows students to develop their skills to prepare for a professional environment [4]. This is why important accreditors like the *Accrediting Council on Education in Journalism and Mass Communications* [5] establish as entry requirements to universities a balance between the classroom and industry.

Likewise, without renouncing the traditional values of the profession, journalism schools must "incorporate the resources and digital logic" to practice professional skills "with, in, on and through the Internet" [6] because "in some cases, students study journalism without the intention of entering the profession. Instead, they learn high-level information and communication skills to advance their liberal arts studies or to pursue a related profession" [7].

Universities are committing to offer new educational strategies and practices aligned with social changes and trends. Through mobile applications, it is possible to educate professionals on how to work with cutting-edge devices and software when requesting information, manipulating the data, and making it known to the public.

B. Final thoughts

The confinement caused by COVID-19 has greatly reduced student interaction; therefore, mobile technology has become crucial. It is important to adapt to social conditions and understand the resources that companies are using more and more as part of customer service or for interaction with employees. Therefore, updating educational paradigms for future creators and information transmitters is vitally important.

The results show a significant improvement in the ease of learning and usability (according to the EUS) when performing a second interview exercise using Chatcontext. Artificial intelligence can impact the intrinsic learning of the tool and favor the development of more natural conversations, allowing the student to extract more information when doing class exercises.

V. CONCLUSION

The use of a robot to practice class activities is not just a call to adapt to socially-distanced education; it also takes advantage of the technological offerings in world markets that promote the digital literacy of students who are preparing to be future professionals.

As Mulrennan [8] points out, students in communication and journalism, when using social networks through mobile devices, can take a proactive role in acquiring their skills, develop more confidence when exploring new technologies, and apply them in various situations. This approach is based on a heutagogical stance that promotes autonomous and self-determined teaching by the students [9]. In this sense, the introduction of a chatbot in academic activities is relevant. It allows students to practice interviews at any time and place without limiting time or repetition of exercises. A greater amount of practice can promote mastery of the technique and the ability to overcome difficulties when faced with varying and challenging answers.

It is important to note that during 2019, Internet users in Mexico increased by 4.3 percentage points and numbered 80.6 million users, representing 70% of the population over six years old. On the other hand, households with fixed or mobile Internet represent only 56.4% of the population [10]. This is an indicator that the university needs to work with various types of technology and online resources for both the school community and society.

This exercise used a robot to extract information during practice interviews. The activity was limited to two different subjects. However, without a doubt, enriching the chatbot with more information and Artificial Intelligence will provide the opportunity for measurements and assessments in taxonomic areas, ease of use, skills development, and implementation in work areas beyond those contemplated in this research project. For example, the reported chatbot could interact with students and offer parameters that allow predicting student behavior based on the questions, their character, how the students ask the questions, and if their style corresponds to formal or informal attitudes. The possible uses of Artificial Intelligence are infinite, so it is relevant to carry out diverse research that impacts Social Sciences and Humanities, where remote learning offers high potential.

Given the results, it is worthwhile to continue exercising this Artificial Intelligence tool and see if the learning and usability levels increase among students in the creative industries.

The data provided by the users facilitate analyses that reinforce the relevance of the tool and lead to understanding its benefits as an innovation in the classroom. Undoubtedly, these times of change in education require new ways to connect at a distance. Using robots can be considered as supports for literacy and comprehension in multiple areas. They offer the advantage of maintaining the students' attention as they engage them.

The use of this type of technology highlights the importance of updating education for future managers. The universities have to offer new educational strategies that encourage students to participate more while increasing their self-efficacy [6]. The future communicators are today's students; therefore, universities have to offer educational strategies relevant to future needs.

ACKNOWLEDGEMENT

The authors would like to acknowledge the financial and technical support of Writing Lab, TecLabs, Tecnologico de Monterrey, Mexico, in the production of this work.

REFERENCES

[1] R. Reen and K. Ramnarayan, "Heutagogic approach to developing capable learners," Medical Teacher, vol. 39, no. 3, pp. 295-299, March 2017, https://pubmed.ncbi.nlm.nih.gov/28019131/ doi: 10.1080/0142159X.2017.1270433

[2] C. Sutcliffe and C. Albeanu, "12 essential self-taught journalism skills" September 2, 2016, Retrieved: August 2020, https://www.journalism.co.uk/news/ten-essential-self-taught-journalism-skills/s2/a557267/

[3] M. I. Hedlefs Aguilar and A. A. Garza Villegas, "Comparative analyses of the Usability System Scale (EUS) in two versions" RECI Revista Iberoamericana de Las Ciencias Computacionales e Informática [Ibero-American Journal of Computational Sciences and Informatics], vol. *5,* no. 10, pp. 44, Dec. 2016, https://doi.org/10.23913/reci.v5i10.48

[4] M. Deuze, "On Media and Entrepreneurship as Ways of Being in the World: a Challenge to Journalism Education" In Robyn Goodman & Elaine Steyn (Ed.), Educación Global de Periodismo en el siglo XXI: Retos & Innovaciones [Global Journalism Education in the 21st Century: Challenges & Innovations], pp. 283–300, 2018.

[5] AECJMC. *Accrediting Council on Education in Journalism and Mass Communications*, 2019.

[6] L. Lugo-Ortiz, "The academia, the media, and the ideal professional: A generalist-multimedia journalist" Communication and Society, vol. 29, no. 4, pp. 271–286, 2016, https://doi.org/10.15581/003.29.4.271-286

[7] J. Foote and F. Wao, "Global Journalism Education in the XXI Century. Challenges and Innovations" (R. S. Goodman & E. Steyn (eds.); pp. 286–307, 2018. Knight Center for Journalism in the Americas, School of Journalism. Retrieved: August 2020, https://knightcenter.utexas.edu/books/Educacion-Global-de-Periodismo-May15-vd-cover.pdf

[8] D. Mulrennan, "Mobile social media and the news: heutagogy where enables journalism" Journalism & Mass Communication Educator, vol.73, no. 3, pp. 322-333, 2018.

[9] S. Hase and C. Kenyon, "From andragogy to heutagogy," *Ultibase Articles*, vol *5*, pp. 1–10, 2000.

[10] Instituto Nacional de Estadística y Geografía [National Institute of Statistic and Geography], "*En México hay 80.6 millones de usuarios de internet y 86.5 millones de usuarios de teléfonos celulares: ENDUTIH 2019*" [*In Mexico, there are 80.6 millions of internet users and 86.5 millions of mobile phone useres*] 2020. Retrieved: August 2020, https://www.inegi.org.mx/contenidos/saladeprensa/boletines/2020/OtrTemEcon/ENDUTIH_2019.pdf

[11] Qualtrics. [Online] https://www.qualtrics.com/, Retrieved: August 2020,

Rethinking Self-directed Learning for Information Managers

- A process model for self-learning materials regarding the degree of complexity -

Gerrit Wucherpfennig, Monika Steinberg, Anke Wittich
Faculty of Media, Information and Design - Information and Communication Department
University of Applied Sciences and Arts Hannover
Hannover, Germany
e-mail: [gerrit.wucherpfennig, monika.steinberg, anke.wittich]@hs-hannover.de

***Abstract* - Self-directed learning is an essential basis for lifelong learning and requires constantly changing, target group-specific and personalized prerequisites in order to motivate people to deal with modern learning content, not to overburden them and yet to adequately convey complex contexts. Current challenges in dealing with digital resources such as information overload, reduction of complexity and focus, motivation to learn, self-control or psychological wellbeing are taken up in the conception of learning settings within our QpLuS IM project for the study program Information Management and Information Management extra-occupational (IM) at the University of Applied Sciences and Arts Hannover. We present an interactive video on the functionality of search engines as a practical example of a medially high-quality and focused self-learning format that has been methodically produced in line with our agile, media-didactic process and stage model of complexity levels.**

***Keywords - Self-directed Learning; Information Management; Reduction of Complexity; high-quality Learning Formats; Constructive Alignment; Motivation; Media Didactic Concept; Digital Wellbeing*.**

I. INTRODUCTION

As part of the QpLuS IM [1] project, the bachelor's degree programs Information Management and Information Management extra-occupational (IM) at the University of Applied Sciences and Arts Hannover will be further developed with regard to their competence profiles, blended learning scenarios and assessments. The focus is on the support of competence development of students through self-directed learning in digital learning scenarios. In this way, the degree programs contribute to a modern securing of skilled labor by addressing different target groups of prospective students. The courses of study support and accompany the development of students' self-control competences as information managers in digital learning formats.

A. Reduction and Complexity

On the one hand, e.g., in the case of technical topics, a reduction in complexity is required in order to facilitate access to more in-depth content with an increasing degree of self-regulation. On the other hand, a flexible deepening of the content by exploring further learning resources (as text, audio, video, animation, website, book, blog, etc.) should be possible at any time, if the learner wishes or if it is necessary for the subject. Within the context of a media-didactic concept for newly conceived, self-directed learning scenarios in the Information Management course of studies (regular and extra-occupational), we develop an agile, multidimensional process model taking into account complexity reduction as an ambivalent construct in learning settings. Our target group, the students of Information Management and Information Management extra-occupational, focuses on mediality (interactivity, multimodality, design quality), adaptive, competence-oriented (low-threshold to profound) information access (complexity, information reduction) and cognitive/psychological dimensions (degree of self-control, attention span and learning motivation). Digital Wellbeing and mental health play an increasingly central role in the context of the educational society, aggravated by the corona crisis, and must no longer be missing as a superordinate cross-cutting theme in learning, working and leisure. The media-didactic concept for self-directed learning described here was already developed before Corona, but the Corona crisis has intensified the focused aspects and made them even more concise in dealing with online teaching.

B. A Media-didactic Concept for Information Management Students

Blended learning and self-directed learning are not new learning/teaching concepts. Nevertheless, it is currently becoming clearer than ever that these traditional teaching/learning concepts must face new challenges in order to be successful and healthy in the long term. Current characteristics, as well as problems in dealing with digital media (also social media) and interaction must be taken up and considered in innovative learning settings in order to support the target group of students (in our case) cognitively and medially where they are competent.

Digital competence or media competence is now so complex, that not all students can always keep up with the immense digital dynamics that can suddenly be experienced at universities due to corona. The variety of tools and the great creativity of the teachers sometimes seem chaotic, over-enthusiastic and confusing from the students' point of view. The high degree of self-control, that is suddenly demanded of students in the context of exams by activating digital learning formats and tools is sometimes perceived by our students as strenuous and as more work than face-to-face courses. The real contact to fellow students and teachers is missing for perfect communication.

From first evaluations, we learn that some students wish to have the pre-corona back. Nevertheless, we will continue the increased use of digital learning/teaching resources in a meaningful way, but hopefully gradually supplement this with more face-to-face sessions. There must now be order in the digital tool chaos, but here at University of Applied Sciences in Arts Hannover, the central choice has already been made for Moodle [2], BigBlueButton [3] and Zoom [4], so that structure is now in place.

Now, we have to reduce the hot-needle emergency online mode with more attention to detail and focus on learning goals and skills to be promoted in order not to lose or regain the trust and interest of the students. The boundaries between work and leisure time have long since become blurred and the consequences can be felt by every individual.

The paper is structured as follows: in Section II, we present the current state of research on self-regulated learning. In the following section III, we introduce our own developed process model for self-directed learning against the background of mediality, complexity and learning motivation. The section is divided into the subsections A (Process model for learning assets) and B (Four levels of complexity). Section IV discusses the importance of digital focusing and reduction, with regard to mini-lectures and digital wellbeing. This section is also divided into two subsections. Subsection A deals with multitasking and overwhelming and subsection B deals with the balancing act of dealing with information and complexity. The reference to practice then arises in Section V, in which our interactive video entitled *How Search Engines Work* is explained didactically, technically and aesthetically. Section VI forms the conclusion and outlook on how digital self-learning materials can be effectively used for information managers in the future in terms of media didactics.

II. State of Research: Dimensions of Self-Regulated Learning

Self-directed learning requires modern conditions adapted to the target group of our students in order to be successful in the currently very dynamic teaching and learning environment. Dyrna and Riedel [5] describe it aptly:

"*Self-directed learning is a goal-oriented, multi-dimensional process in which learners subjectively recognise, master and use the didactic scope for decision making, design and action that objectively exists with regard to the goals, content, sources, methodology, assessment, partners, the path, time and place of their learning. The greater the use of this scope, the more self-directed the learning process is.*"

Besides the specific design of a media learning offer, as well as the methodical-didactical embedding of learning media in a learning arrangement, various personality traits of the learners are also important, they continue to write. [5]

In Constructive Alignment [6] [9], we see a promising approach to generate continuous feedback on learning progress and interaction in the exploration of learning assets.

The Office of University Didactics & E-Learning HdEL Bern [7] cites the degree of self-regulation and immediacy in combining asynchronous and synchronous learning units in a variety of ways: "*The learning process should be diverse and varied. Therefore, (a)synchronous learning scenarios and the degree of self-regulation should vary, be didactically taken into account and used in a targeted manner*". And in a text in the book Educational Psychology it says:

"*Self-regulation describes the ability to purposefully control one's own thoughts, emotions and actions. It is a basic prerequisite for setting and achieving goals. This applies to all areas of life; for sports as well as for professional life, for leisure time as well as for school and studies.*" [8]

Ryan, Richard and Deci, for example, write about the connection and interaction between motivation, self-regulation, social development and wellbeing [10]:

"*Specifically, factors have been examined that enhance versus undermine intrinsic motivation, self-regulation, and well-being. The findings have led to the postulate of three innate psychological needs--competence, autonomy, and relatedness--which when satisfied yield enhanced self-motivation and mental health and when thwarted lead to diminished motivation and well-being.*"

III. Process Model for Self-Directed Learning: Mediality, Complexity and Motivation to Learn

The aim of our media didactic concept is to create varied and flexible learning settings in terms of information density and access (content complexity), interactivity/multimodality (mediality) and self-control. Agile learning scenarios are implemented according to a methodical process model as a loose network of semantically related learning resources of varying complexity, mediality and varying degree of self-control, which are prepared in a motivational sophisticated way and allow for directed exploration. Our target groups are Millenials and Generation Z, who are considered digital natives and actively use social media. Multimedia formats such as Spotify, Instagram, Snapchat or TikTok [11] enjoy sustained popularity and are part of everyday life. Our target group is "*digitally spoiled*" and demanding. Motivation is a basic prerequisite for long-term interest in specialist topics and self-directed learning. Sustainable learning success is only possible if the use of digital tools is also mentally appropriate.

A. Process model for learning assets

Our process model [12] is designed to combine the networking of lightweight learning formats (as uncomplicated access to new topics) and more complex formats enhanced by modality and interaction (in order to deepen knowledge) in a didactically meaningful way in terms of the target group and the learning goals to create an explorative, varied learning scenario. Through the agile combination of learning assets with different degrees of complexity we approach complexity reduction as an ambivalent topic.

The complexity for learning assets is derived from the three following dimensions:

- **Mediality** (interactivity, multimodality, design) degree of modality/mediality (text only, video only, video with audio, etc.) and interactivity (no interactivity, basic activity, branching up to being active/creative yourself)
- **Complexity** of content and subject (reduction of focus, information density), degree of complexity of

the content (basic knowledge, further resources, prerequisites required, ...)

- **Cognitive/psychological** dimension (self-control/motivation/wellbeing), degree of self-control (cognitive aspects, motivation, self-regulation, self-creation of content as the highest degree of self-control and often learning objective)

To start with, the focus is on the motivation of the students, who in the best case are "*triggered*" and become enthusiastic about, e.g., challenging, technical topics. We would like to pick up the students who are e.g., influenced by social media where they are. At the beginning, we focus on short attention spans and then, if there is interest, we deepen our knowledge.

Device-independent presentation and interaction according to the 24/7 paradigm and the "*mobile first*" approach ("*anytime, anywhere, anyplace learner*") are basic requirements for the learning formats to be designed.

B. Four levels of complexity

In order to accommodate research into learning materials of varying degrees of complexity on IM topics, we propose a preliminary, agile categorization into four levels of complexity for learning materials to be created, which will be adapted and expanded step by step. The four levels of complexity are:

A: Social media compatible information for getting started, e.g., IM glossary at Instagram.

B: Multimedia learning assets for teaching basic knowledge e.g., educational films, screencasts with Camtasia [13] and Open Broadcaster Software (OBS) [14] lecture recordings, explanatory videos, podcasts, animations, lecture with audio.

C: A, B or other Open Educational Resources (OER) [15] with in-depth information and interaction (self-active and thinking along, exploration) e.g., via H5P [16], quizzes, tutorials, autonomous creation and publication of media content for the IM curriculum.

D: Branched learning offers (remix, exploration, self-active, thinking along, knowledge transfer) with personalized learning path (Branching Scenario) e.g., via H5P.

IV. Digital Focusing and Reduction: Mini Lectures and Digital Wellbeing

The cornerstone of the project is a dynamic, agile media-didactic concept that is continuously updated. At the center of the media didactic considerations formulated therein are the aspects of digital focusing and reduction against the background of a constantly increasing flood of information.

Various studies have already shown that multitasking, and thus the attempt to process or edit a lot of information at the same time, has a negative effect on concentration and productivity [17]. In addition, several studies have shown the associated effects on the human perception of stress. For example, the research team around Professor Clifford Nass of Stanford University found in their publication Cognitive Control in media multitaskers in 2009 that trying to perform several tasks at the same time leads to mental impairment. In addition to a constant state of stress, the ability to remember also suffers from multitasking [18][19].

A. Multitasking and overwhelming

However, due to the increasing amount of information on digital media, we experience more than ever a kind of permanent state of multitasking, for example when we open ten different browser windows with different information at the same time while working on the computer and checking our e-mails and WhatsApp messages. Psychology professor and computer scientist Gloria Mark of the University of California, Irvine, explains this in the film documentary Always networked - When the brain is overwhelmed [20]:

"People have been doing several things at once for a long time. They make phone calls, listen to the radio... but what has changed in the workplace is that digital media has given them access to more information faster than ever before. People suffer from burnout because they have to constantly focus on new tasks. It's a burden. So we know that multitasking and the interruptions it causes lead to stress and cognitive overload."

In general didactic terms, but also specifically for our QpLuS IM project, the consequence of these findings must be to counteract this development. Especially as a project within our study program Information Management at the University of Applied Sciences and Arts Hannover, a constructive and responsible handling of information must be the focus for students and learners. In order to cushion the problem of the negative effects of multitasking and the processing of too much information at the same time, the QpLuS IM project is developing a media-didactic approach that is concentrated around a formal focus and reduction to the essentials.

Within the QpLuS IM project, digital self-learning materials are produced according to this principle (e.g., mini-lectures). Formally clearly structured and tidy user interfaces are fundamental for the communication of central learning contents. The developed self-learning materials are intended to act as supporting and, especially on basic knowledge, focused supplements to the courses of the study programs Information Management and Information Management extra occupational.

B. The balancing act in dealing with information and complexity

It is crucial that students receive compact information snacks in a tidy digital learning environment, if possible in the sense of "*mobile first*", considering the ubiquitous use of mobile devices. In the learning environments produced, a large amount of simultaneous information should definitely be avoided, so that stress and excessive demands on students are noticeably reduced. However, such a reduction of complexity is a very ambivalent construct. On the one hand, the method of this formal reduction and focusing seems to be the only way to stimulate today's generation of students to a deeper examination of the respective subject matter without excessive demands, and in such a way that they do so out of intrinsic motivation. The challenge here is to produce substantial learning material with digital, reduced means that makes students want more and is not too superficial. The content must therefore be prepared creatively and excitingly despite the reduction. It is essential that a small amount of selected information is concentrated and prepared in as complex a way as possible so that learners begin to understand education as a multifaceted and reflective process. So-called branching scenarios, which can be generated in interactive learning videos with the free and web-based tool H5P [21], allow creative experimentation here. Ultimately, the aim must be to reduce the complexity in terms of information overload in order to keep the stress level of the learners low. On the other hand, this must not undermine the learning process of training multi-layered, complex thinking. On the contrary, the complexity of the information flood should be significantly reduced, but by concentrating on a small amount of information, individual topics can be deepened and complex thinking improved, especially with the help of our model of complexity levels. A positive learning experience and a productive learning process should be the result of such media didactics. The following chapter describes a practical example from our project that takes up these considerations.

V. INTERACTIVE VIDEO: HOW DO SEARCH ENGINES WORK?

In 2019, a professional interactive video was produced as part of the QpLuS IM project, which explains the basic functions and mechanisms of search engines [22].

The idea was to digitally and interactively process a complex topic as a film in such a way that the rough contexts and individual components of the search engines are also easier to understand for beginners through a formally and content-wise focused, reduced processing. The video is based on an analogue model, which was developed by our colleague Monika Maßmeyer and which has already been used several times in her courses in the Information Management study program.

Figure 1. Interactive video on how search engines work; exposition

Figure 2. Interactive video on how search engines work; medium long shot; Duplo figure represents hyperlink

A. *Concept of an interactive learning video of complexity degree D*

In the video the important elements of the search engine such as crawler, searcher and indexer are personified, i.e., they are "*brought to life*" by human actors. The web, i.e., the individual web pages and their structure, for example graphics, hyperlinks or "*dead links*" are represented with the help of Duplo stones.

The aim of the interactive video is to provide users with basic knowledge about how search engines work in a focused, reduced and creative way. With the implementation of a so-called branching scenario, however, the user is encouraged to think actively and can deepen his knowledge beyond that. The interactive video thus functions in the sense of our complexity level D.

With an aesthetically appealing video look, video effects (e.g., glitch) and a playful, humorous presentation as well as a compact length, the aim is to "*encourage*" learners to deal with the topic.An impression of these aesthetics is shown in Figure 1 and in Figure 2. What makes the video special, however, are the individual interactivities. In line with our media-didactic concept, these are as reduced and sparingly used as possible and, in addition, are easy for the user to understand. Thus, there are some interactivities that function as in-depth information pop-up windows. As soon as corresponding scenes are shown in the film, in which important basics of the search engine function are presented, these pop-up buttons appear with corresponding captions.

If, for example, the World Wide Web is visible in the form of Duplo stones at the beginning of the film, a pop-up button with the inscription "*World Wide Web*" appears automatically. The user of the video now has a few seconds to click on this pop-up button. If he clicks on it, a detailed info text appears; if he does not click on the button, it disappears again after a few seconds.

For a superficial understanding of the topic, passive reception of the video without interactivity is theoretically sufficient, but in order to obtain more detailed information about what is shown, the video consumer himself must become active and "*interact*". Thus, interactions are not an end in themselves, but should encourage active self-learning by the video users.

A special feature in our interactive video is the implementation of the branching scenario already mentioned.

Branching scenarios have been used repeatedly in the history of entertainment media and are part of non-linear storytelling. Norbert Braun writes the following in his dissertation on non-linear storytelling [23] :

"The non-linear story is constructed from different branches [...]. Fixed branching points are integrated into each branch of the non-linear story. At these points decisions are made which lead the participant of the story into a new branch of the story. For each branch there is a predefined dramaturgy, which the user lives through until the next decision point."

With H5P, however, there is now a provider that even explicitly offers a Open Source tool for branching scenarios. In addition, branching scenarios can be created manually within H5P's interactive video tool using the *Crossroads* feature. This is also the case in our interactive video on how search engines work.

The possibilities with branching scenarios within interactive learning videos to encourage learners to think actively, self-directed and above all explorative are manifold, but also depend on a video production that is as creative and innovative as possible. We wanted to meet these demands with our interactive learning video and the production was accordingly professional.

The branching scenario in our video confronts the video user with a decision-making question. In order to make the right decision, the learner must have been self-learning in the previous video and have read the interactive info pop-ups carefully, as shown in Figure 3.

If the video user or learner makes the wrong decision, a video sequence is played showing the consequences of the wrong decision.

In this way, the active video user is also more likely to be inspired to reflect on their own learning. To ensure this reflected self-learning, it is important for the video user or learner that the video and the interactions implemented in it are based on a consistent and thus comprehensible architecture and design.

In order to create an innovative and coherent interactive self-learning video, it makes sense to concentrate on the aspect of focus and reduction in order to guarantee a high-quality User Experience (UX). Michael Richter and Markus Flückiger write the following: [24]

"An essential task is to avoid unnecessary complexity, to reduce the functional range of a product to an ideal minimum for the user and thus to optimize the functionality of the product. The technical system should support the user optimally in the execution of his goals and is designed exactly for this purpose. This reduction to the essentials does not come automatically and the decision which functions to offer and which to leave out usually requires some work and coordination. However, the effort pays off in the realization at the latest".

Our interactive video on how search engines work is also based on a tidy and reduced User Experience design.

Thus a manageable number of interactions are implemented in the video with H5P. The learners should not be overwhelmed by a multitude of information and possibilities. Rather, the focused interactions and information should be processed cognitively in a sustainable and concentrated manner.

With these parameters, the interactive video on the functioning of search engines thus fulfills the demand for the three dimensions mediality, complexity, as well as the cognitive and psychological dimension in the sense of our complexity level D.

The logistical, creative and technical complexity of the video makes it clear, that this is learning material of category D. Although this is not always a prerequisite for a complexity level of categorization D, a scenic video with many creative elements and different action sequences requires a certain amount of production time. In this case, the pre-production (brainstorming, idea sketch, storyboard, planning of logistics) took about one month, the filming took four days, five to eight hours each, and the post-production (video editing, sound post-processing, color grading and effects processing) another twenty days. This time should be planned for the production of a professional scenic learning video, especially if you are a small team and have other work to do on the side. Alternatively, this work can be outsourced to an external agency, but this would involve an enormous financial effort.

For the project QpLuS IM, learning formats of the complexity categorization D, such as the interactive video on the functioning of search engines, will be supplemented in future by further productions of the complexity category A, B and C. Thus, a social media glossary of the complexity categorization A is planned for the further course of the project. For this purpose, basic terms from the Information Management and Information Management extra occupational courses of study will be explained briefly and concisely in text and pictures, for example via Instagram Post.

However, our interactive video is to be understood as a prototype to show which media-didactic possibilities are feasible with such a video. A survey of the learning benefit of students through the video has therefore not yet taken place.

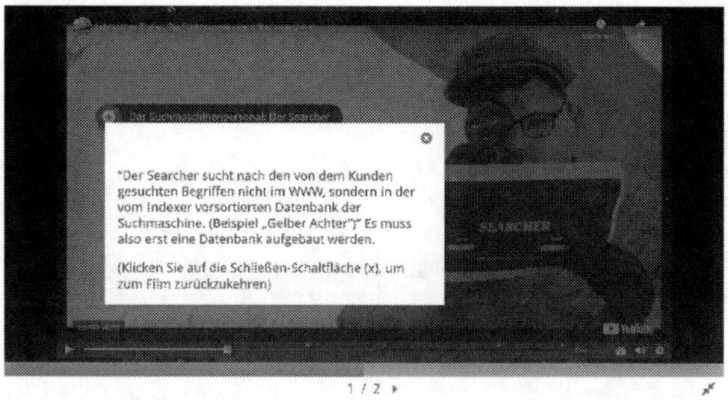

Figure 3. Interactive video on how search engines work; close-up *Searcher; opened informational Text-Pop-Up-Window*

B. *Implementation of interactive branching element in detail*

For the branching scenario in the interactive video on how search engines work, the H5P tool Interactive Video and the Crossroads feature it contains was used. With Crossroads, a branching pop-up menu can be integrated into the video that appears at the selected timecode position, as shown in Figure 4. In this pop-up menu you can now define various time codes with text headings. If the user clicks on a timecode-defined heading, the video jumps to the corresponding timecode of the video. In this way, it is possible to jump to different action sequences in the video. When an action sequence ends, the branching menu reappears and the video user can again select how the video should continue.

In the case of the interactive video on how search engines work, there are two action options available.

Even though H5P is under constant development, there is still the limitation that the official Branching Scenario feature is still in beta and is not included in the Interactive Video feature. In the Interactive Video feature, the branching scenario must be created manually with the Crossroads tool. In this context, it would be welcome if H5P were to offer its users even more consistent and interlinked features in the future. There are also limitations in terms of aesthetics; for example, there are hardly any free design options for text overlays.

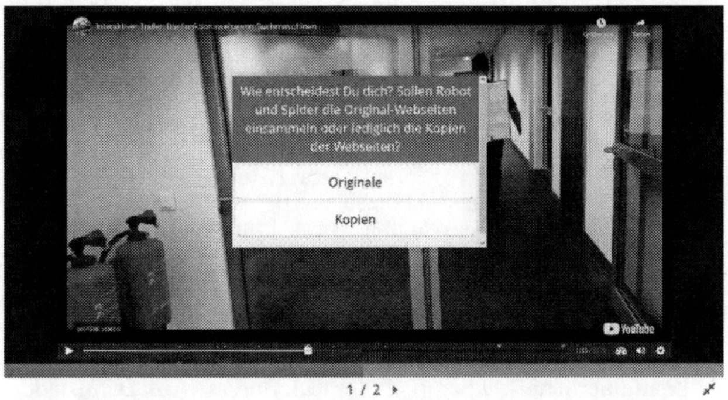

Figure 4. Interactive video on how search engines work; close-up *Searcher; Branching-Scena*

VI. CONCLUSION

Against the background of rapidly changing digital education, especially in times of the corona pandemic, in which self-directed learning is becoming increasingly important, the QpLuS IM project is concerned with the development of an agile, multidimensional process model in the sense of a media-didactic concept for the study courses Information Management and Information Management extra-occupational, which takes into account in particular the ambivalent handling of complexity.

In addition, a **four-level complexity model (A to D)** was developed, which is based on the parameters **mediality**, **complexity** and **cognitive and psychological dimensions**. This model can be used, for example, to efficiently determine learning goals and learning methods in the context of Constructive Alignment. The four levels are:

A: Social Media compatible information for the introduction.

B: Multimedia learning tools to impart basic knowledge.

C: A, B and further OER with in-depth information and interaction.

D: Branched learning offers with personalized learning path.

With the complexity level model, the digitally "*spoiled*" generations of learners and students are not cognitively overtaxed or stressed (in the sense of digital wellbeing), but can acquire basic knowledge in a targeted and reduced self-determined way and, if necessary, deepen this knowledge.

There is already an interactive video about the functioning of search engines available for the courses of studies Information Management and Information Management extra-occupational, a self-learning resource of the complexity category D for practical use. With the planned further learning resources, such as the information snack glossary on basic terms of information management on Instagram, further complexity levels are to be served.

The aim is to create a modern, intuitive and consistent network of digital self-learning materials for the study programs Information Management and Information Management extra-occupational, which can be used in addition and integration to the official courses.

In order to achieve this goal, we want and need to do more research on the importance of self-directed learning, for example how the use of interactive tools like H5P affects the learning behavior of students.

ACKNOWLEDGMENT

The work described in this article is supported by the Center for Teaching and Counseling and is funded by the Ministry of Culture and Science of Lower Saxony as part of the Quality plus - Program for the Development of Tomorrow's Studies funding program. We gratefully acknowledge these contributions.

REFERENCES

[1] QpLuS IM Project, [Online]. Available from: https://q-plus-im.wp.hs-hannover.de/ [retrieved 10.2020]

[2] Moodle, [Online].Available from: https://moodle.de/ [retrieved 10.2020]

[3] BigBlueButton, [Online]. Available from: https://bigbluebutton.org/ [retrieved 10.2020]

[4] Zoom, [Online]. Available from: https://zoom.us/de-de/meetings.html [retrieved 10.2020]

[5] J. Dyrna, J. Riedel and S. Schulze-Achatz, "When is learning with digital media (really) self-directed? Approaches to enable and promote self-direction in technology-supported learning processes [Wann ist Lernen mit digitalen Medien (wirklich) selbstgesteuert? Ansätze zur Ermöglichung und Förderung von Selbststeuerung in technologieunterstützten Lernprozessen],"2018. [Online]. Available from: https://nbn-resolving.org/urn:nbn:de:bsz:14-qucosa2-338278 [retrieved 10.2020]

[6] Constructive Alignment, 2019. Available from: https://www.e-teaching.org/didaktik/konzeption/constructive-alignment/constructive-alignment [retrieved 10.2020]

[7] Department of University Didactics & E-Learning HdEL Bern, "Media-didactic considerations on distance learning and tool use - self-regulation [Medien-Didaktische Überlegungen zu Distance learning und Tool-Einsatz - Selbstregulation] ," Fachstelle Hochschuldidaktik & E-Learning HdEL Bern. [Online]. Available from: https://pbs.twimg.com/media/ET3vkvcXgAAHG5G?format=png&name=4096x4096, [retrieved 10.2020]

[8] M. Landmann, F. Perels, B. Otto, K, Schnick-Vollmer and B. Schmitz, "Self-regulation and self-regulated learning [Selbstregulation und selbstreguliertes Lernen,"] in Educational Psychology [Pädagogische Psychologie], E. Wild and J. Möller, Eds. 2 Edition, Berlin-Heidelberg: Springer, p. 46, 2015.

[9] J. Wildt and B. Wildt, "Learning process-oriented testing in Constructive Alignment [Lernprozessorientiertes Prüfen im Constructive Alignment]," in New Handbook of University Teaching, Part H: Examinations and Performance Checks. Further development of the examination system as a consequence of the Bologna Process [Neues Handbuch Hochschullehre, Teil H: Prüfungen und Leistungskontrollen. Weiterentwicklung des Prüfungssystems in der Konsequenz des Bologna-Prozesses], B. Berendt, H. P. Voss and J. Wildt, Eds. Berlin: Raabe, pp. 1 -46, 2011.[Online]. Available from: https://www.hrk-nexus.de/fileadmin/redaktion/hrk-nexus/07-Downloads/07-03-Material/pruefen.pdf [retrieved 10.2020]

[10] R. Ryan and E. Deci, "Self-Determination Theory and the Facilitation of Intrinsic Motivation, Social Development, and Well-Being. The American psychologist," pp. 68-78, 2000. [Online] Available from: https://www.researchgate.net/publication/11946306_Self-Determination_Theory_and_the_Facilitation_of_Intrinsic_Motivation_Social_Development_and_Well-Being [retrieved 10.2020]

[11] JIM-Study, "JIM Study 2019 - Youth, Information, Media. Basic research on media use of 12 to 19-year-olds. Media education research association southwest [JIM-Studie 2019 - Jugend, Information,Medien. Basisuntersuchung zum Medienumgang 12 bis 19-jähriger. Medienpädagogischer Forschungsverbund Südwest],"[Online]. Available from: https://www.mpfs.de/fileadmin/files/Studien/JIM/2019/JIM_2019.pdf [retrieved 10.2020]

[12] G. Wucherpfennig, M. Steinberg and A. Wittich, "Media-didactic concept QpLuS-IM-Project [Mediendidaktisches Konzept QpLuS-IM-Projekt]," University of Applied Sciences and Arts Hannover, pp. 7 - 13, 2020. [Online]. Available from: https://www.researchgate.net/publication/341900843_Mediendidaktisches_Konzept [retrieved 10.2020]

[13] Camtasia, [Online]. Available from: https://www.techsmith.de/camtasia.html [retrieved 10.2020]

[14] OBS, [Online]. Available from: https://obsproject.com/de [retrieved 10.2020]

[15] Open Educational Resources, [Online]. Available from: https://en.unesco.org/themes/building-knowledge-societies/oer [retrieved 10.2020]

[16] H5P, [Online]. Available from: https://h5p.org/ [retrieved 10.2020]

[17] A. Baethge and T. Rigotti, "Effects of work interruptions and multitasking on performance and health. A diary study among health and nursing staff. [Auswirkung von Arbeitsunterbrechungen und Multitasking auf Leistungsfähigkeit und Gesundheit. Eine Tagebuchstudie bei Gesundheits- und KrankenpflegerInnen]," Dortmund / Berlin / Dresden. BAUA, p. 16, 2013. [Online]. Available from: https://d-nb.info/1037119606/34 [retrieved 10.2020]

[18] E. Ophir, C. Nass and A.D. Wagner, "Cognitive control in media multitaskers," PNAS. September 15, 2009. Vol. 106. No. 37, pp. 1-3 [Online]. Available from: https://www.pnas.org/content/pnas/106/37/15583.full.pdf [retrieved 10.2020]

[19] A. Gorlick, "Media multitaskers pay mental price, Stanford study shows," Standford Report, August 24, 2009, [Online]. Available from: https://news.stanford.edu/news/2009/august24/multitask-research-study-082409.html [retrieved 10.2020]

[20] G. Mark, Interview partner in, "Hyperconnected, the brain in overload [Hyperconnectés, le cerveau en surcharge]," Documentary, TV report, Broadcast: Arte, 2016.

[21] A. Bieberstein, "Create interactive videos with H5P. E-Learning Working Group [Interaktive Videos mit H5P erstellen. E-Learning Arbeitsgrupp]," Technical University of Darmstadt, 2019. [Online]. Available from: https://blog.e-learning.tu-darmstadt.de/2019/07/15/interaktive-videos-mit-h5p-erstellen/ [retrieved 10.2020]

[22] QpLuS IM Project, "How search engines work [Die Funktionsweise von Suchmaschinen],"An interactive Video with H5P. [Online] Available from: https://q-plus-im.wp.hs-hannover.de/einblick-in-die-suchmaschinen-welt-aus-duplo-steinen [retrieved 10.2020]

[23] N. Braun, "Nonlinear Storytelling: Programmed, interactive narrative approach for continuous media [Nonlinear Storytelling: Programmierter, interaktiver Narrationsansatz für kontinuierliche Medien]," Technical Univesity of Darmstadt. Dissertation. P.40, 2003.

[24] M. Richter and M. Flückiger, Usability and UX compact. Products for people [Usability und UX kompakt. Produkte für Menschen], 4th Edition. Springer Vieweg. Berlin Heidelberg. P.16., 2016.

A Conversational Agent for Mobile Assisted Language Learning

CPIAbot as a tool for learning Italian as a second language

Giorgio Robino
Institute for Educational Technology
CNR
Genoa, Italy
e-mail: giorgio.robino@itd.cnr.it

Simone Torsani
Department of Modern Languages and Cultures
University of Genoa
Genoa, Italy
e-mail: Simone.Torsani@unige.it

Fabrizio Ravicchio
Digital Humanities
University of Genoa
Genoa, Italy
e-mail: ravicchio@itd.cnr.it

Abstract — **Learning the language of the host country is one of the most important aspects of social inclusion for adult migrants. Within the migrant population in Italy, it is possible to find a high heterogeneity of language profiles, which differ in level of competence and degree of literacy. This phenomenon is reflected in the composition of the classrooms of the Provincial Centers for Adult Education (CPIA), educational institutions that offer courses of Italian as a second language to adult migrants. To meet the needs identified in a preliminary survey in two CPIAs, a conversational technology was developed: CPIAbot. The system is a multimodal and multi-level chatbot, whose ecosystem is Telegram, to support both the communicative teaching in the classroom and the autonomous learning of CPIA students. For the implementation of the designed innovations, embedded in the technology, an ad-hoc system was developed, integrating a dialog-manager (NaifJs), capable of managing multi-turn dialogues, and other different solutions for the communication with external services, aimed to the management of multi-channel interactions. The contribution, therefore, will describe the technological solutions adopted, insisting on their link with the linguistic needs that have emerged from the context.**

Keywords-Multimodal/voice chatbot; Conversational Agent; Task-oriented dialog manager; Mixed-initiative bot; Conversational AI; Teachers/Students mobile platform; Social inclusion for adult migrants; Italian L2 Learning; Adult Literacy.

I. INTRODUCTION

The social inclusion of migrants poses the problem of learning the language of the countries of arrival (or transit), since language is the main means of interaction with the host society. In Italy, in particular, the migrant population has very different linguistic and social profiles, including low educated adults [1]. This phenomenon poses important challenges to the Provincial Centres for Adult Education (CPIA), the institutions in charge of offering language courses [2]-[4], where the heterogeneity of linguistic profiles is reflected in the composition of their classrooms. Within the class groups, in fact, it is possible to find students with different linguistic backgrounds [5], levels of competence and, in different situations, people that suffer social isolation and do not speak Italian outside the language class [6]. Moreover, a preliminary survey in two Ligurian CPIAs showed that, in line with the provisions of the Common European Framework of Reference (CEFR), the teachers' teaching is oriented towards a communicative approach and the topics addressed, as well as the activities proposed, are relevant to the experiences lived by students outside the classroom.

In order to respond to the needs expressed by the context of reference, embracing the Mobile Assisted Language Learning (MALL) approach [7]-[9], the idea was born to develop an educational technology, CPIAbot, which can support teachers during the lessons and students in their autonomous learning, blurring the classroom boundaries. The conversational technology described below, therefore, aims to constitute a support tool that, promoting interaction based on natural language, can be a bridge between different educational scenarios.

The importance of research on tools that support language learning through mobile devices, as pointed out by Kukulska-Hulme [10], lies in the possibilities of exploiting the ubiquity of such devices to explore new teaching options for groups of people with high mobility. Specifically, conversational interfaces have, today, the possibility to establish themselves within MALL technologies both thanks to the learners' confidence with online text and voice, synchronous and asynchronous, conversations, and thanks to the development of speech recognition technologies and the growing computing power and ubiquity of mobile technologies.

On the other hand, the relaying of conversational technologies, especially if expressly oriented to language learning, requires interdisciplinary work and a wide range of skills. Similarly, the operational development or system integration of each component of the instrument requires specific study to ensure sufficient quality in the user experience and in the didactic value of the technology. This has been particularly evident in the development of CPIAbot, as it aims to reach an audience that is heterogeneous in terms of literacy levels and language skills. On the other hand, the limitations and challenges of the described experience, highlighted within the contribution, may constitute future strands of research.

This contribution, therefore, aims to describe a conversational technology, developed ex novo and expressly designed for the language learning of adult immigrants, highlighting the relationship between the needs of the specific context of reference and the technological solutions implemented.

The global research question is: *What effectiveness can a chatbot have in replicating/supporting the action of a CPIA teacher inside and outside the classroom in L2 pre-A1 teaching?*

In Section 2, a state of the art of MALL tools developed for Italian as a L2 will be presented. In Section 3, the innovativeness of CPIAbot will be described, focusing on the shift from the Graphic User Interface (GUI) to the Conversational User Interface/Vocal User Interface (CUI/VUI). In Section 4, the adherence of the chatbot characteristics with the context one will be addressed, detailed widespread in Section 5. In Section 6, a reflection on some technical and UX issues will be explained, while in Section 7 the teachers' feedback will be detailed. Finally, in Section 8, preliminary conclusions are presented.

II. EDUCATIONAL APPs FOR IMMIGRANTS AND REFUGEES IN ITALY

In Italy, it is possible to find interesting examples of apps specifically designed for immigrants and refugees, even with low language skills, that share some common elements.

Most of the software designed for learning Italian as L2 from mobile devices is free of charge. A second feature that these apps have in common is the fact that they are made in collaboration with local realities, which offer language courses to adult immigrants. Finally, in accordance with the m-Learning principles [11], mobile apps for Italian as a second language allow users to access multimedia contents every time and everywhere and are oriented to the personalization of learning.

An example is "Presente" [12], realized by CPIA Bologna and Regione Emilia-Romagna, whose main characteristic is to have, in addition to communicative exercises focused on listening and reading, a database of useful sentences organized in daily life situations. Similarly, the exercises in "Ataya" app [13], focused on the four skills (read, speak, listen, write), are divided into domains related to daily life. "Fare parole" [14], instead, is an app oriented to the graphemic and metaphonetic competence and provides exercises with a binary feedback focused on listening and writing.

A peculiar example is "Q-CPIApp" [15], built on the Learning App platform by the teacher of Lodi's CPIA, in order to provide the students exercises available on their smartphones. The activations are focused on grammar and lexicon and are organized in levels.

All the described apps are characterized for intuitive interfaces and ease of use that allows the learner's autonomous exercise, with short and engaging interactions, within the classroom and outside it.

The limitations are related to the binary feedback provided within the exercises, the weak relation between the interaction and the user's context, the lack of the students' interaction tracking (beyond the single session) and the lack of systems for vocal input management.

It is possible to find some of these elements in brand new apps recently developed.

"LinguaCuisine" [16], for instance, is an app aimed to teach Italian to adult immigrants providing cooking recipes. The main innovation is that the user can upload personal content that will personalize the learning experience.

Another peculiar example is "Studiare Migrando", realized thanks to the collaboration between the Scuola di Lingua Italiana per Stranieri (ItaStra) of the University of Palermo and the Institute for Educational Technology (CNR). The focus of the app is language learning for adult students that are attending compulsory school in CPIAs. It is based on a truly e-Learning environment aimed to support students with high mobility (often due to external factors) [17].

A brand new app, "Mondly", presents innovative and disruptive elements. The first innovation that distinguishes it from the previous app is the automated tracking of the user. An algorithm, indeed, tracks errors in order to present the failed attempt items during the same exercise or in another one. Mondly, in addition, embeds a chatbot that allows students to practice language within authentic situations. It is important to notice that users can insert even vocal input while training with the chatbot. Mondly is a "freemium" app and, in the free version, users can explore different resources/units, but just one dialog for lexical domain [18].

CPIAbot, as detailed below, stresses the margin of innovation in different ways:

- It provides a conversational and multimodal interface,
- It supports student to access resources or services with single simple commands, while they are experiencing a learning scenario (formal or informal),
- It offers adaptive feedbacks and different multi-turn dialogues
- It allows teachers to easily assign exercises and to monitor their students' interaction with the chatbot.

In brief, the contribution of CPIAbot to the MALL approach is double. On one side, the conversational interface promotes interactions in L2 in the whole User Experience, to access resources and services or to explore multi-turn dialogues. On the other side, CPIAbot represents a system that supports hybrid learning environments that actively engages students and teachers: the former can easily interact with information useful in the context they're experiencing or can explore autonomously automated exercises and the latter can assign assessment and monitor the students in their bot usage.

It is important to notice that CPIAbot differs from other systems, like Duolingo and Babbel [19], focused on a completely informal autonomous learning.

The relation between the chatbot use and the learning path designed by the teacher is deep, since the teacher's mediation in the use of any resource for learning is fundamental for the low-educated adult learners and, in general, for the students with low level of competence.

III. A LANGUAGE-FIRST TOOL FOR LANGUAGE LEARNING

The main innovation of CPIAbot is the language-first user interface paradigm, also called Conversational UI (CUI) /Voice UI (VUI) [20], which involves interactions based on natural language. This is a completely different and innovative approach, compared to the typical one of mobile apps on smartphones, where the user navigates a decision tree through menus, touching buttons on a visual layout (the usual web GUI). The choice to adopt a CUI/VUI paradigm derives from two preliminary considerations. On one hand, with the spread of the conversational paradigm within everyday systems and devices requires the research on educational technologies to relate to these interfaces. On the other hand, while in GUI based language apps the target language is used on the exit point of interaction, when a specific exercise starts, within the CUI systems, the language is the entry point of the interaction with the tool.

Our linguistic-based interface is therefore a challenge on which we expect important feedback in the experimentation phase with students.

IV. CPIABOT: FUNCTIONAL ASPECTS OF EDUCATIONAL ACTIVITIES

The adherence of the tool to the characteristics of the specific context required a design and development effort, aimed at matching particular requirements:

- Accessibility (CPIA students must be able to use CPIAbot from their own devices)
- Ergonomics (a multimodal and multi-level chatbot to support learning in heterogeneous classes)
- Adherence to the teaching approach (interaction in natural language and possibility to use CPIAbot as a support for communicative activities)
- Hybridization of learning spaces (possibility of CPIAbot to act as a link between the classroom lesson and the individual learning of the extra-school).

Compliance with each of the listed parameters involved the use of specific applications or the development of ad hoc software, as none of the (mobile) apps already available was able to meet the functional specifications required by the project [21].

The result, CPIAbot, is a conversational server application on cloud, developed in NodeJs programming environment, which interfaces to Telegram servers through the Telegram Bot API [22].

The CPIAbot's software architecture is schematized in Figure 1.

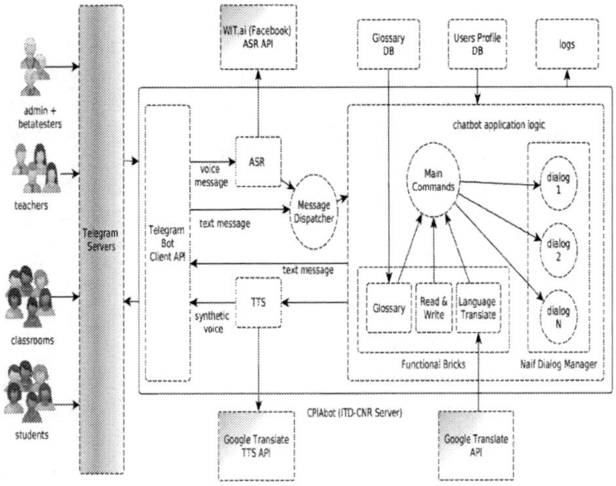

Figure 1. Architecture of CPIAbot

The illustrated architecture is the structure on which the technological solutions presented in the following paragraphs have been implemented.

V. CPIABOT: TECHNOLOGICAL FRAMEWORK

The technological solutions, conceived and developed for each of the parameters indicated in the previous paragraph, are illustrated below.

A. Accessibility: The choice of Telegram instant messaging app as the chabot channel

In order to facilitate the access to the developed system for the CPIA's students, it was decided to develop a chatbot within the instant messaging app Telegram.

Downstream of an analysis of the best communication channel for the development of a conversational application, Telegram was found to have more features suitable to the conceived technology with respect to the other apps analyzed: Google Assistant voice assistants, Amazon Alexa (especially through smart-speaker voice interfaces) and WhatsApp. Therefore, the most suitable platform for the development of the application turned out to be Telegram for different reasons.

Costs saving: Telegram app is a free software whose client-side code is open-source; it does not require the purchase of dedicated hardware and the Telegram application can be installed on any personal computer, already available in the classroom, or on smartphones in the possession of students. In the case of Amazon or Google voice assistants, instead, it is necessary to purchase expensive hardware devices, with a cost linear with the number of classes in which to use the devices themselves.

Low System Requirements: Telegram is a lightweight app that can also be installed on mobile devices with older Android/iOS operating systems.

Feasibility: Whatsapp is the most used mobile chat messaging app in Italy, that is why it would be the preferred channel for the development of chatbots, but they are here feasible only through the Whatsapp for Business platform, now available in private beta. In addition, the APIs of the business platform allow the exchange of text messages (SMS-like) but do not allow to manage multimedia content such as audio, images and video.

B. *Ergonomics: A multimodal and multi-level chatbot for heterogeneous classes*

To face the heterogeneity of the CPIA's classrooms, CPIAbot has been conceived and developed as a multimodal and multi-level chatbot. CPIAbot can be defined as a multimodal chatbot, as the interface allows users to interact through different channels. Using multimedia content in the paratext facilitates the decoding of the written text and makes the system easy to use, even for low-educated adult learners.

Three elements characterize the multimodal interface of CPIAbot: written interaction, oral interaction, and multimedia contents.

Written interaction: Telegram allows for written interaction with the chatbot, otherwise impossible with a Google and Amazon conversational application; especially cantered on the use of smart speakers (it is partially possible even when using assistants via smartphone)

Oral interaction: In CPIAbot the student can interact either by typing through the keyboard or by speaking, through a voice message or a video message. The audio recording is processed by a speech recognition platform, which converts the user's voice into text. For the speech recognition task we used the Facebook/WIT.ai API service, one of the few available free of charge for the Italian language.

Multimedia contents: The processing of the user request produces a response to the user which can be textual, vocal or an integrated multimedia content; for example, an image (also with subtitles), a video, an audio recording or an animation.

The answers to the user are translated into speech with a synthetic voice, thanks to the use of a Text To Speech platform. The synthetic voice in Italian language used is that provided by the Google Translate Speech cloud platform.

The multimedia interaction concerns not just contents in output (to the user), CPIAbot architecture, indeed, is built to allow users to upload images and video files, besides audio and text. By example, CPIAbot can process an image submitted by a learner, trying to understand the content of the picture and triggering a dialog (future development). Telegram allows the use of many types of multimedia contents (audio, images and video), which is not possible through Alexa and Google smart speakers (Amazon Echo/Google Home). It would indeed be possible just with smart display devices (Amazon Echo Show or Google Nest) but the high cost per device remains an issue.

CPIAbot, on the other hand, can be defined as a multi-level chatbot, since the outputs of the system, as well as the channel with which they are transmitted to the user, can be differentiated according to the level assigned to the user by your teacher. This is expected to be an important feature in the integration of CPIAbot within multi-level classrooms, supporting the personalization of content and activities, with the aim of reducing the workload of the teacher.

C. *Timing Management: output pauses and input silence*

Another peculiar element of CPIAbot, that could support the personalization of learning activities within heterogeneous classrooms, is the timing management. The management of timings in the interaction with users is an element of differentiation of CPIAbot, compared to other reactive-only chatbots (operating just in pull mode): the chatbot, for each message issued, can be programmed to insert pauses (of an arbitrary number of seconds, depending on the student's learning level) to allow the learner to have sufficient time to read or listen to the content provided by the chatbot.

It is also possible to concatenate multiple timeouts in sequence, engaging the student to continue the conversation or forcing him to end the dialog.

D. *Adherence to the didactic approach*

The adherence between the characteristics of CPIAbot and the communicative approach, to which teachers' teaching is oriented, emerges on two levels.

On one hand, in fact, the language-first paradigm of the chatbot orients the student to interact with the system in the target language, even using very simple expressions, instead of continuing the interaction through menu navigation (as described in the previous paragraph).

On the other hand, CPIAbot's resources allow the student both to have support for their communicative needs and to measure themselves in simulated dialogs, pushing them to exercise their communicative competence in everyday situations (even if simulated).

That is why CPIAbot provides two types of interactions: short "user initiative" interactions and dialogs with "bot initiative" interactions. In the first mode, the student, like other users, can invoke single function (here defined as *user requests*), useful to support both teaching activities and the use of L2 in daily life, by students. It is the user, therefore, who guides the conversation. In the second mode, the student activates a multi-turn *dialogue*, which proposes a lexico-grammar or a communicative task. In this case, the conversation is controlled by the chatbot, which proposes different conversation turns, prompts and content depending on the stimuli entered by the user. By virtue of the coexistence of these two human-bot interaction modalities (reactive and proactive), it is possible to define CPIAbot as a "mixed initiative" chatbot.

The request message that the user sends to the bot is processed by a sentence processing procedure (the *main state* dispatcher) that matches the natural language sentence, expressed by the user, with available user requests or dialogs.

a) User requests

The application provides primitive functions to support the understanding and the production of the Italian language. These primitive functions are always available to the student; these are single-turn sequences (where there is no specific dialogue context, i.e. there is no "conversational state").

Below, we offer a brief overview of the functions implemented (all the examples of invocations of functions are translated into English to facilitate the reader's understanding)

Write (Scrivi), displays the written text corresponding to the speech that the user has sent to the bot with voice message or video message. The function enables read-write skills, facilitating sound/sign association. Example:

```
write supermarket
```

Read (Leggi), activate the playback, through the available synthetic voice, of a text written by the user with the keyboard. This function also enables read-write skills, facilitating sound/sign association. Example:

```
read supermarket
```

Syllable (Sillaba), similar to writing, but breaks down a word or phrase into its constituent syllables. The function facilitates the sound/sign association with division into syllables. Example:

```
syllable salt
```

Spell (Compita); scan one-word letter by letter. This function can be invoked either verbally or in writing and in the latter case, it is indicated, for each letter, whether it is written in upper or lower case. Example:

```
spell tomatoes
```

Translate (Traduci), allows users to translate from the Italian language to one of the 104 languages available on Google Translate or, vice versa, from a foreign language to the Italian language. The interlanguage translation can be used in the understanding of terms/phrases in a text, or for translation from source language to target language to support oral production. Example:

```
translate in German good morning
```

Word (Parola): A simplified glossary was created that provides static (photos) and animated (gifs and videos) multimedia material. The lexical database collects the terms indicated in the Syllabus [23] for the domains "work" and "purchases" chosen for the bot experimentation phase. The CPIAbot glossary currently contains about 500 glosses, inserted in 24 semantic fields (groups). The glossary is a subset of the total list of glosses that the Syllabus proposes for the Pre-A1 level (~900 terms) and A1 level (~1000 terms). Each term has an associated data structure, in which the following attributes are stored: description, usage examples, multimedia content (an image, or video or animation), audio recording, grammar notes, category and group, language level. The attribute "description", in particular, is co-constructed incrementally by CPIA teachers through a collection of simplified definitions of glosses (suitable for Pre-A1 and A1 level learners), provided in crowd-sourcing mode.

When invoked, the function returns a multimedia output, and the word insert as parameter of the user request, is displayed with a picture, a gif or a short video, accompanied by a synthetic entry describing it together with a sequence of short sentences.

The glossary can also be queried with semantic filters with respect to categories and groups of words and/or grammar rules, thanks to the ***Give me words*** user request. The function has been designed primarily for use by the teacher in the classroom. Example:

```
give me six words in category work, singular
```

b) Multi-turn Dialogs

Besides, the peculiar feature of CPIAbot is the contextual multi-turn dialogues (we call it just *dialogs*), which perform lexical and grammar exercises (repetitive tasks) and real scene simulation dialogues.

Repetitive task dialogs

Listen and repeat - Practice the pronunciation of words, with repeated exercises. The student listens to a word extracted randomly from the glossary and reproduced in a synthetic voice, then has to repeat it. The student can select words from the entire glossary or from different groups of words in the glossary, divided by level of pronunciation difficulty (these levels have been defined in collaboration with the CPIA teachers).

Read and repeat - Practice the sound/sign association through repeated exercises. Like the previous exercise, but instead of listening to the sound of a word, the student must read an entry from the glossary presented in writing.

Listen and write - Practice the sound/sign association, through repeated exercises. The student listens to a word and then has to write it on the keyboard.

Guess the word - Supports vocabulary acquisition with image-word association. The learner must guess which word corresponds to the picture selected randomly by the chatbot. The exercise can draw on all the words in the glossary or one of the 24 groups defined in the Syllabus.

Simulated dialogs

The dialogs consider the authenticity of the communicative situations proposed, also in reference to the social practices of the students. The conversations, therefore, are based on the daily life of the learners in Italy and calibrated to their communicative needs. The dialog "Let's shop" is an example: in this dialog, the learner is called to assist a fictitious character in choosing the place where to buy food. After a short contextualization, in which the fictitious character illustrates the task (shopping) to the user, the chatbot proposes some short questions about the place where the student prefers to accompany the protagonist to buy what he needs. At the end of the dialogue, the chatbot asks the user to identify, between two images, the one representing the chosen place.

All the structures of CPIAbot's dialogs have elements in common. The dialog flow is constructed to provide adaptive feedback to the student, allowing them to access resources/contents that support the interaction if the user's input does not reach a predetermined level of correctness or does not contain the necessary information to proceed with the conversation.

The teacher, therefore, can integrate the dialogs with the chatbot within the design of the learning unit, aimed at pursuing the objectives identified.

Since all of the dialog types described require the ability of the conversational system to maintain the context in the different turns of the conversation, to realize such multi-turn task-completion dialogs, a special dialog manager, called *NaifJs*, has been developed in ITD-CNR.

c) A dialog manager for task-completion dialogs

NaifJs is a dialog manager that implements dialogue management with a Finite State Machine (FSM), released as open source (Git: https://github.com/solyarisoftware/naifjs), where each *input state* is a node of "understanding" and local processing of input sequence patterns, and where each *output state* is a node of content production with some backend elaboration and messaging to user. Each dialog is activated programmatically with the setting of an initial state that performs some kind of logic (L, in Figure 2), presents a message to the user and can store contextual memory variables (M). The output message to the user can be a textual description of a scene, a voice message, an image or audio/video content, followed by a question (prompt) to the student.

NaifJS supply to in JavaScript developers a simple DSL (Domain Specific Language) that allows to program stateful dialogs using simple function statements, as shown in Figure 2, to manage dialog flow life-cycle (`start`, `end`), to change state (`goOut`, `goIn`), to match an input pattern (`match`), to output contents (`say`, `tts`), to manage timeouts callbacks, to manage dialog memory (`setvar`, `getvar`).

In the dialog flow, the output state typically activates a subsequent state (input state), in which the dialog manager analyzes the user's response (a sentence in Italian language) and performs a contextual interpretation based on a Pattern-Matching (PM). The dialog manager is agnostic with respect to the Natural Language Understanding (NLU) mechanism and for simplicity and efficiency; the parsing has been implemented with the use of regular expressions.

In the case of a positive pattern match, the input processing node performs some processing and a response is given to the user (textual, with synthetic voice or other multimedia audio/video content).

The current state can evolve into a new state or might not change (loopback), based on a dialog flow programmed by the designer. The dialog flow finally ends, according to the application logic and the dialog ends.

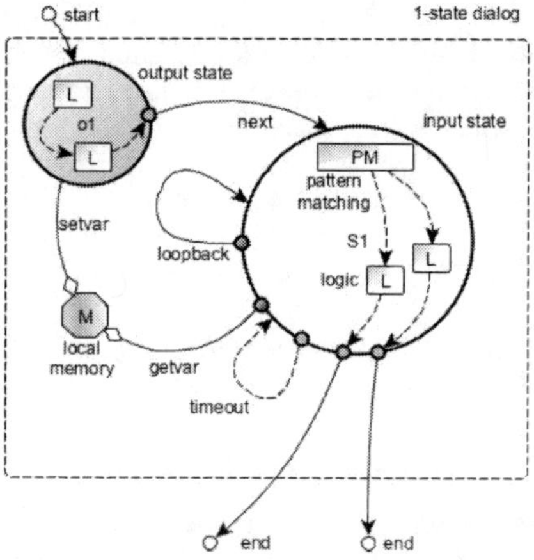

Figure 2. Naifjs dialog manager. Dialog with a single input state (on the left). 2-states dialog (on the right).

To complete a specific task (as a language exercise), the multi-turn conversation is implemented as a network of micro-dialogues, called *dialog units* (Figure 3), each containing a graph of nodes that allow conversation flows in a specific domain. These dialog units are concatenated modules, which can receive input parameters. Each dialog unit has a short-term memory: temporary variables with local visibility to the unit itself.

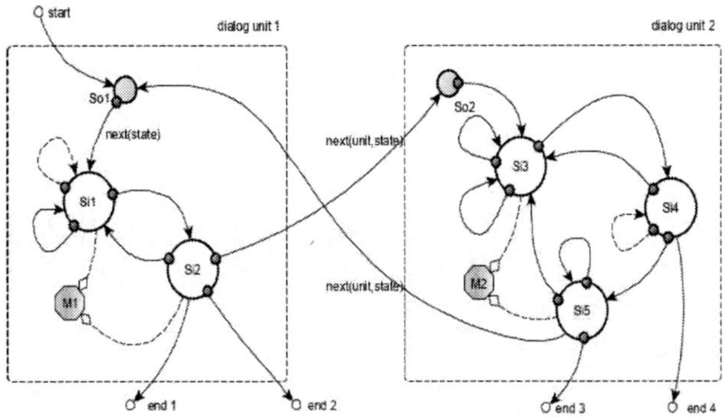

Figure 3. Multi-state (5 states) and multi-unit (2 units) dialog example with Naifjs dialog manager.

E. *Hybridization of the learning environment*

The hybridization of the learning environment of Italian L2 is a process that intersects two dimensions. On the one hand, the hybridization of learning is guided by the teacher, within the classes, for instance on the aspects of L2 that students may have encountered incidentally in the extra-school time (words, expressions, syntactic constructions, etc.) [24]. On the other hand, in an inverse process, the teacher attempts to extend the didactic action beyond the lesson hours, proposing to the students structured activities to be carried out autonomously, even at lower levels [25]. In this, CPIAbot can act as a mediator able to facilitate remote communication between the teacher and his students or allowing the teacher's monitoring of his students' interaction with the system.

The prerequisite that enables such processes is the User Unique Identification (UUID). In Telegram, in fact, registered users can be easily and uniquely identified. This allows, through profiling mechanisms, to customize the experience for each student, as well as enable the monitoring of interactions and their analysis. The univocal identification of the speaker is instead a problem in interactions with Google and Amazon devices, with which there is, to date, no mature technology available to identify the voice print of the individual speaker in front of the smart speaker, positioned for example in the classroom, where the number of students can be high and may vary over time.

In CPIAbot, therefore, the UUID potentialities are exploited to allow the creation of different account types: (1) student accounts, to be used by students inside and outside the classroom; (2) teacher accounts, to be used by teachers outside the classroom; (3) classroom accounts, to be used in the classroom by a teacher and his students. Each one of these account type can perform peculiar actions in the system:

Students' usage: the conversational agent is designed for personal use inside and outside the classroom with access via smartphone.

Teachers' usage: the cloud-based database and logging system allow the bot to keep information about student activities both outside the classroom and within the class group. For in-classroom activities, the conversational agent can act as a teacher's assistant in the classroom during lessons. Through the class account (each classroom has his unique account), the teacher can use all the features of the bot on the classroom personal computer, often connected to an Interactive Whiteboard (IWB), to propose exercises and games to be done in groups or as individual exercises to be done later "at home".

With the CPIAbot push mode (see below), teachers can send notifications messages and messages containing activable exercises to single students and/or virtual classrooms.

A teacher, interacting with CPIAbot through simple commands, can create virtual classrooms naming these with a personal chosen *classname* (e.g. *3C*) and the teacher can group students in the specified classroom with simple command messages to the agent.

Each student part of (virtual) classroom *3C* just has to click buttons inside the received message to activate the corresponding dialogs.

a) Report

Furthermore, teachers can remotely monitor students' chatbot usage and obtain information on the exercises done by an individual learner, or statistical information on the progress of the specified class, just using simple commands in natural language. Teachers can also get a report specifying a period of days/months from now. Example: report for the last week activities of the classroom 3c; report for the last 2 days' interactions of the student Giorgio Robino.

```
classroom 3C report 1 week
student Giorgio Robino report 2 days
```

b) Pull and push messaging

CPIAbot mainly performs a reactive interaction (*pull mode*): the chatbot is always listening to a user request, which is typed on the keyboard of the device, smartphone, tablet or personal computer. The programmer, for example in relation to the student's language level, processes by the conversational agent, which responds immediately, or at a configurable time, to the user's request in a similar way to a man-to-man conversation.

A proactive interaction (*push mode*) is also developed in CPIAbot, thanks to a Telegram feature (currently not available on Google and Amazon smart speakers) which contacts the user in a deferred time (sending a *notification* after the end of a dialogue session). In the push mode, the chatbot can send unsolicited notifications or start new conversations with the student (triggered by a backend logic or *human-in-the loop* teachers messaging). In this scenario, the student receives notifications on his or her device, in which the agent proposes diverse activities to the student, such as an exercise, a topic conversation, aimed at achieving one of the training objectives.

Among other uses, push activable messages, along with the report function, helped teachers to fully-remotely interact with students during the COVID lockdown period, caused by COVID pandemic, allowing them to propose and monitor distance activities even with the lower educated students.

VI. Technical Issues, User Interface (UI) and User Experience (UX) Open Points

The implementation of the functions and dialogues designed traveled in parallel with the preliminary tests within PreA1-A1 level courses of the two CPIA involved. These preliminary tests revealed critical points concerning the use of the chatbot by learners with low levels of competence in L2.

A. Speech recognition

The Automatic Speech Recognition (ASR) Facebook/WIT.ai technology platform, integrated via cloud API into CPIAbot, has an excellent level of understanding of speech input from Italian-speaking beta-testers. In tests carried out so far with a set of 20 beta-testers, adults speaking Italian fluently, the Single Word Error Rate (SWER) was less than 7%. Testing with foreign learners, the speech recognition system performances degrade a bit, revealing a higher WER in case of incorrect pronunciation. Another general open point in speech recognition is *syllables recognition*. The used ASR is not able to recognize single syllables, part of Italian language dictionary. This is a common issue all available ASR in the market have. Following this limitation, CPIAbot current version is not able to correct learner syllables pronunciation.

B. Push to talk and push to listen buttons

The voice interaction using the Telegram app is enabled by a *push-to-talk*: the student has to press a recording button of the message to be sent, at the same time he has to speak keeping the button pressed and releasing it until you speak, ending the message. Similarly, to hear the voice response of the bot, the user must press a button to activate the playback of the bot response (*push-to-listen*). In comparison to a smart speaker *wake-word / continuous mode* UX usual by example with Google Home smart speakers ("*Hey google, what's time is it?*"), the push-to-talk / push-to-listen interaction modality is a bit unnatural and is a friction element with poorly literate (computer literate) learners. This is a telegram UI limit, not a CPIAbot limit, nevertheless this kind of interaction requiring the user to explicitly press a button to talk and listen, is interesting from a linguistic/educational perspective because it forces the learner to be very focused on the voice interaction sequences, when chatting with the virtual assistant.

C. Language-first for lower-educated adults

After a first experimentation without any button, we introduced a disambiguation menu to simplify usage. Users can now interact with the bot just speaking or writing any word or any sentence; the bot reply with a short list of options, suggesting buttons that activate related contextual user request, as ***write***, ***read***, ***translate***, as shown in Figure 4.

Figure 4. Examples of disambiguation menues

The final UI was successful in teachers and students' feedback, achieving a versatile and adaptable interaction, that allows a full natural language interaction for advanced users (with language level >= A1) and a simplified experience for PreA1 students (with buttons suggestions).

VII. Teachers Feedback

The experimentation of CPIAbot within the PreA1-A1 courses of two Genoese CPIAs was planned for the spring of 2020 when, due to the COVID lock-down, all Italian educational institutions suspended their lessons. It should be noted that the distance teaching carried out by the teachers during the lock-down was an emergency solution. The teachers, therefore, sought operational solutions to meet sudden and changing needs of the context, requiring a period of adjustment to build a real design of the teaching actions. In this framework, CPIAbot was immediately used for the possibility of sending group assessments, or customized for the individual student, which can be activated without having to navigate complex learning environments and is usable from their mobile devices. In a mirror-like manner, teachers used the monitoring functions integrated in the chatbot to monitor student activities. At the end of the academic year, unstructured interviews were carried out with six teachers who continued to use the chatbot even during the COVID lock-down.

The final question of the interview allowed teachers to give free feedback on CPIAbot. The analysis of the answers showed that, in general terms, teachers consider the chatbot a useful tool for teaching Italian as a foreign language, while highlighting different aspects. Among the elements emerged in the teacher's answers, it is possible to find the representation of CPIAbot as a good tool for teaching vocabulary, thanks to the multimedia contents. Another element that emerged is the role of stimulus for the students, while another teacher underlined the flexibility and the portability of the tool. This came together with the grade of detail of the report about the students' activities, available within the system. Finally, another important element, elicited by different teachers was the importance of a preliminary phase where the teachers mediate the students' use of the system during classroom activities.

VIII. CONCLUSIONS

Learning Italian is one of the key steps for the integration of adult migrants arriving in or temporarily transiting through our country. Among the institutional responses to this specific linguistic need are the CPIA, which offers L2 courses aimed at achieving different levels of competence. To meet the needs of the CPIA context, CPIAbot, a conversational educational technology, has been conceived and *ad hoc* solutions have been developed, in order to tailor the characteristics of the system on the users' ones.

Accessibility to the system by students, for instance, is facilitated by the ecosystem in which we chose to develop the chatbot, i.e. telegram, an open source instant messaging app, free of charge and not requiring high system requirements to be installed on mobile devices.

The attention to the heterogeneity of the classes has been translated into the creation of a multi-modal and multi-level chatbot, to allow students with different degrees of competence (and literacy) to interact with technology. The UX, in fact, includes written and oral human-bot interaction, occasionally supported by multimedia resources, and the multi-turns dialogs are tailored to the linguistic competence of the student.

The adherence to the communicative approach, adopted by teachers and aligned with the CEFR guidelines, is implemented in the chatbot on two levels. Firstly, a conversational "language-first" technology, such as CPIAbot pushes the student to interact in natural language with the whole system. Secondly, the content and the activities proposed by the software are oriented to the communicative needs of the adult immigrant.

Finally, CPIAbot embeds features that support the hybridization of the learning spaces, because it bridges the formal and non-formal dimensions of learning. In particular, CPIAbot enables the teachers to set up, manage and monitor activities that consider the autonomous learning of the students, thanks to the UUID system and to the consequent account type differentiation (Teacher, Student, Class). This element played an important role in the (not expected) usage of CPIAbot during the COVID-lockdown period, when teachers could interact and monitor their students thanks to the features embedded in CPIAbot.

CPIAbot, therefore, is a language learning technology that tries to merge the advantage of the mobile/multi-devices oriented systems with the conversational approach. The former represents a solution that supports the expansion of a personalized learning path outside the classroom, the latter represents an interface that promotes the use of the target language as a mean to interact with the system and not only as the object of a specific exercise.

In conclusion, waiting for the implementation of the experimental phase of the project, it is possible to say that the developed technology, CPIAbot, contains within itself the prerogatives of a tool usable within the heterogeneous classrooms attended by adult students and could be integrated with a communicative oriented didactic, thanks to its peculiar architecture and interface.

ACKNOWLEDGEMENT

Since the CPIAbot chatbot was developed within a project of the Institute for Educational Technologies, in collaboration with the teachers of the Centro-Levante and Centro-Ponente CPIAs, the authors would like to thank the people who are contributing: G. Trentin (Project Manager), L. Bernava (ITD Technician/CPIAbot contributor), E. Spadaccini, P. Cataldo, G. Rocchi, C. Zappalà, E. Simeoli, A. Gavino, G. Saitto, C. Lazagna, M. Castello, F. Pironi, F. Amato (teachers).

REFERENCES

[1] ISTAT, "Vita e percorsi di integrazione degli immigrati in Italia." (Life and integration paths of immigrants in Italy.) 2019 [Online] Available from: https://www.istat.it/it/archivio/230556 Retreived: October 2020.

[2] M. Catarci, M. Fiorucci, and M. Trulli, "L'ABC della cittadinanza."(The ABC of citizenship.) Milano, IT: Franco Angeli, 2014.

[3] F. Martini and M. Bartolini, "La Liguria duale dell'accoglienza."(The dual Liguria of hospitality.) Genova, IT: Genova University Press, 2020.

[4] MIUR, "10 passi verso i CPIA."(10 steps towards the CPIA.) [Online] Available from: https://www.istruzione.lombardia.gov.it/wp-content/uploads/2010/04/miur-1881-9dic2013-all-ocr.pdf Retreived: October 2020.

[5] A. Borri and G. Masiero, "IDEA: interazioni dialogiche e affini. una proposta di didattica ludica in classi eterogenee di adulti."(IDEA: dialogical and related interactions. a proposal of playful didactics in heterogeneous classes of adults.) Italiano LinguaDue, vol. 9, no. 2, pp. 506-523, 2018.

[6] P. Nitti, "Un'indagine sui corsi di lingua seconda erogati dai centri di accoglienza in Piemonte." (A survey of the second language courses provided.) Educazione Linguistica. Language Education, vol. 7, no. 3, pp. 413-438, 2018.

[7] G. Duman, G. Orhon, and N. Gedik, "Research trends in mobile assisted language learning from 2000 to 2012." ReCALL, vol. 27, no. 2, pp. 197-216, 2014.

[8] A. Kukulska-Hulme, “Mobile Language Learning Innovation Inspired by Migrants” Journal of Learning for Development-JL4D, vol. 6, pp. 116-129, 2019.

[9] A. Kukulska-Hulme, J. Traxler, and J. Pettit, "Designed and user-generated activity in the mobile age" Journal of Learning Design, vol. 2, no. 1, pp. 52-65, 2007.

[10] A. Kukulska-Hulme, “Mobile Language Learning Innovation Inspired by Migrants”. Journal of Learning for Development-JL4D, vol. 6, no 2, pp. 116-129, 2019.

[11] UNESCO, UNESCO Policy guidelines for mobile learning. [Online] Available from: https://unesdoc.unesco.org/ark:/48223/pf0000219641. Retreived October 2020.

[12] Presente App [Online] Available from: https://play.google.com/store/apps/details?id=presente.edizionilalinea.it&hl=it. Retreived November 2020.

[13] S. Pasta “Hybridising media education and social pedagogy: the (missed) opportunity in educational intervention with refugees in the ‘Italian reception system’ “ Research on Education and Media, vol 11, no. 12, pp. 38-44, 2019.

[14] Fare Parole App [Online] Available from: https://play.google.com/store/apps/details?id=it.ervet.fareparole1&hl=it. Retreived November 2020.

[15] Q-CPIapp App [Online] Available from: http://www.cpialodi.edu.it/wordpress3/percorso-alpha-prea1/ Retreived November 2020.

[16] P. Seedhouse, P. Heslop, A. Kharrufa, S. Ren, and T. Nguyen, “The Linguacuisine Project: A Cooking-Based Language Learning Application”. The EuroCALL Review, vol. 27, no. 2, pp. 75-97, 2019.

[17] G. Fulantelli, V. Pipitone, D. Taibi, G. Todaro, M. Arrigo, and D. La Guardia, “Le Tecnologie Digitali per Rispondere ai Bisogni Formativi dei Migranti Forzati.”(Digital Technologies for Responding to the Training Needs of Forced Migrants.) In Didamatica 2018. AICA-Associazione Italiana per l'Informatica ed il Calcolo Automatico, pp. 313-322, 2018.

[18] L. Fryer, D. Coniam, R. Carpenter, and D. Lăpuşneanu, “Bots for Language Learning Now: Current and Future Directions.” Language, Learning and Technology, vol 24, pp. 8-22, 2020.

[19] J.P. Bajorek, “L2 Pronunciation in CALL: The Unrealized Potential of Rosetta Stone, Duolingo, Babbel, and Mango Languages”. Issues and Trends in Educational Technology, vol. 5, no. 2, pp. 60-87, 2017.

[20] R. Moore and R. Arar, “Conversational UX Design: A Practitioner's Guide to the Natural Conversation Framework.” New York, NY: ACM, 2019. doi: 10.1145/3304087. 2019.

[21] F. Ravicchio, G. Robino, G. Trentin and L. Bernava, “CPIAbot: un chatbot nell’insegnamento dell’Italiano L2 per stranieri.”(CPIAbot: a chatbot in teaching Italian L2 for foreigners.) In G. Adorni e F. Koceva (a cura di), Atti di Convegno Didamatica 2019, BYOD, realtà aumentata e virtuale: opportunità o minaccia per la formazione? pp.77-86. Milano, IT: Edizioni AICA. 2019.

[22] F. Ravicchio, G. Robino, S. Torsani, “A conversational assistant to support immigrants’ learning of Italian as l2: CPIAbot”. In press. [Online] Available from: https://ijet.itd.cnr.it/article/view/1142. Retreived: October 2020.

[23] A. Borri, F. Minuz, L. Rocca, and C. Sola, “Italiano L2 in contesti migratori. Sillabo e descrittori dall’alfabetizzazione all’A1.”(Italian L2 in migration contexts. Syllabus and descriptors from literacy to A1.) Torino, IT: Loecher. 2014.

[24] T. Magnaterra and M. Pentucci, “Le tecnologie e la didattica dell’Italiano.”(The technologies and teaching of Italian.) In “Tecnologie per l’educazione” a cura di P. C. Rivoltella and P. G Rossi. Pp. 252 –262, 2019.

[25] C. Lai, “Autonomous language learning with technology: Beyond the classroom.” Londra, UK: Bloomsbury Publishing, 2001.